# CHARLIE GRAY

# At Least I'm Not The Frog

*A Zany Memoir Of Alcoholism & Recovery*

The following is a true account of my struggle with alcoholism and identity, my subsequent recovery, and my emotional renaissance. To maintain their anonymity, some names have been changed and I have combined two treatment centers into one, in Chapter 8: Palm Beach Retreat. Actual names of individuals and names of treatment centers were used with express written permission.

First edition

Cover art by Euan Monaghan
Illustration by Eva Polakovicova

This book was professionally typeset on Reedsy.
Find out more at reedsy.com

*For Mom & Dad*

# Contents

# Preface

To my fellow alcoholics and addicts, it is my hope you are able to find yourself on these pages, so that you, too, may discover a more beautiful, purposeful path of life. If you're a loved one or friend of someone battling this affliction, I hope these pages are a source of solace for you as well, to see that there is, indeed, a light at the end of the tunnel.

# Acknowledgement

So many people helped make this book possible, and I would like to name a few of them individually. I could not have accomplished this without their support and guidance. I am *immensely grateful* for each of you:

Brodie, Trella, and Taylor, *my girls*.
Kendra, Courtney, and Devin, *my other girls*.
Mallorie, *my inspiration*.
Ransom, B. Will, Cory, William, and Kyle, *my boys*.
Granny Norma Jean, Granny Doris, Dave, James, Jeremy, Teresa, Mai, Pam, Ronnie, Marnie, Amanda, Dena, Chris, Sarah, Bill, SJ, Kathy, Dillon, *my amazing family*.
Cody and Jeremy, *my patrons*.
Sarah, Charles, Euan, and Eva, *my creative team*.

We did it, y'all!

# 1

# My House on The Hill

*March 2010*
*Clinton, Missouri*
*23 Years Old*

Pouncing with the grace of a cat into my living room, I spin a dashing circle and gulp carefully from my mug of wine. I am mindful to tread easily around the haphazardly strewn headshots. By tomorrow morning, I need three picked as my final selections and sent to Jean, my agent. I'm struggling to find the perfect set. Tilting my head, I peer at each photo for a long moment.

While I'm not thrilled at how feminine I appear in some, I am over the moon to be sifting through headshots. It's as if the planets are aligning and I'm fulfilling my destiny. I chose to sign with Infinite Talent in Kansas City, based on their clientele, and I am confident they will provide me with plenty of work. It was my top pick of the agencies I auditioned for, and I was extremely impressed with the photo shoot for my headshots.

Mid-morning sun streams through the sliding glass door as I

take a rest on the fireplace ledge and sip wine. I am especially proud and validated. It was only a few months ago that I missed an internship at the Actors Theatre of Louisville in Kentucky by one slot, and thought my acting career was over before it had even begun. I had sat on this very ledge and wept, devastated. In hindsight, my reaction was a bit melodramatic.

Graduating from Drury University last August, under the tutelage of Broadway veteran Robert Westenberg, I assumed my path to in-demand theatre thespian would be quick and easy. I was woefully wrong. Back to the drafting lab I went, however, and crafted a new plan. Securing work in Kansas City will allow me to pad my resume, and from there I will decide which coast to further pursue. I am particularly interested in landing a role on a soap opera; it's not that I'm a fanatic, merely they seem to provide steady work.

Draining my wine, I step up the lone stair, into the kitchen, and round the corner to the garage fridge. There are two boxes of Franzia left by my Dad's girlfriend, Tahnee. She's handy like that, leaving wine and weed after a visit. Twisting the knob, I top off my mug, gazing out the garage door. I forgot to close it last night before I passed out, but no matter. No one will ever know; it's usually only me at home nowadays. Dad spends most of his time in Kansas City with Tahnee, and Brod crashes at Taylor's house, her boyfriend. Which is *great*. I have plenty of alone time to explore truth and life as an earnest Bohemian.

The air is chilly, and I wander back inside to the kitchen, where I stare vacantly out our other sliding glass door. An outdoor patio connects the two rooms, offering a spectacular view of our back pastures and tree line. Zoning out for a while, I hold my mug with both hands at chest level, then catch my reflection in the hall mirror and clear my throat.

2

"Alright, one cigarette and back to work, chap!" The wine has me buzzing and my British accent is in full force.

Blasting Robert Pattinson's *Let Me Sign*, I draft an email to Jean at my laptop in the dining room. It is late, nearing midnight, and I put quite a dent in the Crisp White Wine Franzia box. In all fairness, it took as much to narrow down my top three headshots. Unable to convince myself of the need for a brooding model shot, each photo shows me smiling. Two with teeth, one without. I followed suggestions and chose three different outfits, poses, and backdrops, using one as a closeup. It is my favorite, and very authentic to who I am as a person: not too glamorous, but definitely with a sense of taste. Handsome, but not swoon-worthy. Cute.

Before clicking send, I lean close to the screen and proof for typos; the wine has made my fingers heavy. Satisfied, I send it off and walk through the wide dining room arch to the front door. Stepping onto our front porch, I slide down a column and light a cigarette. Cold night air attempts to nip at me, but the wine keeps it at bay.

I feel electrified. My shoulders begin to bounce, and I let it flow, dance washing over me like a wave. My torso twists and I tap my feet, hearing the beat in my mind. It is pulsing, causing me to rise, clapping, and stepping side to side. I throw my head back and spin in circles, weaving from the walkway to the grass. Our country lamp gleams brightly from the corner of the yard, and I hold my arms out, spinning faster and tighter now, working my way toward its halo.

Dixie, my hound, scoots in from the backyard, wagging her way around me, blind and happy to boogie. I bop over and pat a rhythm down her back as she licks my arms. Breathless, I fall to the ground beside her and watch the night sky. She nestles near me and I hear her tail thumping the ground.

"What're you thinking, girl?"

She sniffs my cheek and sneezes in my ear.

"Oh, thank you! It's all gonna be golden, huh? It's gonna be alright, huh? Yeah."

We lay like this for a while, a pastime of ours. Dixie is older now, pushing nine, and showing her age a bit. But despite her graying beard and blindness, she still acts like a puppy. She has a voracious appetite and is always pleased to see me. I'm not supposed to allow it, but this winter I let her come inside on exceptionally bitter nights, and I usually cook her a whole chicken once a week; I've found she prefers Ina Garten's recipe. It's the little things; she is the duchess to my duke at our house on the hill.

I soak up the stars with her by my side, content and eager.

*****

Tay, my youngest cousin, flops on our oversized, squishy chaise chair in the living room. I call to her through the server's window between the kitchen and where she sits.

"Should I do some mashed potatoes? The ones in the bucket thing?"

Her eyes widen with delight. "Yes, do those!"

I laugh and continue mincing garlic in preparation for our dinner. It is a usual Thursday evening, with my Aunt Trella busy bowling on the league for her bank, whilst we cook and fangirl over *The Vampire Diaries*. It's most likely not the show for a nine-year-old, but then again, Taylor isn't your average nine-year-old.

Her father, my Uncle Tom, passed away in February of last year, and it was a sudden blow to the entire family. I was in rehearsal when Trella called to tell me he'd had a massive heart attack, and by the time he'd been found, it was too late to resuscitate him. I was shocked, but my immediate response was for Tay. Losing a parent at such a young age is now an unfortunate event we have in common, and I grieve not only for her father's passing, but that she will grow up without him. It makes for a cheated childhood, I think.

She's bright, and I've never found the need to have child-like conversations with her. From very early on, we have held intelligent, articulate discussions. It's a different brother-ship than I have with Brodie, but it feels similar in that they both need an older, wiser "Bub" to confide in. Someone in the family to listen and remain calm, no matter what the situation.

They're important people in my world, and I'm thankful to be home at this time of their lives. For Tay, we've gotten through the first year without Tom, and her spark is re-igniting; and Brod, without the suppression of a stepmother, is blooming into such a vivacious little woman, it is an honor to witness the transformation. Life is nice on the hill.

"Bub, it's starting! I'll pause it so we can fast forward through commercials!" she calls, jumping up to grab the remote off the Papasan chair.

"Excellent idea!" I holler back. "I'm about to put the chicken in the oven, have a cig, and that should probably give us enough time."

"Yup!" she agrees.

I rinse my hands at the sink and trek to the garage for more wine and a smoke. Tay joins me outside, and we walk the stone path from the house to the barn. The weather is warmer than usual for late March. Avoiding the rose bush, Tay does pirouettes off the path onto a raised peninsula of trees at the edge of our drive. She comes to a stop at the tip and pats the statue head of St. Francis of Assisi. He was here when we bought the place, and overlooks our drive as it winds up the hill to our house. Tay is very fond of St. Francis.

"Oh, St. Francis," she says, her hand resting on his head. "What a beautiful evening."

I chuckle and turn back toward the house.

"Shall we to our vampires?" I ask.

Tay shrieks with laughter and sprints across the yard. I smile, amused, and snuff out my cigarette beside the gazebo. Later tonight, after I've put her to bed, I'll partake in a bowl on this gazebo and enjoy the stars. Tay was right, what a beautiful evening, indeed.

*April 2010*
*Clinton, Missouri*
*23 Years Old*

It is a bright, warm day, with a slight breeze in the air. Birds chirp pleasantly from the pasture as Tay lays sprawled on the grass with Dixie. Brod, Trella, and I lounge on the patio, our feet propped on the table. The trees are beginning to bud, my yard is growing a greener shade of yellow, and I clap my hands, anticipating summer.

"Oh, the weather is getting so nice!" I sing-song. "What should we do for your birthday, girls?"

My Aunt Trella and Brod share the same birthday. Due to my Mom's heart-shaped uterus, a cesarean was required for delivery, and Brod's birth date was planned as the ultimate present. It is a rarity, and the doctors did not discover Mom's condition until I was almost a month late. I like to think that's where my patience with others started.

"I don't know," Brod answers, hidden under large sunglasses and a mane of blonde hair. "I can't believe I'm turning seventeen."

"I can't believe I'm turning forty-one, y'all!" Trella exclaims.

"Well, you don't look it," Brod says.

"Thank you, Brod!" Trella beams.

"It's gonna be hard to top your Dad's fiftieth!" Tay muses, rolling onto her stomach.

"Oh, I know, that was so cool!" I say.

Last week, my Dad celebrated his fiftieth birthday with a magnificent event at our local Elks Lodge. It was planned by Tahnee and my Aunt Dena, who is married to my Dad's brother, Chris. Growing up, I used to call her "mean Aunt Dena," although I don't know why. She's always been kind, growing quite maternal to Brod after Mom died. Chris is the rebel maverick on my Dad's side, who sneaked me packs of cigarettes when I started driving, experiencing my first taste of freedom. He's a riot.

"I don't think I want anything big," Brod decides.

"Me either, Brod," Trella agrees.

"We could just hang out here, per usual, and I'll grill or something," I offer.

"That sounds good," Brod says.

"Works for me!" Trella grins and stretches.

We relax, listening to the sounds of nature. I feel so content and joyful here with them, in this moment. Missing that internship was a blessing in disguise! Things truly *do* happen for a reason; and who would want to miss this?

Eventually, Tay grows bored of laying in the grass and meanders off to the northwest pasture. There is a bucket of apples next to the gate, and she enjoys feeding Tucker and Kate. We have seven equines in total, three horses and four mules. Tucker is my beautiful Sabino, a retired western pleasure show horse; Kate is the family pet and never ridden.

I was not an athletic child growing up, but I made up for it with my horsemanship skills. At the tender age of three, my Dad tied me to a saddle on the back of a mule, and off we rode. While I cannot recall it, I'm sure that's the day I fell in love with trail riding. It's a relationship, developed over time, with its own language and nuances. I have had the privilege of sharing this relationship with two equines: Tucker, of course, and my first mule, Jack.

He was short, round like a barrel, with enormous ears, a dull black coat, and a knotted tail, but I loved him with all my heart. He was the mule my Dad trusted to put me on at such a young age. Jack was what horse folk call "dead broke," which means it was extraordinarily difficult to startle him. He was just super chill, perma-stoned. And although he may not have been much to look at, he was amazingly smart and always knew when I was around, even if he hadn't seen me. I rode him until I turned ten, and it was a grave, dark day in my youth when he disappeared. Grandpa never said it outright, but I'm certain there was a reason I didn't have a chance to say goodbye.

I smile, reminiscing about Jack.

"Where's that j?" Brod asks.

"I've got it in my cigarette pack," I say, flipping them open and retrieving the partially smoked joint we toked on earlier.

"Fire it up," Trella giggles.

I get it smoking, and then pass it to Brod.

"Thank you, sir!" she chortles in a British accent, and pinches the joint from me. She's new to the world of marijuana, and it's hilarious to watch her learn the culture. I don't mind her smoking weed; I rather prefer it over her getting drunk and losing control. And we're both far too vain to become involved in hardcore drugs. Besides, the rest of my family has been smoking it since they were her age, and we're all a perfect mess.

"Have you heard anything else about that series in Fayetteville, Bub?" Trella asks, taking the joint from Brod.

"I'm pretty sure I got it—they're going to meet me in Springfield for a read-thru type thing, and I should know by then if it's not going to work out. But the character is pretty easy, he's the manager of the group, so I'm just flustered a lot. Which can be funny, if I play it a couple of ways."

"You'll get it, Bub," she beams again, luminous when surrounded by her kids.

"And it's filmed in Fayetteville?" Brod asks.

"Yup, the writer and director, Brian, is using his apartment and a couple of places around town to shoot. It's a super small budget, I mean I'm not even getting paid. It's not through Infinite Talent. But it's work, and who knows? Maybe it will turn into something?"

"That's right, you never know!" Trella echoes.

"Well, it sounds like a lot of fun! I can't wait to watch it! It'll be like when you made that movie and we got to see the premiere in Columbia," Brod says.

"Oh, that was so sweet! I wasn't a large part in that, but a good supporting part. I didn't get to go, though, remember? I had a play at Drury—wasn't it shown in an old theatre or something?"

"Yes, it was really cool," Trella says, her eyes wide. Tay must get her wide-eyed excitement from Trella.

I blush and turn toward the pasture.

"This makes me really happy, guys. Talking like this. It makes me feel like I *really will* be an actor."

"Oh, Bub," Trella says sweetly, "even if you're not an actor, we'll still love you!"

The moon is scarcely visible in the dark night sky, but the stars twinkle brightly. After the girls left, I felt bored and busted out the vodka, pouring myself a stout drink. There's a bit of weed left on the living room table, and once I get a strong buzz going, I will put some in my pipe and smoke it, thank you very much. I pull a long drag from my cigarette and wander onto the gazebo, taking a seat in the swing.

It is the ideal place to sit and gaze at our front pastures, split in two by the drive, which snakes up the hill to a thin, circular driveway in front of the house. Three tall oaks grow in the center of the circle drive, providing shade. I sigh peacefully; I love my home.

We bought it a couple of years after my Mom died, with my Dad's *first* replacement wife, Suzie. It was the only good thing that came from my Dad's marriage to her. She was an acutely troubled woman, and very demeaning to Brod, but she picked a damn fine house. It is a ranch home, built in the mid-'70s, made of red brick, and outfitted with white columns. The rooms are wide with tall ceilings and full of windows. It is only two stories: the main floor and the partially finished basement, but it is quite sprawling. My family and I can usually be found in the massive kitchen and sunken living room, though. There is another sunken, formal living room, but it's reserved for Christmas and special occasion photos. We're a family that likes to eat and veg out.

The starlight reflected on the pond is hypnotizing and my mind drifts. Should I be doing more? Should I seriously start to consider a backup plan? I've received auditions through Infinite Talent, but I've yet to book a gig. I'm living at home by the grace of my Dad, and at some point, I'll need to show an income. I wonder: what about regional work? Another drink is required if I'm to ponder further.

Heading to the sliding glass door in the kitchen, I hiccup, trip over a stick, and crash to the ground. My glass goes flying into the grass but doesn't shatter. *I* have busted the hell out of my elbow, pain sears through my arm, and I scream out.

Dixie lopes around the corner, smelling for me.

"I think Bub's had enough to drink, old girl, what about you?" I ask her and step into the kitchen.

In the light, I wince at my gash, smeared with blood, skin, and dirt.

"Great. Lovely."

Walking to the bathroom off the kitchen, I turn on the faucet and clean my wound. Dousing it with peroxide, I cover it with a bandage. My drunk ass belongs in bed, but I should drink water first. And eat a pickle.

*May - July 2010*
*Clinton, Missouri*
*24 Years Old*


"Watching *Pride and Prejudice* again, are you?" Brod quips through the server's window.

"But of course," I answer softly.

It is late, around eleven at night; Brod must be crashing here tonight. She flips lights on, making her way through the kitchen, down the hallway, to the back of the house, where our bedrooms and shared bathroom are. The shower turns on, and I turn back to my movie.

Thirty minutes later, Brod hops into the living room, shower fresh.

"Do you have any weed?" she asks hopefully.

"Yup," I answer.

"Let's go on a smoke drive down the gravel road!"

"Okay!" I say excitedly.

As we make our way down the drive, Brod loads an old sprocket with weed and takes a hit. I switch on music, taking a left. The gravel crackles soothingly under my tires as we cruise down the road, passing the makeshift pipe back and forth. We stop before the abandoned bridge and I reload the bowl.

Brod takes a hit, lost in a daze out of the window. Night air whistles through the trees as Gnarls Barkley breathes *Open Book* through the speakers. We listen in the moonlight.

"I think I just had an out-of-body experience listening to that song," she says, still fixated.

"Yeah?"

"Yeah, it was crazy, Bub! I was standing over there, by that bush, watching myself smoke and, like, when Gnarls Barkley was breathing, I was breathing with him! But it wasn't scary, it was eerie, in a good way."

I guffaw. "Oh my Lanta, you're stoned!"

She turns slowly toward me, a puzzled expression on her face, then erupts in giggles. Deciding we've smoked plenty, I head to the house. Brod bounces her feet and sways her head with the music, flinging her hair around the seat.

"Mm, we've got cereal back home, huh?" she trills.

"And Granny's potato soup!" I exclaim.

She braces herself on the door and gapes at me as though I've told her there's gold hidden in our basement.

"Oh. My. God, Bub! Yes, that's so perfect! *So You Think You Can Dance*, Granny's soup and cereal, and then I'm passing out. Oh, this is so glorious!" she cries, closing her eyes and thanking the heavens.

While she rummages in the pantry, I scroll through our DVR to *So You Think You Can Dance*; season five wrapped last summer and it was the most inspiring TV event we've ever watched.

"Go to Kayla and Kupono, you *know* which one!"

She brandishes a wooden spoon at me through the server's window.

"You're a hot mess right now and I'm loving it! You remind me so much of *me* when I first started smoking," I chortle.

"Monstrously delightful!" Brod squeals, kissing her fingers and exploding them in the air. She's referring to Granny's home-made potato and sausage soup, and I agree wholeheartedly.

"Wait, leave it out, I want some, too," I say, swinging around the small corner between the kitchen and living room.

We munch on crackers while preparing a midnight feast, then sit crisscrossed on the floor in front of the TV, like when we were kids. It was such a good decision, to stay sober tonight. Well, at least from alcohol. Yesterday morning, I battled a hangover sent from the depths of hell and vowed to kick the sauce for a bit.

If I'm being honest with myself, I *was* drinking rather excessively; I have a tendency, when bored, to run to the bottle. Henceforth, I believe I will fare better with the pipe and herb.

"I—am—so—full!" Brod collapses back on the rug and exhales loudly. Blonde hair cascades around her wildly. "Bub, I don't think I can walk to my room," she says seriously, rubbing her stomach. "I ate too much!"

I fall back beside her. "Just walk very slow and very careful, dear. Slow and careful." I sound like an elderly British lady.

She hoists herself up with the aid of our big wooden coffee table, gradually standing.

"Oh, Bub, I can't do it! It hurts!"

I am lost in a fit of laughter and absolutely no help. She cackles, squinting down at me.

"I'm just gonna have to walk hunched over to my room," she says, shuffling up the stair and down the hall. "I'm fucking Quasimodo!" she yells from the dark of our rooms, and I lose control again.

*****

Granny's white truck crests over the hill; I take a quick hit from my bowl, then tuck it away in the end table drawer. Granny knows I smoke weed, but there's no reason to advertise the bowl. She's helping me plant flowers and bushes around the house today. Dad has decided to list the house for sale, and while it breaks my heart, I understand. The recession has been tough on him, but he's persevered. He is a constant source of perseverance and determination.

Around my junior year of college, I began to appreciate my Dad for the man he is. Far from perfect, but a loving, happy-go-lucky, fun-seeking dude. It took a long time for me to remember his carefree playfulness of my youth; it took even longer for me to realize *I* was the one who stopped playing.

Granny steps around the hood of her truck. She has on cutoff work shorts and one of Grandpa's old work shirts; she is radiant.

"Hi, babe!" she says with a wave, walking toward my flowers

and tiny starters: hostas, a rose bush starter, iris buds, a lilac starter, and some marigolds. "These are beautiful, hun."

"Thanks! I think it'll brighten the place up."

"I brought a bag of food for Dixie, should I put it in the garage fridge?"

"Oh, she'll be stoked! Yeah, you can put it in there."

Granny walks to the passenger side and grabs a large, resealable bag full of thinly sliced meats. This is the same food she feeds her two dogs, Sonny and Cher, and Lord help anyone who tries to explain it isn't dog food. Cher was once my sister's, but moved over to Granny's after Brod got her license. I'm extremely confident Cher is satisfied with the deal; Granny has an excellent way of spoiling those she loves.

"Hey, sugar," Granny coos to Dixie, who is wagging and sneezing all over her. "Granny brought you some food, yeah."

Closing the fridge door, Granny claps her hands.

"Where should we start?" she asks, putting her hands on her hips and surveying the yard.

I walk us toward the gazebo. "Let's stand here and look around, and see if any ideas pop out to us."

She follows me along the stone path and I am reminded of yonder days when we'd play "adventure" in the woods behind her house. I would lead the way with a stick, wearing a cape, and feeling fearless with my co-captain, Granny. She has an amazing imagination and can play "make-believe" all day long.

"We could do some irises in the old trough in the alcove between the living room and the patio of Dad's room," I say, gesturing to the back of the house.

"That's a good idea," Granny answers. "And maybe some marigolds over by St. Francis, that'd be nice next to the stone."

"Oh, good job, Granny!"

15

We giggle and take a seat on the swing, gently gliding back and forth.

"Are you sad your Dad's selling it?" she asks softly.

"I am. I really, *really* am. It's not *just* a house to me, it's so much more. It's like the rock of stability for Brod, Tay, Trella, and me. It's just so peaceful, I feel so *content* here. And we've been here for so long, like, where will my home be now?"

Granny rubs my back, soothing me.

"You'll always have my home, hun."

I lean onto her shoulder and let her scratch my head; this has been a source of comfort since before I can remember. A faint breeze blows through the trees, rustling their leaves.

"Well, let's give this old gal a facelift," I say, and Granny chuckles. We rise from the swing and set off.

*****

Dad's truck turns into our drive, hitched to a trailer carrying a tiny green boat. I grin; it will do perfectly for picking yonkapins from our pond. When dried, they're fantastically ugly and cringe-inducing, yet people love to put them in their dried flower arrangements. It is all part of my "make money while still trying to act, but don't get a traditional job" plan. Amazingly, my Dad is supportive.

"We can probably just carry it to the water," he says, stepping out of his truck.

"Okay," I answer and help him unload it near our small dock. "Cool, I'm gonna go grab a knife and some string and start whacking them down."

"There's plenty out there for you," he says, motioning to the pond. It's in our southwest pasture and almost an acre big.

16

"Yup, they go for a little over two bucks each, which is fucking crazy, but cool."

Dad chuckles. "Really? Wow, well you've got a helluva crop!"

We stand side-by-side, taking in the pond, its water lapping softly against the dock. My Dad is giving me a fair amount of time to try and become an actor; I was worried he would make remarks about me getting a job or going to school for nothing, but that was rude of me to think. I was projecting my fear onto him, for he's nothing but supportive, understanding, and hopeful that my dream comes true. I am immensely thankful my Dad has always accepted me, constantly easing my doubts. Frightened, I attempted to dodge him after coming out as gay, but he blew up my phone until I finally answered, my stomach in knots. Ultimately, we had an average, boring conversation, and it was one of the most moving, beautiful conversations of my life. It meant nothing had changed. I'm also acutely aware that not every individual is guaranteed a relationship with their Dad after coming out, but my Dad's love for me is too fierce to be doused by something as insignificant as who I sleep with. We're more than that; we've been through more than that.

He shuffles his feet and turns to his truck.

"Tahnee and I are heading to South Carolina for a week or so, taking the RV."

"Oh wow, you guys are going there a lot lately, huh? Working on a big deal?"

"It could be," he answers. "I hope it is."

"Me, too," I say genuinely. "Well, I'll just be here picking yonkapins."

We snicker and he walks to his truck, backs out, and waves goodbye. I wave him off, then turn and stroll up the drive to the house. There is a box of Crisp White Wine calling my name, I do believe. A few sips of the vino and I shall slice some yonkapins.

I scream, beating the side of the boat furiously with my ore. A snake is bathing on one of the lily pads where I'm chopping, and I almost didn't notice.

"Out, devils! Away, serpents! Be gone with you! Go back whence you came, trollops of hell!"

Slapping the water with the ore, I give another forceful holler, hoping all my noise and commotion will frighten any lurkers hidden in the shadows. Satisfied, I sit down and light a cigarette.

"Shit, that was intense," I reflect, unscrewing the lid of my water bottle, which is actually full of wine.

My efforts are paying off, however. An hour's work and I have collected forty-three yonkapins. They are lined up neatly in the front of the boat, each roughly three feet long. Having sailed a small portion of the pond, I anticipate at least six or seven hundred in total. At two bucks a pop, that's not an ugly penny.

I sizzle out my cigarette in the water and throw the butt on the floor of the boat. The sun is beginning its rest for the evening, and I need to shower, start a load of laundry, then cook Dixie and me some dinner. I think we'll have lasagna tonight, and I'll start a roast for tomorrow; it's Thursday and that will be easy for Tay and I to munch on while we watch *The Vampire Diaries*.

*****

"So what exactly are we doing with them, Bub?" Tay asks, standing amid the yonkapin-covered garage floor.

"Well, I need to hang them upside down to dry and harden, which should take about a week. So we need to tie string right

18

above where I snipped them, and then hang them from the ceiling rails in here and the barn. I'll just leave the garage door open while they're drying."

"How many do you have now?"

"I think there's about two hundred in here and a hundred in the barn. I've still got to get more from the pond, once they're a bit bigger. Here's some string and scissors, I'm going to the barn to get those sorted out and ready."

"Okay," she chirps and sets off to work.

Entering through the barn's side door, I pick up my loaded pipe from the shelf. I must have had a strong buzz going the other night, for these are messily flung over the floor, shelves, and lawnmower. Organizing them on the floor, I smack my lips, thirsty.

Finding my water bottle of wine, I take a pull from it, then lift the utility door and let the light in. This is *not* the work I thought I would be doing this summer. I *thought* I would be shooting commercials and photo spreads for businesses around Kansas City, but I've yet to get work through Infinite Talent.

It's not their fault, though. I'm given plenty of auditions, I just can't seem to book anything; my voice is too high and feminine, making it hard to believe me as rugged or manly. I sound gay, and it blocks me from jobs. I've tried using only my lower register, but I come off flat and dull. I can't win, and it's starting to weigh on me. While I've always embraced being gay, I've never felt it was my defining characteristic, yet I'm so often judged by this one facet of my being. It is so baffling to me.

Taking another gulp of wine, I begin clustering bunches together in the gravel outside of the barn. I spot Tay working diligently in the garage and smile. She's happy to do about anything, as long as we're hanging out.

After she finishes her task, Tay joins me in the barn and we finish up, then head in for dinner. As we're walking up to the house, she glances at the mass of yonkapins hanging in the garage.

"That's going to look really creepy in the dark," she giggles.

*August 2010*
*Clinton, Missouri*
*24 Years Old*

'90s Alternative Hits blare from the speakers of the TVs in the living room and kitchen. With my large wine glass, I amble from room to room, pausing every few steps to stop and weep. It is overly dramatic and flamboyant, but it's how I feel. The house has been on the market for a couple of months, and I have a sinking suspicion it will soon sell. And a part of my heart will be hacked from my chest and discarded in the dirt, to bleed out and shrivel in the sun.

I hiccup and giggle, amused at my penchant for melodramatics. At the core of it, though, lives the truth: selling this house will be akin to losing a family member. I have strong emotional investments here, and I'm not eager to have those split open. But it *will* happen, and I need to prepare myself, thus I'm saying my goodbyes.

As I step down the stair into our formal living room, I have nostalgia for Christmas and the warmth of my family. Gathering in this room, Tay sorts presents to each person before the frenzy of unwrapping begins. We laugh over gag gifts and fawn over treasured ones. Granny's Christmas feast waits in the kitchen, and the merriment spills into our sunken living room and dining room.

Smiling, I take a seat on the ledge of the hall and cross my legs. This was the first room of the house in which I smoked a cigarette; my family took an RV road trip the summer before my Freshman year of college, and I stayed back to work at Walmart. They were gone for two weeks, and in that first week, I had a glass of wine, watched *The Four Feathers,* and smoked a cigarette.

It's odd how some memories can be so clear, while others are lost in the void. Perhaps I felt independent for the first time, knowing I was a young man about to embark on his college education. Whatever the reason, I spent the remainder of their trip cleaning, spraying air freshener, and fanning the open windows. My brief moment of rebellious independence turned out to be more worrisome than I'd expected.

I walk downstairs to the basement, sucking down my wine as though I've just run a marathon. The creak of the stairs comforts me and I open the door to our unfinished portion. Six tie-dye shirts lay on plastic, spread between boxes of books and old clothes. I gasp.

"I completely forgot I made these!"

A week or so ago, I got a wild hair and decided to make the girls and me tie-dye shirts to wear to the lake and pool. I believe I purchased a fifth of vodka that night, as well, which explains why they've been abandoned down here.

"Cute," I say, looking them over. Two are pink, magenta, and yellow, two are blue and green, and the last two are a combination of all the colors. Not much of a theme, but at least there are options.

Sloshing up the stairs, I decide to hop on Craigslist and browse local auditions. I have one gig booked for this month, but other than that I'm dry. Although, I'm not sure if I'd even call it a gig; I'll be repping for a phone company at an IndyCar race. Jean reached out to me and said a local phone company had browsed the agency's website for attractive young models and requested me, among a few others. I'm stoked and flattered, but it's not exactly acting.

Filling my wine glass to the brim, I shuffle to the dining room and fire up my laptop, hopeful a jewel awaits me online.

*October 2010*
*Clinton, Missouri*
*24 Years Old*

The leaves have begun to litter our patio, and I enjoy crunching them under my feet. Yawning deeply, I stretch, greeting the day. Morning sun peeks over the tree line; I inhale the damp scent of dew, absorbing fall. These are some of my favorite days, cool crisp mornings followed by the last of the summer's mid-day warmth.

Dixie snoozes in her doggie palace, nestled on a cushion. I take a seat near the edge of the patio and light a cigarette. I'm prepping for an audition in Kansas City tomorrow and have spent the last few days tanning, cleansing, and drinking gallons of water. My skin *is* refreshed, but I'd love a box of wine.

The gig is for an insurance company, and I say a silent prayer that, for once, I will be chosen. There's minimal dialogue, my character spends most of the thirty-second spot confused, and I've made a funny bit out of the script. Of course, forty other guys probably feel the same way.

Gradually and poignantly, I am concluding that an acting career isn't in my stars. It was a dream, a creative outlet, but nothing more. A delusion, perhaps, for why would I expect a gay boy from the sticks of Missouri to make such a splash in the world?

"Probably not the pep talk to give yourself a day before an audition," I whisper, exhaling smoke.

Dixie hears me and rises from her sleeping quarters. She sneezes, sniffs the air, and then plods over to where I sit.

"What're you doing, girl?" I chortle to her, scratching her neck and ears. She licks my neck and I rest my head on her back.

Birds sing to one another in the distance and I watch the sunrise. It is beautiful, the simplicity of the morning, and a sense of hearth and peace melts over me. Maybe I'm not supposed to make a splash, but I sure can appreciate the majesty of Mother Nature.

Chuckling to myself, I pat Dixie on the back, heading to the garage for sunscreen. I'd like to be a shade more tan before going on camera tomorrow.

*December 2010*
*Clinton, Missouri*
*24 Years Old*

"What channel should I put it on?" Brod hollers from the living room.

"Just a Christmas one," I yell back, standing at the basement door and assessing the stairs. There are twelve of them, but they're not too steep and the ceiling is high; how in the hell did Brod and I finagle the tree downstairs last year? We kept it intact, but for the life of me, I can't remember how.

"There's like fifty of them!" she says exasperated.

"Is there a '90s one?"

"Yup!" she chirps and I hear Mariah through the speakers.

Brod bounds through the kitchen to the door where I stand.

"What are you doing?" she asks in an aristocratic British accent.

"How did we get the tree down there last year?"

"Oh, my gosh!" she doubles over with laughter, in stitches. "You don't remember?"

I stare at her, grinning and lost. "I guess I don't."

"We were so stoned, and you kept yelling 'pivot' like Ross and it kept falling apart. We made it, like, halfway down, and then you gave up and tossed it the rest of the way! We put it back together after that."

"Oh, yeah! Yeah, that's right! Well, shit."

We trod down the stairs to the far corner, where we've left the tree to stand for a year. It is eight feet tall, with multicolored pre-lit lights and frost on the edges. Brod and I purchased it four years ago, and I love it. We've kept our collection of ornaments on it for nearly three years, adding a few here and there. Mainly, we use the decorations Mom displayed when we were kids. New pieces were added by Granny and step-wives over the years to create a smattering of Christmas cheer.

"I think I hear Trella and Tay!" Brod says, and I hear footsteps upstairs.

"We're down here," I call up to them.

The stairs moan as they make their way down. Peeling out of their coats, they lay them on the bed by the laundry area. Tay's cheeks are rosy from the cold.

"Bub didn't remember getting the tree down here last year," Brod teases, swinging open the door to a side room where we store the boxes of festivity. It is dark and old-timey, reminding me of a saloon door in the Old West.

"We threw it," Trella chortles. "But it held up okay."

There is another round of giggles.

"I think Tay can carry the top and I'll carry the bottom, it's connected by the lights, but we can separate it enough to carry it," I suggest.

After hauling the tree and Christmas boxes upstairs, Brod, Trella, and I step to the garage for a quick smoke. We leave Tay in charge of popping popcorn as we're going to craft several of our own pieces this year.

"So has Dad said anything more about real estate school?" Brod asks, taking a seat in a camping chair near the window.

"Yeah, I'll start in a couple of weeks. But I also applied for a bank in town, UBT. Leanne works there, and thinks I'd be a great drive-thru teller. Trella was actually the one who told me about it," I say.

"I think it's an excellent idea!" Trella says encouragingly, lighting a fat joint.

"Besides, it's winter and there's not much auditioning going on right now," I offer.

It is not my dream to become a real estate agent or work for a bank, but desperate times call for desperate measures. In all fairness, my Dad has been extremely lenient and patient, waiting for my big break. Some extra money will be nice, too.

"And it's good hours," Trella says.

"This is true, no crazy schedule," I agree.

"But it's just for now," Brod says sweetly.

Melissa Etheridge plays through the door and Trella rocks her head.

"It's my girl!" she sings, rushing into the house.

I finish my cigarette and sigh. I haven't actively sought out an acting job in two months, and my contract with Infinite Talent expires in three months, unless I'm renewed; it is doubtful they will offer to take me on for another year, as I've only secured two jobs through the agency. However, I'm not sure entering the corporate world is a safe decision for my soul.

Shaking off my thoughts, I round the corner to the kitchen and find Brod with a handful of popcorn, and Trella scooping out of the bag.

"I'd rather eat the decorations, too," I say, digging in.

Every light in the house blazes: it feels bright, warm, and merry. My employment situation can be damned, I'm enjoying this Christmas! Its spirit is rampant in this moment, as we bop to the music and hang up old ornaments. It's almost as if Mom is with us, smiling and laughing over what would look best and where. I am reminded of the Christmas before she died, when she danced around the house draped in garland with Brod and me. We played disco music, oddly, and rattled the railings of our staircase; it is one of my fondest memories.

Now is a time to be happy, a time to celebrate and revel with my family. Fiddly-dee, I will work on grown-up problems tomorrow.

*August 2011*
*Clinton, Missouri*
*25 Years Old*

Shutting off the engine, I sit in Martha, letting the silence envelop me. Flicking my tie around absentmindedly, I snap off my name tag. It is my eighth month at UBT, and I've been offered a promotion: to float between two local branches as their personal banker. It is a pay raise with a commission incentive, and I am thankful for the opportunity.

Banking turned out to be a much more challenging and exciting job than I anticipated, although I could not have picked anything further from my degree. From scripts to balance sheets, late-night rehearsals to early morning opening procedures, I am quite out of my element. It's fulfilling, albeit I feel a profound lack of creativity or inspiration. I try to refrain from imagining my life as a banker indefinitely. It is a daunting and bleak thought, for me. I find adhering to a routine stifling and wonder how long I can keep up the charade of being content and satisfied.

Sighing, I crawl out of Martha and go inside to change and pour an adult beverage. I'll smoke a cig, sip my juice, and water the plants. Which usually turns into watering the trees and St. Francis, as well. It's been so hot lately, and I feel bad for him, baking in the heat all day. I try and find the positives in my life, and with the orange juice and vodka, Daddy's helpful juice, I'm usually able to see a silver lining. This is a transitional period of my life, and that's fine. I'll weather this storm, surely. With my juice, I'll be a-okay.

# 2

# Electronic Daisy Carnival

*April 2012*
*Clinton, Missouri*
*25 Years Old*

Pausing *Downton Abbey*, I step softly to my phone charging on the wall outlet near the TV. Careful of my neck brace, I lean down and see a message from my best friend from college, Anne. Grinning, I read it with excitement:

*"Dearest Lassie of The Glen! All is a go for EDC and your birthday—I'll call later to go over the details! Love, Lassie of The Gale."*

Using my pointer fingers, I do a happy dance in the air. My neck is healing well, and feels much stronger, but there's no reason to push it. Honestly, I'm lucky to be standing, at all.

A little over a month ago, I flipped my SUV, Patty, end-over-end eight miles from my house. Rounding a curve, I lost control and flew off the edge, missing a giant propane tank by fifteen yards. I suppose that's what happened, for I remember very little. There's a brief memory of sitting in an ambulance and seeing Trella, and then being strapped to a gurney wearing a halo-type thing in the life flight.

It wasn't until the early hours of the morning, when the obscene amount of vodka coursing through my system subsided, that I became coherent. Trella was with me, feeding me ice chips and waiting in stunned silence. At the time, the doctors were not sure if I would need surgery to fuse the three fractured vertebrae or a couple of months in a neck brace. Fortunately, my neurologist prescribed the brace, with two months of easy rest and recuperation.

My recovery time has been quite enjoyable, definitely aided by the hydrocodone bottle in my name. I've caught up on the latest TV and movies while cooking myself delicious and nutritious feasts. Based on the circumstances, I have abstained from drinking any form of alcohol since my wreck; my body and mind needed a break from the sauce. Naturally, my family is thrilled with my decision; in turn, I am pleased and bolstered by their support.

However, I have no intention of refraining from my beloved vodka indefinitely. Once I'm healed and back on track, I think it's perfectly acceptable to drink again, albeit much more responsibly. In retrospect, I can see how *insanely* blessed I am to have walked away from that accident, hurting only myself. Next time, God forbid there is a next time, I could hurt someone else, and *that* thought is haunting. I must cease to drink and drive. It is foolish, selfish, and dangerous. Never mind the fact I am facing DUI charges, as well. This makes my second DUI in two years, and I fear jail time is imminent.

I dash out a reply to Anne and resume my regularly scheduled programming:

*"Dearest Lassie of The Gale, I quiver with anticipation! Please let's chat and sup soon! Love, Lassie of The Glen."*

*June 2012*
*Las Vegas, Nevada*
*26 Years Old*

"Enjoy your trip to Vegas! It was fun partying with you!"

I unfasten the seat belt and grab my backpack from underneath the seat in front of me. Standing, I realize how much I drank on the flight. Rather than feeling sluggish or numb, though, I feel alive. Euphoric. It's my first time visiting Las Vegas as an adult and I don't plan on sleeping until my return flight.

Disembarking from the plane, I anticipate meeting Anne and her Dallas friends. I've met two before: Kole, cute and gay, with dark eyes and hair; and Grant, handsome but definitely not my type. Nor Anne's. Poor guy, maybe he'll catch a break in Vegas.

Grant is in charge of procuring the drugs, mainly ecstasy and some coke. I prefer weed mixed with vodka, but figure I'll have at least one drug-fueled night. It seems the natural thing to do when in Vegas. Maybe I'll make "drug night" my second night; I'll be tired and in need of some pick-me-ups.

As I head toward their arrival gate, I wonder how many of the crowd are here for the epic event that is Electronic Daisy Carnival. I've experienced a few raves in my time, but nothing as gigantic as EDC: a three-day extravaganza of electronic music complete with carnival rides at the Las Vegas Speedway. Quite the event to celebrate my twenty-sixth trip around the sun. It's a planned surprise in that I only know the location and the shows.

"Lassie!"

I hear the faux British lilt before I can place her.

"Lassie, where are—oh there you are! Matilda, darling, how was your flight?" I ask Anne in my own mock British accent.

"Oh, Jeremy Fisher! 'Twas devilish. And yours?"

"I drank," I answer with a mischievous grin. "But where are the others?"

"Kole is grabbing his luggage, and Grant's in the bathroom. I think the plan was for us to get in line for a taxi."

It's been almost a year since I've seen Anne and she's as beautiful as ever. She's wearing her hair longer, and it suits her very nicely.

"Is it just Kole and Grant? I thought Marissa and Leah were coming, too?"

"Yeah, I'm not sure what happened there. Marissa called Grant and said they weren't going to be able to make it but that's about all I know. It's always very mysterious with that gang."

"Must be a trust fund thing," I say as Kole saunters over. He winks at us and pulls three airplane bottles from his tote.

"Thirsty?"

Las Vegas is bright and hot, the air heavy with booze, prostitute perfume, and grease. Yet I have a profound feeling of being right where I'm supposed to be as we walk down Fremont Avenue. The energy around me burns with joy and lowered inhibitions; I'm soaking up as much of it as possible. I find the glittering chaos alluring and calming.

"I'm thinking we should check-in, smoke a blunt, eat some dinner, and then see what Vegas has to offer," Grant says as we arrive at a hotel called The Golden Nugget.

"Is this our hotel?"

I gawk at the flashy decor, impressed.

"We'll be here for the first two nights, then we're staying at The Paris," Anne answers, making her way toward the swinging doors.

"The Paris? Oh, wow! This is a fancy trip, guys!" I don't hide the amazement from my voice. They have gone all out for my birthday and I'm truly appreciative.

As Kole and Grant check-in, Anne and I stop at the lobby bar to order Manhattans.

"So Kole is super into you, you know?" Anne says, smirking.

"Yeah? I mean, he *is* cute, but after Pete, I'm not sure I want to do the whole long-distance relationship thing again. But, I dunno, maybe we could test the waters and see where it goes."

"I mean, I'm sure he's down."

"Oh, he'll be down," I chuckle, deciding to change the subject. "Was Grant able to find everything?"

"Yes, thank God! I still can't *believe* he flew with it all, I was so nervous! But it was necessary. There's quite a bit of E and some good weed, but never enough coke."

"Amen," I agree.

*****

Springing out of bed the next morning, I step silently to the bathroom and immediately take a shot of vodka. I was clever last night and placed it on the sink before everyone fell asleep, knowing I would be the first one awake and in need of a buzz to kill the hangover. Turning on the shower, I take another swig and replay last night. After our blunt and dinner, we went zip-lining down the strip, followed by bar-hopping. My last coherent memory happened around 1:30 in the morning. Checking my phone, I see that it's 9:28; perhaps I got more sleep than expected.

Stepping into the warm water, I hear the bathroom door open.

"I just have to pee."

It's Kole. Did we hook up last night? A memory flashes in my mind, but I can't grasp it.

"Have a shot, did ya?" he asks, and I hear him pissing.

"I did. One. I's firsty. Wanna grab some breakfast?" I counter, not wanting to elaborate on the fact I'm already drinking.

"Sure, can I jump in there with you before we go?"

"Yeah, but no grab-ass, you hear? I've got a very important meeting and I shan't be late!"

Kole and I stroll down Fremont Avenue, and I notice how different it seems in the sunlight. Everything appears sharper without the glare of neon lights. With fewer people, the sidewalks feel more open, too. The air is already exploding with heat and I'm glad I had a few sips of vodka; I'll be able to eat breakfast, which will help me pace myself throughout the day. Tonight is our first night of shows, and the plan is to drop some E before Benny Benassi.

"How about here? I bet they have good beer," Kole says, pointing toward Hennesey's Tavern.

"That'll do."

The tavern is fairly empty and we choose a seat on their shaded patio. Kole orders a dark, disgusting beer, and I settle for the house Bloody Mary with a dash of vinegar.

"Are you excited for tonight?" Kole asks, flipping through the menu.

"I am! I feel like it's going to be a lot more exciting than Lights All Night since it's an open venue."

Kole laughs. "Yeah, Lights All Night wasn't the greatest first experience for you. How much E did you take that night?"

"Oh, wow, I guess I had forgotten about all that! Yes, that was terrible. I'm not sure, three or four probably."

I shudder, remembering my first rave. I had flown to Dallas to party with Anne and her trust fund gang for a two-night rave. The entire week before I could hardly focus at work from sheer excitement. Anne had found a connect for primo E, and I was dying to try some. I had dropped it once in college, with my friend Sarah, however, I think it was speed, as all I did was walk circles in her boyfriend's apartment for five hours. Not exactly the high I had been expecting. Unfortunately, my second encounter was none the better.

At the beginning of the night, I had taken one pill, as Anne assured me that was plenty. However, two hours later, I still felt sober as a lark, so I popped another. And another, thirty minutes later. Since everyone around me was rolling their balls off, I naturally assumed my DNA did not allow for me to get high from ecstasy. I was wrong. During the last set of the show, it hit hard. The first hour was glorious: I put vapor rub on my shoulders and finally understood what it meant to *become* the music and lights. I was *at one* with the moment. It soured quickly, though. I spent the remainder of the night, and most of the next day, hovering three feet beside my body. I had no thoughts or feelings, I was simply existing. No more than four or five words escaped my lips that day.

"Don't worry," Kole says, bringing me back. "If you don't feel it after the first one, we'll just drink and smoke and do coke."

I giggle. "First world problems."

After finishing our breakfast and another round of drinks, Kole and I head back to The 'Nug. I was careful to eat the perfect amount, just enough to keep me going but not enough to get in the way of my drinking. A nice vodka glow cocoons me as we walk, and I'm thankful I asked for a double on my last Bloody Mary.

"You know, I think I may have to pass out for a bit. We've got a long night ahead of us," I say, watching a man zoom across the zip-line.

"That's probably a good idea. And you know Anne will sleep until four or so, she and Grant played Black Jack until the wee hours."

"Oh did they? I had no idea! When did I turn in? And was I okay?"

"Yeah, you were fine," Kole laughs. "I think we went to bed a little before three."

"Cool. Well, shall we to the suite, then?" I ask.

"We shall," he smiles.


I'm in the bathroom with my vodka bottle again. Having slept off my Bloody Mary's from earlier, I was in need of something to wet my whistle. Anne and Kole are at dinner, and Grant is hooked on the slots; I have the suite to myself.

I call it a suite, but in reality, it's an overly large hotel room with a half-wall divider and three queen beds. The bathroom is luxurious, though: there are marble his and her sinks, and a walk-in shower with a waterfall head. A painting hangs behind the toilet, and I believe it is supposed to be of a surreal, sunny sky, but reminds me of a pelican dancing ballet. He is named Chesterfield McIntosh, and I've asked him to refrain from judgment regarding my drinking.

I take two more shots, salute Chesterfield McIntosh, and get in the shower. I don't think it would be wise for me to drink my usual amount, the ecstasy should be enjoyed on its own merits. Besides, I'm sure there will be many blunts to smoke before the show starts.

I'm pulling on my shirt as Anne and Kole arrive back from dinner, looking well-rested and fed.

"Oh, Lassie, what a delightful shirt," Anne says dreamily, her British lilt in its lower register.

"Why thank you, Lassie! How was dinner?"

"Lovely. Absolutely lovely. Now I shall scrub my ass!"

Kole giggles from the other side of the room. "You two talk crazy to each other! I always forget about the 'lassie.'"

"Yes, yes," Anne says absentmindedly, grabbing her bag and making for the bathroom. "Let's do drugs in an hour."

"Let's," I say.


The line for our bus has two pixies, an elf, and around eight or nine go-go dancers. I stare around numbly, feeling very stoned and mildly drunk. We took our happy pills fifteen minutes ago, and figure it will start to take effect while we're en route. The bus will take us from Fremont Avenue to the Las Vegas Speedway. In the center of the track, they have placed several stages, carnival rides, and other attractions. As to what the other attractions could be, I do not know, although I'm mightily excited to find out.

"This way, Lassie," Anne beckons, and I'm present again.

Moving toward the bus doors, I hear Nicki Minaj's *Starships* booming through its speakers. It is the perfect soundtrack for the perfect moment. I take a seat in the middle of the bus next to Anne and move to the music. I can't help myself and it takes over.

"Lassie, Lassie, *Lassie!*" I say softly.

Anne sways next to me, grinning. We didn't choose to dress extravagantly; it's much more enjoyable to roam the crowds, outfit-seeing, than it is to keep up with a costume. She wears a black tank with dark jean shorts and I have on a white v-neck and blue shorts. Another lesson I learned from Lights All Night was to wear closed-toe, comfortable shoes. Anne and I have both purchased disposable show-shoes.

I sit back and listen to the hum of the bus around me, eager for the night's festivities to consume me.

Entering the gates, I can feel the E beginning to spread throughout my body. It's as if a golden river is being poured over me: I feel tingly, bubbly, and radiant. As I snake my way down the stairs with the crowd, I clasp Anne's hand.

"Oh, pigeons," I whisper, "I'm about to be really, *really* high."

The sun is setting over the stands as we meander around the attractions, which are glorious, old-fashioned carnival booths. I am considering a ring toss game when I hear Grant roar.

"Swings!"

I turn and spot the cause for his excitement. A massive, merry-go-round of swings sparkles brightly, its neon bulbs and mirrors twinkling to the beats. Our wrist bands provide us with unlimited rides during the shows, and we make our way toward them as if being called home.

Kole and I take two swings near the front, while Grant and Anne find a pair one row back. I'm surprised by the number of empty seats and hope we can take more than one turn. We begin to move and I lean back, watching as stages, rides, and people slowly sail by. I'm not sure which artist is playing, but they've drawn a writhing crowd, and their bubble show is mesmerizing, as though I'm chasing sound bubbles as we spin. I am definitely peaking, and it is unlike anything I have ever felt before. The lights and sounds throb around me, and I feel weightless and dreamy.

"I think I've found the meaning of life," Kole says beside me, his sunglasses still on.

"I'm listening," I answer, holding my arms out to fly.

"Well, it's all about experience, isn't it? Like, why go through life and not try all that you can? So I figure this is a very heightened experience, yeah? I mean, obviously, we're on drugs, so there's that. But even if we weren't, we're still super overstimulated, right? Light shows, beats, people. This, right here, this moment, is the meaning of life."

He's quiet after this, and we swing a few rotations in silence.

"I think you're right, Kole," I say, looking out over the rave. "If I've only got a limited amount of time on this earth, I'd like to spend it in moments like these."

I glide under a dome decorated with small, blinking lights set to the rhythm of Benny Benassi. His stage isn't far, and I settle myself down to watch the spectacle. Having taken another happy pill, I can maintain the sensation of floating by holding very still. I pause here for a while, hovering between space and time, then decide I'm tired of floating and move through the crowd. There are only a few hours left of tonight's festivities, and the masses aren't showing any signs of slowing down. All around me people are dancing in a frenzied, EDM vibe that seems both exhausting and exhilarating. I never can tell if they're able to keep up this stamina from their love of the music or drugs. Probably drugs.

I hear laughter around me, and I can absorb the magnificent sound bubbles of joy. The energy tonight is shinny and infectious. So *this* is what a rave is supposed to be. My Dallas friends weren't kidding, E stands for epic. I have been elevated to an epic echelon, and it's eclipsing any other experience before it. Raucous laughter overtakes me and I spin circles, ecstatic.

*****

A fan blows on me as I wake in our hotel room. I am not in a bed, though. Rather, I've made a pallet on the floor with extra pillows and blankets. I raise up and look around, wondering why I didn't sleep in my bed. I see Anne sleeping in her bed, and Grant in his, but there is no sign of Kole. We were sharing a bed, and I notice I didn't use any of our pillows or blankets as they're still neatly made. The plot thickens.

I move around the room as quietly as possible, trying to find my phone and piece together the early morning hours. The shows ended right before sunrise, and we caught a bus back to Fremont Avenue shortly after. Grant had the brilliant idea of doing a bit of coke before boarding to continue our revelry. As the bus ride is my last memory, I'm assuming we did continue, and with plenty of alcohol.

I find my phone, the time is 4:47 in the afternoon. I'm grateful I don't feel hungover or weird, however, we need to move quickly if we want to pre-party before tonight's show. I clear my throat, walking to Anne's bed.

"Lassie, dear, wake up," I say gently, and squeeze her arm. She breathes deeper.

"Lassie, you needs must wake up."

She opens one eye. "Water."

I smirk and grab her a glass of water.

"What time is it?" Anne asks.

"Almost five at night."

"Oh, my God, it's almost five?" I hear Grant say hoarsely from his bed. "Shit, we better hurry up!"

He jumps out of bed and sprints for the bathroom wearing only his boxer briefs. I raise my eyebrow at Anne, drinking her water, and she winks.

"Oh 'twas crisp and nourishing," she says, smacking her lips.

I stretch out on her bed, staring up at the ceiling.

"Lassie," Anne starts, "what would you say to hanging around Vegas tonight? Just you and I? We can eat dinner somewhere nice, my treat, and then gamble or see a show or something?"

"You know, Lassie, I think that is a fine idea."


We have chosen Hakkasan in the MGM Grand for our birthday dinner date. A very posh restaurant, it has a black and blue motif, while the seating and walls are a merge of Eastern and Western decor. Our booth is bathed in bluish-gray light and secluded. Anne orders martinis with three olives.

"Do you perhaps know why I was sleeping on the floor this afternoon?" I ask, perusing the menu. The food is Cantonese and the descriptions sound delicious.

"You went up to the room before the rest of us, and you were afraid Kole was going to come back and try to fool around. You pulled me aside and told me you were going to make a pallet. I think Kole heard but wasn't upset, he ended up finding someone else to entertain him."

"Right on," I say. "That's good, I was a wasted Wendy last night and needed to sleep. But I had so many epic moments.

It was a really moving night, honestly. It's like for a minute, I had life figured out, but then I forgot the secret when I woke up this morning."

"Lassie, I know. I was under the dome last night, and I had this really beautiful emotional experience. I just felt so much self-love, you know?"

I know exactly what Anne is talking about. Last night's combination of music, lights, and drugs left quite an imprint on me.

"It was really healing, actually," I begin. "I mean it was sensory overload but I think that helped."

Anne nods her agreement. "I feel like rolling has helped me grow as a person. Obviously, it's not something to be overindulged in, but I think microdosing could have its benefits."

We spend the remainder of dinner talking about life, purpose, and hopes. It's easy to talk like this with Anne, for we have always been on the same plane. As we're finishing our meal, I order us two double shots of vodka. Anne responds with a devilish grin.

"Grant gave me a bag before they left for the show, it's got *several* bumps for us!"

I gasp. "This is excellent news!"

"Here," she cups the baggie and a compact mirror in my hand with a wink. "I've thought of everything. Go do a line in the bathroom while I pay for dinner and then I'll do one after."

"Oh, Lassie," I say, rising from my seat, "I feel so classy and shit doing coke! And you paying for dinner! Fancy as hell!"

Anne poses, rock 'n roll, and I make a bee-line for the men's room. The handicapped stall is unoccupied so I close the door, pull out the compact with the coke, grab my license, and break up a nice, fat line. Within a few moments, I'm humming my way back to our table with a feeling of delight and invincibility only cocaine can provide.

"Your turn," I say, passing the goods to Anne.

Fifteen minutes later, we are walking down the main strip of Las Vegas, elevated on expensive vodka and Dallas coke. We have purposefully avoided making any specific plans, as years ago we discovered some of our most memorable nights were those that happened organically.

"Shall we go watch the fountain display at Aria?" Anne asks, absentmindedly touching her nose.

I stop dead in my tracks and turn to Anne.

"Lassie, I just realized something. We've evolved! Remember when we used to throw up *every time* we did coke? We didn't tonight! You scratching your nose just reminded me!"

Anne takes a sharp breath. "You're right! And we didn't last night, either. I hadn't realized! Maybe we should find somewhere and do a little more, to celebrate?"

"And take shots!"

It doesn't take long before I spy with my coke eye a bar. I motion for Anne to follow, confident we can do the quick change with the compact again.

"You go first this time," I say as we enter, and she disappears to the ladies' room.

The cooler temperature of the bar is refreshing and I watch as people dump their coins into flashing, dinging machines. Of all my many vices, gambling is not one. I require instant gratification *every* time, which a slot machine cannot guarantee. Drugs and booze are better suited for my type.

Anne breezes up to me and lays her clutch on the bar counter. I place my hand on top of it, turn on my heel, and weave through the crowd to the restroom. We do this with no more than brief eye contact and a swift nod.

This bathroom is more crowded than the last, with only one stall open. I take my bump and check my phone: it's 10:30. The night is still young and it is exhilarating.

As I return from freshening up, I notice Anne has ordered shots with a double vodka backer.

"You read my mind, I worked up a powerful thirst from all that walking."

"Lassie," Anne says, "let's finish these drinks and then go to Aria. I feel like the fountains will be life-changing."

I raise my glass in approval. "Lead the way, I have no fucking clue where we're at."

Anne and I stumble our way to Aria and stand gazing at their hypnotic fountains. Streams of water leap, twirl, arch and collide, illuminated in colors of blue, purple, and green. We are in an ideal state of mind for such a display. I give Anne a droopy glance and realize her interest is held by something else entirely. A group of twenty-somethings stands in a circle not far from us, talking animatedly and blowing smoke in the air. I catch a whiff of marijuana.

"Oh, Lassie, they've caught my interest, too. Shall we introduce ourselves?"

Without waiting for her answer, I begin walking over. Perhaps it's the mixture of intoxicants, but it feels like a very solid idea. There are three in total, two girls and a lanky guy. I find no reason to be cautious.

"Hello, tree friends," I introduce myself. "My friend and I were wondering where you came upon such a delicacy?"

They look to one another, then to Anne and I, assessing.

Sensing no threat, a girl on the left answers. She's shorter, with bouncy auburn hair and a toothy grin.

"The streets, man. You guys wanna smoke some of this?"

"I thought you'd never ask," Anne answers coyly.

Our group of vagrants moves to a shaded area, hidden from the public by decorative landscaping, and forms a circle, passing the spliff.

"Are you in for EDC?" the guy asks, tall and slim. He has shaggy brown hair and sky blue eyes.

"We are," I say. "Just skipping the show tonight to see Vegas."

"Us, too!" the other girl squeaks. She's of average height and build, but sounds strangely tiny, a bit like Minnie Mouse. I suppress a grin.

"I'm Anne," she says and hands the spliff to me.

It is a potent strain of weed and rolled very nicely, with a hint of lavender.

"I'm Jacob, Emma," he says, pointing to the shorter of the two, "and Rea."

"I'm Charlie," I pass the spliff to Rea. "Very nice to meet you guys. What are your plans for tonight?"

"We're going to see where the night takes us," Emma answers with a saucy smile. "You two care for some drinks?" she indicates Anne and me.

"That sounds lovely," Anne answers in her faux British lilt. There is a moment of confused silence followed by an eruption of laughter. We have grown accustomed to this response.

I sit alone on the balcony, smoking a cigarette. I'm fairly certain smoking isn't allowed, yet it's nearly three in the morning, and I figure most people are either asleep or too drunk to notice. I hear Anne laughing inside with our tree friends. We are currently in their hotel room at Aria. Meeting those three by happenstance was a gift of fate. Gazing at the city lights of Las Vegas, I reflect back on our evening.

Once our spliff was finished, we embarked on a tour de force of bars around the strip and Old Vegas; Jacob, Emma, and Rea kept pace with us excellently, and we decided to split our remaining coke among the five of us. After trading turns in the restrooms, we ran on sheer joy, loping around Vegas while dancing, giggling, clutching, and slipping. Emma, very pleased with how the evening was shaping up, vowed to secure more drugs along the way, and she did not disappoint. A cocktail of pills, coke, and ecstasy was collected, most of which I sampled. Honestly, despite the high level of intoxicants swirling within my body, I feel present and alert. I drank just enough throughout the night to stay plastered, but never fell into the abyss that is a blackout.

I hear the glass door sliding open and glance over to see Rea. She has a long, slim cigarette in her hand and walks in a haze. I'm fairly certain she busied herself in the bathroom banging a few pills, as she was gone an inordinate amount of time.

"Enjoying your night?" she asks in her helium voice, lighting a cig. Her eyes are glassy, but her speech is not slurred.

"I'm basking in the warm glow of life right now."

"It always leaves too soon," she says quietly.

I look over at her, and she strikes me as wounded. Her eyes are wide but lack expression, reminding me of a doe.

"That's what makes it so sweet," I reply. "It wouldn't be the same if it was endless."

Rea and I sit in comfortable silence. As I listen to the roar of the city, I am hit with a sense of inadequacy. As wonderful and moving as this trip has been, I have seen how small my life truly is. And how much bigger, how much greater it *could* be. It's bittersweet: I *am* proud of my accomplishments, but at twenty-five, well, twenty-six now, I had expected to be further, to have achieved more. My life is stunted, and it took this trip for me to notice. I haven't been able to see the woods for the trees, and I'm just now grasping how unfulfilling my life has become. I have no purpose, no meaning. I sigh. These thoughts are too deep.

Rae seems far away and I know she's lost in her mind as well. I stand and excuse myself.

Opening the glass door, I call to Anne.

"Lassie, this Lassie needs to sleep. Shall we to the commons?" My British accent is slurring.

Anne, slumped on the couch, tilts her head slightly. "Oh but, Lassie, we shall."

*****

Finding a seat at my departure gate, I check my phone: it is 11:57 in the morning and my flight leaves in an hour. I will have time to eat a banana, drink water, and pull myself together before I board the plane. The trip to the airport took all the energy I could muster; I'm sweating and winded. Needless to say, I spent the last night of EDC drinking and dancing far more than my body appreciated. Dehydration and fatigue have definitely caught up with me. I think five days is too long in Vegas.

As I wait for my heart rate to simmer down, I watch people pass by. Some are rushing, no doubt late for a connecting flight, while others meander along bored, waiting for their journey to begin. Chatter and excitement fill the air, the static of chaos stinging my ears. I rub the back of my neck, and my head feels heavy.

Taking a deep breath, I hold it in for a moment and then exhale steadily. I'm twitchy and clammy. In the back of my mind, I know a drink will steady me. I refuse to drink right now, though. I'm flirting with alcoholism and rather than feeling nervous, I am intrigued, which frightens me.

I close my eyes and sip water. Regardless of my stance on booze, my twenty-sixth birthday was a complete success and I feel a small bit of accomplishment. Perhaps I'll lay off the drugs and booze for a few days, and re-evaluate my life. Or maybe just the drugs.

# 3

# Mary Skittles & The Food Network

*March 2013*
*Kansas City, Missouri*
*26 Years Old*

"Charlie, get the fuck out! No one wants you here!" Ali screams, pushing me out the door and attempting to slam it shut.

"What the fuck?" I scream back, throwing my weight against the door. "You don't even live here, you pill-popping bitch! *You* get the fuck out and go back to Tennessee! You're fucking greedy, you're lazy, I know you're stealing from Alec and he's the last bridge you've got, you dumb bitch!"

My heart is beating wildly in my chest, and I can feel my hands shaking violently. I am on the brink of losing control.

Alec stumbles out from the bathroom, tears streaming down his face.

"Go, Charlie. Just go. I can't do this anymore, with either one of you."

My breath escapes me and I pull my hair in frustration.

"Go! Go where? This is fucking nuts, guys! Fucking nuts!

Yeah, no, I should go—this is insane and toxic and we're all gonna die living like this. Fuck it, you're right, I'm out! Ali, you're still a fucking piece of shit bitch and I hope you get everything that's coming to you."

Alec shuffles back to the bathroom and closes the door as Ali weaves to the couch. I walk toward the freezer, grabbing every pack of cigarettes I can find along the way.

"Yeah, fuck you, Charlie, you drunk ass loser, grab that vodka! Run back to Clinton now, run to your Daddy! You fucking pussy!"

Tucking the gallon of vodka and a couple of Gatorade bottles into my backpack, I head for the door. Before closing it, I turn to Ali one last time.

"Just stop stealing from him and leave him alone. You're killing him, Ali. You need help, we all do, but you especially."

I shut the door and run to the elevators as she rises from the couch in a rage. When I reach the downstairs lobby, I scroll through my phone until I find my cousin Marnie. It rings three times before she answers.

"Hello, Charlie—are you okay?" she asks, confused.

"Marnie, I think I might be an alcoholic and I need help," I sob on the cold street corner.

\*·\*·\*·\*·\*

*June 2013*
*Eugene/Springfield, Oregon*
*27 Years Old*

Built in the early '70s, Mayfield Manor operates as housing for those making the transition from a psychiatric ward to

49

"normal" life. It is quite dilapidated, and in the shape of an *L*, with numbered rooms leading to the mess hall at its ninety-degree angle. Picnic tables and weathered outdoor chairs litter the inside of the *L*, while overgrown hedges act as a wall between the facility and the operating, responsible public.

I sigh, unloading my loan backpack from the taxi which has taken me from the Estelle Strat Memorial Unit to this next phase in my recovery. I feel very far away from my boozy loft in downtown Kansas City.

"Charles Gray," a voice calls from the doors to the mess hall. A skeletal woman with thin, stringy hair holds a clipboard, eyeing me with a bored expression.

"Hello," I say blandly.

"My name is Patty, welcome to Mayfield Manor. Follow me and we will complete your intake process."

I take a sharp breath at the word intake; it has, unfortunately, become a reoccurring event in my life. Beginning with the thirty-day treatment center I recently completed, Calvin's House, followed by my stint in the psychiatric ward, I can only hope this third time's a charm.

As I follow Patty into the mess hall, I see a cluster of plastic tables and chairs surrounding a large, '90s TV set. Patty opens a door to the left of this with a set of keys hanging from her neck, and we enter a back office. A series of desks are placed along the outer walls, with a single, battered desk holding an ancient computer in the center. It is behind this desk that Patty settles herself. I seat myself in the chair opposite her, folding my hands in my lap.

Patty remains silent, staring at the computer with the same bored expression shown earlier. I clear my throat and peer around the room. Several stations are piled high with folders, papers, and laundry. Clearly, this is a state-funded facility, and from its appearance, at the end of the receiving line.

Finally, Patty flicks her eyes toward me.

"It says here you were admitted to the Strat Unit due to suicidal thoughts. Are you still feeling suicidal?"

"No, I never really was," I begin. "I was drunk at the time and in a motel room without any—"

"Yes, I see you were treated for alcoholism before going to the Strat Unit," Patty cuts in, her eyes snapping back to the monitor.

"That's correct," I answer, deciding Patty is probably more accustomed to short responses.

"Drinking or using drugs is not tolerated at Mayfield. You may smoke cigarettes in the designated areas. Your stay here will be between three to five days until you're assigned a case manager. Here is a copy of the rules and meal times. Please read and sign that you have received this information."

I skim the rules as the term "case manager" turns over in my mind. How delightful, I've reached a new low.

After signing and initialing the usual documents, I slide them to Patty.

"You will be in room one. Follow me."

Patty leads me out of the mess hall screen door, and into a room at the end of the *L*.

It is a total and complete shit show. Orange and green shag carpet clashes perfectly with the nicotine-yellow walls. A mahogany dresser, which came straight from a dumpster, stands next to a window with crusty blinds. As for the pièce de résistance, it is a sagging and stained mattress nudged up against the far wall.

I place my backpack on the mattress and turn to face Patty.

"Your bed linens are in the dresser. Dinner is at five," she turns on her heel and leaves the room.

I lower myself to the bed and gawk blankly around the room.

"I'm in Oregon. I have no fucking money. I think I'm homeless? I'm—"

The weight of my circumstance falls heavily upon me, and my breath quickens. The heat of tears rises, but I push them down. I've cried enough and it doesn't seem to be doing any good.

Sitting at the picnic table nearest to my "suite," I light a cigarette when a large woman seats herself at the table with me.

"Hi, I'm Mary. But people call me Skittles," she says, casually making reference to her short hair. An interesting choice of color, it does indeed appear as though she tie-dyed it with a box of Skittles.

"Hello, my name is Charlie."

"You're new, huh? I got here two days ago. I tried killing myself by overdosing on Xanax and gin. My Mom, fucking bitch, found me and called the cops. I guess I tried fighting them so they'd have to shoot me. It's kind of a blur."

"Oh," I reply, genuinely at a loss for words. This is more than I want to process at the moment.

"Yeah, it was pretty fucked up, but whatever. I get super manic and sometimes hear voices. I've been here three times before. The rooms and bathrooms are shit but the food's not too bad. So what's your story?"

At this, Mary Skittles lights a cigarette, a hungry glint in her eye, as though these are the conversations for which she lives. I hesitate for a moment, then decide there's nothing to lose. Honesty usually feels better, anyway.

"Well, I'm beginning to suspect that I'm a terrible alcoholic.

You see, I drank myself out of the sober house I was living in. And after that, I used what remaining money I had left to buy a gallon of cheap vodka, some pickles, and rent a motel room for a couple of nights. Once the vodka and pickles ran out, I knew I had to do something to keep a roof over me, so I called CAHOOTZ, super drunk, and said I was suicidal. I was spiraling. And, now, well. Here I am."

I glance around at my bleak surroundings and sigh. "Fuck."

"Yeah, I get it. I've been on and off meth for years," she says.

I am just about to ask Mary Skittles if she has any significant amount of sober time when I feel a tap on my right shoulder. I turn and see a rather short, stout woman with cropped black hair. Her gaping, dark eyes protrude ominously with an uneasy gleam, reminding me of the wild eyes horses make when spooked. She stares at me with a vacant intensity.

"I know you," she whispers, moving closer to me; at once I feel uncomfortable and threatened.

"Uh, I'm sorry, I don't believe we've met."

"I know you, oh yes. Yes, he told me. You've done it, haven't you? Where'd he go?" she rattles, pacing around the table. I am unsure if I should stand or remain still. She begins to speak louder and work herself into a frenzy.

I dart my eyes to Mary Skittles and she shakes her head. "She's bat shit, dude."

*****

I awake and lay gazing at the stained popcorn ceiling. It is my second day at Mayfield, but feels more like my second week. Yesterday was one of the strangest days of my life. Or year. Kelly, the woman who thought she knew me, had a breakdown after

53

dinner, rolling on the ground and talking to "him," whoever the hell "him" is; in an instant, she would switch from crying to anger to hysterical laughing. This episode was not a complete waste, though. During it, I was able to slip beyond the bushes separating me from the outside world, and miraculously spotted a bar, Mike's Corner. It made my heart race, and I vowed in that moment to locate money, someway, somehow, so I could get good and drunk.

I check my phone, 10:14 in the morning.

"How to get money?"

Pulling my shoes on, I peer out the window and see Mary Skittles.

"I wonder," I whisper in my British accent.

Popping a squat beside Mary Skittles, I pull out a cigarette. Her multi-colored hair shines brightly in the sun, and I feel like I should call her Tonks instead of Skittles.

"What are your plans for today?" I ask casually.

"I dunno, prolly hanging around here avoiding dumb fucks. You?"

I flash a charming grin and take my chance.

"Well, I am planning to go on an adventure," I answer mischievously, and ensure no one is listening, "a drinking adventure."

Mary Skittles grins. "Oh yeah?"

"Yeah, there's a bar not too far from here. I saw it when Kelly was losing her shit last night. Wanna go? We'll have plenty of time to sober up before dinner."

I'm nervous she will want to be compliant, that her last episode put her on the straight and narrow.

She takes a beat. "Sure."

I grin and run off to change, feeling elated I'm only moments away from vodka.

We seat ourselves at the bar and wait for service. It is placed in the center of Mike's Corner, wooden and circular, with seating for roughly twenty patrons. On the right side of the bar is a set of booths, their napkin holders shining dimly in the light; to the left is an open space used for dancing, and two aged slot machines. The green carpet is worn and stained from years of shuffled dancing and sloshed drinks. Damp air mixes with the smell of cigarette smoke, stale beer, and grease. I breathe it in deeply, the smell of my people. In the hazy light, I scan the rows of liquor. My choices are slim, however, I find what I'm searching for quite quickly: a large bottle of Oregon Falls vodka.

My mouth waters.

The barmaid throws two coasters in front of us. "What can I get you?"

"Double vodka water, Oregon Falls, please."

"I'll take a Bud Light," Mary Skittles answers through a mouthful of bar-mix.

"Sure thing."

The barmaid busies herself making our drinks. I watch her, with bleached-blonde hair and caked-on make-up, she has the dried appearance of a lifelong barfly. Is this a glimpse of my future?

"Fitting," I mumble as she places our drinks on the coasters. I cannot get mine to my lips fast enough. Swallowing my first, treasured drink, vodka's fiery sear floods me. I am content at last.

Several hours later, I find myself quite inebriated on the outside patio, smoking with my new bar friends. It is nearing four in the afternoon, and I've lost track of Mary Skittles. Once she stopped buying me drinks, I no longer had use for her and found other, more sharing companions.

I snuff out my cigarette and head to the graffitied men's room. Washing my hands, I catch sight of my reflection in the mirror and freeze, gazing at myself for a long moment. The man staring back at me is hard to recognize.

"What are you doing?" my voice is hoarse and raw.

A wave of loneliness washes over me; a loud ringing pierces my ears and I begin to sweat. Despite finding vodka, this is exactly where I *don't* want to be. My natural instinct is to drink more, achieving a blackout, but I don't have the funds. Revolted by the man in the mirror, I flip my switch and say fuck it all. If I have to, I'll mooch, charm, or seduce, but be *damn sure* I'll drink.

\*\*\*\*\*

I blink open my eyes, realizing I'm not at Mayfield, but in bed with another man. Head pounding, I glance over at him. He is young, with copper hair and tanned skin. The room is dark and cool, with a large fan oscillating in the corner.

I lay very still and try to remember how I ended up in this random man's bed. My last memory is of sitting on the floor of my room at Mayfield, drunk, surfing YouTube videos. The beat of my heart thumps harder and my skin grows clammy. Shit. I was successful in getting blackout drunk, per usual.

Sliding out from underneath the blankets, I rummage on the ground for my clothes. Putting them on gingerly, I gauge how to handle the situation. I have no recollection of meeting this man, nor any idea of his demeanor. This could be an absolute shit show.

Cautiously, I clear my throat and tap him on the arm.

"Um, good morning."

The mystery man's eyes flutter and he smiles. "Morning."

I smile back and notice he has kind, brown eyes. "I, um, don't remember very much of last night. Everything is blurry and then, boom, blackout. Shocking, I'm sure. Where am I exactly?"

He laughs. "Yeah, we were all pretty toasted last night. We're at my place, not too far from the bar where we met."

"Oh, nice. The bar."

Usually, I would stay and chat with this attractive mystery man, yet I feel a sense of urgency to remove myself from this ordeal. I need to shower the entire experience off, literally.

"Well, I'm really hoping we had an epic time last night. But I need to get back to Mayfield—I have a job interview this afternoon. And I, uh, smell like a vodka bottle. And old carpet, strangely."

Disappointment flashes across his face, and he crawls out of bed, slipping into a pair of boxers.

"Alright, give me a few minutes. Wanna pick me up? I've got a bit of coke left from last night."

I rub my jaw, suddenly aware. "So *that's* why my jaw hurts! We did coke, I was coked out, grinding my teeth. No, thank you, I'm good on that shit. But do you have any weed?"

Chuckling, he shakes his head no, pulls a small bag from his pants pocket, dumps it on his dresser, and begins to break up lines.

"So do you remember my name?" he asks over his work.

I smirk, caught. "Listen, I can barely remember my own name

right now, I'm sorry."

"It's Luke."

"Hi, Luke. I'm Charlie," I say as he snorts a thin white line.

"Hello, Charlie," he wipes his nose and begins dressing

"You can drop me here," I say a block away from Mayfield.

Luke slows the car. "Can I get your number?"

"Honestly, dude, my life is a hot ass mess right now. I really don't think that's a good idea, no. I do appreciate you driving me back, though. And asking for my number, that's very sweet of you."

"Alright, worth a shot. Well, take care of yourself."

"Yeah, you too. Thanks, again."

I exit the car and began walking toward Mayfield. My heart pumps out of my chest, and my nerves are firing on all cylinders. As I approach the garbage-looking picnic tables, I catch sight of Patty. She is not pleased.

"Mr. Gray," she cracks sharply, "your ride is here. And you're very lucky it is, as you were about to be discharged for violating the rules! I thought I had explained to you that drinking is not tolerated. You have ten minutes to pack your belongings."

"Okay." But how did she know I'd been drinking? What did I do last night?

As I walk in the direction of my suite, a kind woman with graying hair smiles at me.

"Hello, Charlie! It's nice to meet you! My name is Elizabeth and I am from Lane County Behavioral Health. I will be taking you to the Marriott for respite. Do you need help packing?"

I am caught off guard by the words "Marriott" and "respite," but decide to wait until we're both in the safety of her van to inquire.

"No, thank you, I have very little to pack."

After throwing my clothes and phone charger in my backpack, I jump in the passenger seat of her van. It smells pleasantly of vanilla.

Elizabeth tosses her hair in Patty's direction and gives me a grin. "Are you excited for the next chapter of your journey?"

"Yes, I do believe I am," I answer, instantly liking her vibe.

*****

I yawn loudly and fling the covers to the floor. After leaving Mayfield, Elizabeth treated us to a fresh meal, and then checked me into my actual suite at the Marriott. It is my third morning waking here, and blissful compared to my previous housing. She has assured me I will be crashing here until my apartment becomes available. The suite, along with my future apartment, will be financed through Lane County Behavioral Health; I'm unsure on the specifics but don't bother to ask for fear of disrupting a good deal.

"Oh, to be a ward of the state," I whisper, and crawl out of the massive king bed.

The suite, 104, is kept on standby for Lane County, and a few modifications have been made, such as a bookshelf holding a variety of Christian-themed books and DVDs, and inspirational quotes stenciled across the walls. They've also ensured only plastic cutlery and paper plates are available. I peruse their inventory momentarily, and then wander to the kitchen. It is all one large room, broken into three by a purposefully placed dining table and couch. The kitchen has a stove top, microwave, dishwasher, and a full-sized refrigerator. There is a fancy flat screen on the far wall, visible from both the couch and the bed.

I flip on the TV and begin to pace as the Kardashian's chatter in the background.

A drink crosses my mind. Or a bowl. Or a pill. Anything, really, that would give me a buzz. While I *should* be focusing my time and mind more productively, I am hyper-consumed with getting wasted. My escape to Oregon is rapidly turning into a fucking disaster. The purpose of me fleeing Kansas City in the middle of the night was to find sobriety and clarity, yet I would give anything to have *neither* at this moment.

A chill pricks me. I have squandered so much of my potential by behaving as a self-absorbed, bratty drunkard. I am an educated twenty-seven-year-old with nothing to show for it; I willingly handed over my job at the bank to spend more time with a vodka bottle. Seduced by the sauce, I have abandoned any plan of bettering myself. My fingertips begin to tingle and my tongue is made of sandpaper. What a horrid time to be sober!

I sink to the floor and sit, stunned. Too many emotions break over me, and it's as though I'm vibrating. The loud ringing in my ears returns, along with the sweats, and I close my eyes tightly. Maybe I could take a walk and find some money on the ground and then be able to buy vodka? Or maybe I could make up a story about losing my wallet and pander a few bucks off unsuspecting individuals?

I stand in a flash, rushing to the mirror. Pale and flushed, but that's easily remedied. I am confident I can think up an elaborate lie on my walk to a gas station. Throwing on a pair of dark jeans and a gray polo, I spritz on cologne and make for the door, smiling. In a couple of hours, I will be walking back into this room with pickles, chips, and a bottle of vodka. I am determined.

The night air is warm as I sit outside of the Marriott, watching my cigarette smoke curl around the street lamp. I have two more packs, a fifth of vodka, a jar of pickles, and two bags of chips waiting in my suite. It took several attempts, at three gas stations, but eventually, enough people bought my story of traveling into town and getting mugged at the airport. My theatre degree at work, for once.

My stomach warms and my lips begin to feel numb; I was careful to drink sparingly, just enough to catch a strong buzz, five large pulls. Rationing will make my life easier by spacing out my need to lie and pander. This is proof of spiraling out of control, and I'm taking it much better than expected. As long as I can find a way to drink, coping should be easy enough.

*****

Wind chimes sing from my phone as I kick the sheets off, drenched in sweat. The Sahara Desert covers my mouth and eyes. I blink as my head splits in two. Unable to remember how many half-pints I drained last night, I rub my eyes and groan. Elizabeth is picking me up later today for a session, and I have dragon vodka breath.

I raise my head ever so slightly from the pillow and feel nauseous.

"Fucking perfect, Charlie. I'm so proud of you," I whisper scathingly. "Well, you gotta work through it. 'Cause, um, you gotta."

Lightheaded, I stand and take stock of the room: half-pints and salad containers are littered on each surface. My stomach lurches and I dash to the toilet, dry heaving. Retching four or five times, I take steady, long breaths, trying to find balance.

Hands shaking, I blow my nose and begin pouring the contents of each remaining half-pint into an empty pint. By the end, I have three-quarters of a pint and smile.

Inhaling and exhaling deeply, I swallow a mouthful. I chatter my teeth slowly while rubbing the top of my mouth with my tongue; it is strange as hell but seems to help the booze stay down on a sour stomach. After a few minutes, I take another gulp and repeat the process. A shower and confession to Elizabeth shall do me well.

"Are you hungry?" Elizabeth asks brightly on the drive to her office.

I smile softly and peer out the window, steeling myself.

"You can probably smell it on me. I've been drinking, so I don't have much of an appetite. I'm really, really sorry and I understand if you need to kick me out."

Elizabeth sighs. "Oh, Charlie, I would never kick you out because you're struggling. You're being honest about your alcoholism, and I appreciate that."

"I just won't stop! It's all I want to do, it's all I think about. As long as I have a bottle, I'm fine. But as soon as I run out, the shit hits the fan and I'll do anything to get more. I'm starting to seriously scare myself."

"Was it easier when you were in treatment and sober living?" Elizabeth asks.

"Yes and no. I was contained with lots of people around, so I believe that made it physically easier. But mentally, it's always there. Sometimes it's only in the back of my thoughts, but it's always there. Unless I'm drinking. I only feel peaceful and content when I'm drinking. It's just like, the sun is brighter when I'm drinking, you know? I feel in tune with the world around me and it's freeing and relaxing. But I drink a lot, and that can't be good, no matter how you cut it."

Elizabeth nods and taps her index finger lightly on the steering wheel, processing everything I have unloaded.

"The good news is that you're not the only person who has felt this way. Would you be interested in attending an AA meeting? Or talking with someone from AA?"

"Honestly, I haven't really checked AA out all that much, but I'd be open to a one-on-one conversation."

"Well, I'm very pleased you're willing to talk with someone and I think I know just the person. She's a colleague of mine, I'll see when she can grab you for coffee or lunch."

"Thank you, Elizabeth," I say, placing my hand gently on her arm. "You're being very kind and I appreciate it."

*July 2013*
*Springfield, Oregon*
*27 Years Old*

"You'll be in the second building, in the first upstairs apartment. It's quite spacious, with a large kitchen, living room and bedroom. It even has a little nook between the kitchen and living room that's so cute. You can put your computer there, once Janis has it ready."

I smile at Elizabeth from her passenger seat. We are driving to my new apartment in Springfield, Oregon, and I'm super excited to leave the Marriott. As splendid as my stay was, I'm eager to feel like a normal human being again, with a normal apartment.

"And Eric will meet with you once a week, do you remember Eric?"

"Is he the guy who led the luncheon the other day?"

"He is," she beams. "He's a great guy, he's been with Lane for years now and everyone is very fond of him. He's in recovery, as well. I figured he would be a good check-in option for you since he's been through similar situations himself."

"Cool," I say genuinely. "So he just stops by and we chat for a bit?"

"Uh-huh. He's essentially doing a wellness check, to make sure you're doing okay each week. I realize you're not as limited in capabilities as some of our other patients, but I thought a weekly check-in was still a good idea."

"I do, too. It'll help me stay motivated and determined."

During my two-week stint at the Marriott, I decided to make the best out of my life in Oregon. It is a beautiful state, and there's no reason I cannot start over here. Once I have my computer, I will update my resume and begin applying to banks in the area. A job will give me purpose throughout the day, hopefully keeping the alcohol at bay.

As Elizabeth turns onto F Street, I see an apartment complex emerging.

"There it is," she says, reading my mind.

It is quaint, with a fresh coat of white paint and blue trim. There are five buildings, each with two apartments upstairs and downstairs. Bushy landscaping, gnarly trees, and sporadic flowers spot the fenced lot. It is reminiscent of a retirement community.

"Peaceful," I muse as she parks.

"Oh yes, it is very peaceful here. It's one of my favorites, we have a few apartments around Springfield. This one is great because it's close to the park and river."

I grab my backpack from her backseat and we walk up the

stairs of the second building and turn right. Elizabeth puts the key in the lock and the door creaks open to reveal laminate flooring and a musty kitchen. It is indeed roomy, and the nook *is* sweet. I turn to Elizabeth, tears in my eyes.

"It's perfect. It's just what I need right now—nothing flashy, just somewhere to restart my life. Thank you so much, Elizabeth!" I hug her, causing *her* eyes to go misty.

"Oh, this is what it's all about," she says. "Well, I'll leave you to it. I made sure there were cleaning supplies and toiletries for you. You've got your food card, yeah?"

"Yup!" I answer and pull it from my wallet.

"Good deal. Okay, Charlie, I'm going to head off. I'm really proud of you, and I hope you enjoy living in your new apartment!" she exclaims, enthusiastic for me; it is humbling and flattering.

I chuckle. "Yes, I'll start scrubbing and then head to the grocery store!"

My phone dials, on speaker, and I wait anxiously for Granny to answer.

"Hey, babe!"

"Hey! What're you doing?" I ask excitedly.

"Sitting on the back porch, what're you doing?"

"Well, I just got into my new apartment!" I burst.

"Oh, wow! Do you like it?"

"You know, it's not bad," I say, picking up the phone and walking the space. "The rooms are big and open, and there's a cute nook with a small table that I can put my computer on. The living room and bedroom are bland but okay. The kitchen has lots of counter space, too!"

Granny giggles happily. "Are you gonna do some cooking?"

"I am! I was gonna try some recipes from The Food Network, since it's all I really watch lately."

"Do you have a washer and dryer?" she asks.

"I think there's a small laundromat-type thing in the main building. I could sure use Dad's quarter bucket right now," I chortle.

"Yes!" Granny agrees. Her voice is light and merry; I am so pleased to bring her happy news. As of late, I've had only sad tidings to share.

"Are you happy, hun?"

I can hear the breeze blowing through the trees in the background and I ache to be on her back porch, enjoying the afternoon in her company.

"I'm very hopeful right now, Granny. I'm happy most of the time, honestly, but sometimes I think about all I've lost and it's a lot to handle. Not Mom, exactly, just the life I'd built before coming to Oregon."

Granny sighs and I give her a beat.

"You know, babe, the life you built before going to Oregon was kind of a mess. You were drinking all the time, and trying to hide it, but you couldn't. And I know you and Alec loved one another, hun, but you're both so troubled right now, and that doesn't mix well. You need to take care of yourself and worry about love later. You'll find the right guy, I just know it, but I don't think it's Alec."

"Granny, you say all the time that you're not smart, but I think you're one of the wisest people I know."

She laughs loudly into the phone. "Oh, hun. Your Grandpa always said I'm clever as a fox, I just hide it. But I don't know."

"I do, Grandpa was right."

"Well, do you need me to send you some quarters and

cigarettes?"

"Oh my lands, yes, that would be amazing! Thank you!"

We chit-chat for an hour or more, while I clean and mess around my new space. She is vivacious and animated, sending me off to the grocery store with several dinner ideas. I'm going rogue and cooking lamb.

*****

Perching on the edge of my couch, I gaze intensely at the UPS van, willing it to stop at my apartment complex. Granny mailed money and cigarettes a few days ago, and my package should arrive this afternoon. The turn signal blinks on and my heart does somersaults.

Dashing out the door, I meet the delivery woman at the bottom of the stairs with a smile.

"Thanks!" I call, taking the steps two at a time up to my apartment.

Ripping it open, I find a carton of Marlboro Lights, a large resealable bag of quarters, and five hidden twenties. Oh, Granny!

Dizzy with the excitement of smoking a good cigarette, it suddenly dawns on me that I can buy vodka. My smile fades and I stand very still, as if momentarily petrified. My mind, however, is sprinting. It's been a week and a half since my last drink, but only because I haven't had the means, nor did I want to hustle. My fortune has changed, though. One bottle, a cheap one. I can put it in the freezer, and limit myself to a certain number of shots when I drink. And I can't drink every night. And I can't drink before five in the evening.

My mouth waters and a sheen of sweat rolls down my back.

My heart and breathing quicken. The tips of my fingers begin to tingle, and I inhale sharply.

"Okay. Okay. Okay. Okay. Just fucking go buy it, get it over with, and then figure out how to drink it. Okay. Okay."

I am in a tizzy, frazzled, and full of chaotic energy. But somewhere, buried within me, is a ball of excited merriment: soon, I shall be in my proper, enlightened state of mind. I will feel content and peaceful; it will allow me to gain insight into my current situation and determine the best means of escape.

Granny won't know, and I refuse to spend the entire amount on booze. It'll be my secret sauce to life.

*****

Passing the downtown shops, I glance at my reflection in their windows. Shaggy hair, cargo shorts, a white tee, and flip-flops. If I only felt as wholesome as I look. I've now gone through the majority of the money Granny sent me, and not on laundry. Needing to free myself from the walls of my apartment, and perhaps my own shame, I have set off to Willamette Heights Park to regroup.

Victor, my sweet, gay, middle-aged next-door neighbor caught me as I was leaving, to make sure I was doing okay. Apparently, my fainting spell last night woke the complex. I suppose it was fainting, but I'm not sure. One moment I was walking away from taking a shot at my freezer, and the next I was flat on my back in a cold sweat. The echo from my floor ratted me out, and Victor was worried I'd hit my head.

I laid there for a while, staring up at the ceiling in the moonlight. There was a feeling of dread that I can't seem to shake, even today. I feel clammy inside and out. It is dread of where this behavior will lead me. It's bizarre, to know I'm making poor decisions, yet rather than altering the course of my life, I prefer to watch the wrecking ball from the sidelines. Is this giving up?

"Is this giving up?" I mock myself in a whisper. "You're so dramatic."

I flip from one extreme to another, and it's exhausting. A few articles have advised finding balance and living in the moment, although I'm not sure how that works; it probably doesn't help that I sift through them in a maudlin mood. I'm hoping a nice sit by the creek will provide insight. I miss the country, I miss my house on the hill. It all seems so far away: my home, my family, myself. It's getting harder and harder to remember why I thought disappearing to Oregon in the middle of the night was a good idea.

I'm homesick, I'm drinking too much, and I have nothing to do. Adrift and unmotivated, which allows for more guzzling, and less accountability. My coveted recipe for debauchery and loss of dignity. Scrumptious. Bowel destroying.

Entering the park, I step carefully as to avoid goose shit, and find a clean bench to rest on. Scratching my leg, I hear my cargo pocket crumple and rummage in it, pulling out five, fifty dollar bills. In a snap, a memory from a few nights ago knocks me in the teeth. I slept with Victor and Alex for two hundred and fifty bucks. My body tenses; I think they used their webcam to video it, as well. This is a new level of whoring for me. I've used men for money before, but I've never allowed them to take pictures or videos. I'm not a porn star, and it's never taken me *this long* to remember an event of such severity. Am I putting holes in my brain? Am I unleashing a dormant, sexually deviant split personality? Am I creating this, or fulfilling my destiny?

I groan and punch my fist into my hand. So I've turned into a common, boozy little slut again. Never a dull moment, never a moment's peace. I have such a shitty mantra.

"Oh, fuck it," I say, scratching my ear. "Fuck it, I'm gonna drink, drunk, drank."

*November 2013*
*Springfield, Oregon*
*27 Years Old*

"Happy Thanksgiving!" Brod, Tay, and Trella sing through my phone, on speaker.

"Happy Thanksgiving!" I exclaim, thrilled to be on the phone with my girls during the holiday. We may be two thousand miles apart, but right now they feel near.

"What do you have planned for today?" Brod asks brightly.

"Well, I'm watching the parade and cooking one of those turkey breasts that Granny got me. And I'm making green bean casserole and mashed potatoes!"

"You make the best mashed potatoes," Tay gushes and I giggle.

"It's a secret recipe from Granny Doris," I quip. "I was gonna take some food downstairs, to Hattie."

"Oh, how's she doing?" Trella asks with concern.

"You know, I don't think she's doing well," I sigh. "It seems like she's needing more oxygen but still smoking. Which I get, she should do what she wants, but I know it frustrates her daughter."

Hattie is my elderly downstairs neighbor. After living here for about two weeks, we met at the base of the stairs and began talking. She's as sweet as the day is long, smokes like a chimney, and wheels around an oxygen tank. She's slipped me money here and there, aware of my struggles with the bottle. Her father was a drunk, and she has a sympathetic bone for those struck by the plight of drink.

"Well good, she'll probably be so happy to see you!" Brod says.

"Yeah, but other than that I'll probably just chill. It's rainy and cold here. What's it like there?"

"Cold," they all answer quickly.

"Are you doing okay?" Brod's voice is neutral, but I know there's a deep amount of worry there.

"Honestly, I am. It's the Shockers—every time I wanna drink, I just get a pack of them and eat them, and it seems to work. It's like I'm conditioning my mind like a dog or something."

"Whatever works," Trella interjects pleasantly.

"But other than that I just loaf a lot. I haven't drank in a couple of weeks and I'm finally sleeping normal, it's a miracle. I swear, I will never take pure, sober sleep for granted again! It's so amazing."

I hear them giggle, and it's as though I'm with them on the patio of the house on the hill. My heart yearns to be home with my girls.

"So Dad's gonna come there around Christmas," Brod says.

"Yeah, he texted me the other day about it. I don't know, I felt kinda weird at first, like kinda guilty, you know?"

"Yes!" Brod answers emphatically.

"But then I got really excited. I dunno, maybe we'll talk about me moving back home?"

"Is that what you want to do?" Trella inquires.

"I think so. I feel like it'll be easier to start over where I'm familiar. I can just live with Granny and go from there."

Moving in with Granny will provide safety. I can help take

care of things around the house, and she can help take care of me; Lord knows I'll need supervision. It will also bring her great joy to have me under her roof.

"Yeah," I decide. "I really think that's what I'd like to do, but I'll wait and see what Dad thinks when he gets here."

"Oh, that would be so nice," Trella coos. "You can help me clean the banks for extra money until you find a job."

"It'll be nice to just hang out again, too," Tay offers earnestly, piercing my heart.

"It sure will!"

"Hey, Bub, we've gotta go eat but we'll call you back later, okay?" Brod says, and I can tell she's leaning close to the phone.

"Sure thing, talk to you then!"

"Love you!" they chime.

"Love you, too!" I return.

Tilting my head, I take a sharp breath and sigh; I *must* move back to Clinton. Only a few more weeks and I'll be with them, home, where I can start over. Oregon was a mere recess from life, a chance to recharge my batteries. I will move home and attack life with full force, claiming the existence I've always wanted.

# 4

# Of Apps & Men

*September 2014*
*Springfield, Missouri*
*28 Years Old*

The clock strikes seven in the evening, and I breathe a sigh of relief. Another day is done, which means one day closer to the weekend, and a reprieve from adult life. My gusto from earlier in the year is winding down, and I find myself drinking more and more. I know it's not a wise tactic, but it makes me feel alive and young while providing me with entertainment. I should probably find another hobby, but that would require effort.

"Are you in balance?" Liz asks, kneeling in front of the vault.

"I am!" I exclaim. "And thank goodness, I thought I was off forty bucks, but I found it."

"Good job, Charlie!"

I take my till out of the drawer and slide it into the vault. After locking it, I shut the vault door and turn the dial. Liz and I usually close the bank, and we've worked out a smooth and efficient routine.

"Did you get any apps today?" I ask as she changes the date on the customer island.

"I got one credit card app, and it's in review. But I can't talk anyone into refinancing their mortgage lately, I don't know what my deal is!"

"Hey, at least you got an app. I got zilch today, but I did open a solid checking account."

"And you've got the Ireland mortgage closing later this week, so I'd say you're good."

"True," I agree.

Liz shuts off the lights, and I clip the rope to wall, separating the bank lobby from the Walmart shopping area.

"Alright," Liz grins at me, "let's go get some sushi!"

I follow Liz to our favorite sushi spot, Ocean Zen, and we request our usual booth. She orders Cabernet and I ask for water. Rarely do I drink in front of my co-workers. They are under the impression I refrain from alcohol most of the time, as it doesn't agree with my stomach. Or some bullshit like that, I can't remember exactly what I said. After the madness of drinking and popping pills with my co-workers at my first banking job, I decided to take a calmer approach this time around. They're also a much calmer group of individuals.

"How's the dating life going?" she asks, scanning the menu.

"Ugh," I sigh. "It's alright. There just doesn't seem to be much out there and it's a lot of work. Which I didn't expect, but it is."

"I feel like I would've been too emotional to use those Apps," she says.

"You would have been, *trust* me," I answer. "Honestly, I think it's a lot of drugs, too, 'cause everyone kept asking me if I 'liked to party,' and I was like, 'sure.' But what they *meant* was 'do you like to do lots of meth and then screw for days?' And I was like 'oh that's flattering you wanted to have sex with me for days, but no thank you.' So there's that."

Liz cackles and smiles at the waiter bringing our drinks. "Ah, well. He's out there somewhere, you just haven't found him yet."

"Hmm," I muse. "So how's Colin doing back in Seattle?"

Her face grows radiant. "He's great! He'll be here in a couple of weeks, and we're really excited to be living in the same apartment again!"

Liz came home to Springfield a few months ago, transferring from a branch in Seattle. She's three years younger than me, cute as a button, and super sweet. We bonded on her first day, and she's filled a void for me; I was getting quite lonely before we met.

"You guys are adorable. You met working on a cruise ship, right?"

She fixes me with a sassy stare, her dark eyes glowing with memories. "Yes. And it was amazing. I thought he was so sexy and smart and figured he didn't even notice me. Then one day we were working together, and it was just so steamy, Charlie! Like, oh my, gosh, I'm not that kind of girl, but with him, I was. And we've been together ever since."

I am in awe of her, as she grins to herself, so wholesomely in love. It is reassuring this still exists, that two people can fall absolutely head over heels in love, be so in tune, that living states apart is but a small nuisance. I admire this display of love.

"Do you think he's going to propose when he finally gets here?" I ask.

"You know, I really do. We've shopped for rings and he's talked to my Mom and Dad. We've talked about it several times, too. So I'm thinking it'll happen pretty quickly once he gets here."

"Right on! Oh, you're so lucky you're past the dating stage, I'm so jealous!"

Liz gives me a sympathetic look and tilts her head. "Have you ever thought about moving to a bigger city? Like Chicago or Portland or something?"

"I have, and I tried living on the West coast in Oregon for a bit, but I managed to find my way back to Missouri sooner than I'd anticipated."

She takes a sip of her wine. "I just feel like there'd be more options for you there, you know? And transferring through the bank is way easier than you'd think, I could help you out!"

Liz sets off an idea in my head, a way out. Starting over in a new city could be just the thing I need to swear off the bottle, once and for all. I could meet a guy, fall in love, do gay, sporty things, and get in shape. We could send out Christmas cards with our cat, showing how toned, tanned, and trendy we are. We'd live in a super luxurious loft and dash around the city partaking in sober, hip activities. My life could finally be epic.

I give her a mischievous, sideways smile. "Now, Liz, I think you're onto something there."

*****

*March 2015*
*Springfield, Missouri*
*28 Years Old*

"Thank you," I say to the taxi driver, stumbling out of their car. It's almost one in the morning and my heart is pounding; every time I use Gropr for a hookup, I feel as though I'm walking to my demise. He said it was the blue house with the green porch light on. I walk a few paces and spot his description.

As I step up his front stairs, he opens the door, wearing tight shorts and nothing else.

"You made it!" he says excitedly, ushering me into his entryway. "Hi! I'm Travis."

He extends his hand to shake, but as I reach for it, I trip over the door ledge and fall on my side, laughing hysterically. "Whoops! So sorry, I can't seem to find my balance tonight!"

He helps me up and pats my ass. "No worries. Mitch over there has had a lot to drink, too." He motions to his dining room table, on top of which a guy is sprawled, wearing a tank-top and boxer briefs.

"Hey, buddy! Do you wanna take a shot?" he slurs, waving at me from his table-bed.

"Always," I chortle.

Travis leads me through his living room, which is bathed in pinkish light from lamps covered with scarves, to the dining and kitchen area. It's spacious and bright, with large cupboards and counters. To the left of his refrigerator, I see the makings of a minibar and help myself.

"Top shelf brands, eh? Right on!" I exclaim, pouring three shots.

"Oh, no, I'm not drinking. I like to partake in other substances," he answers with a roguish grin.

"Ah, yes. Tina. I don't party quite that way, but I'm equal rights," I slam a shot and hand one to Mitch, who tosses it back merrily. "Wait, I think I meant to say equal opportunity. Damn it, now it's not funny."

"I don't get it either way," Travis giggles, and lights an incense. "So you wanted to smoke a bowl?"

"Oh yes, of the weed, please and thank you!"

He points behind Mitch, to a side table near the back door. "Help yourself, but I warn you, it's strong."

"Lovely, thank you," I chirp and smile at Mitch. His eyes are as glazed as a doughnut and I find him immensely attractive. He's dark and slim, with pouty lips and thick eyelashes.

"You wanna smoke, bud?" I ask, my British lilt trilling.

"Jolly good, chap!" he sways upright, chuckling.

"You should be careful of Travis," Mitch blurts.

He sits across from me on the hot tub of Travis's back porch. Earlier, Travis torched a massive bong of meth and is now whipping up a four-course meal with his tweaker friends for the six of us. Wondering how I got myself into this situation, I followed Mitch to the porch, vodka bottle and weed pipe in tow. I am so drunk I feel sober, something I've experienced only once or twice in my life. I should leave, but can't bring myself to call a taxi.

"Why should I be careful?" I ask, slightly jarred.

"Wherever Travis goes, trouble follows. Believe me, I know. And he usually doesn't invite many people over from Gropr." Mitch stares forward while talking and an eerie feeling settles over me.

"It's not that he's bad, but he's definitely not good. I'm kinda stuck here with him for now, until I can figure something else out, but you shouldn't get yourself attached to him."

I take a long pull from the bottle, shuddering slightly. "So, are you like his boyfriend or boy toy or something?"

"Both, when he wants me to be. Neither, when he wants me to be. He has his moods."

"Hmm," I say. "So, but, what do you mean you're stuck here?"

"It's a long story, but I'm actually from Alabama. I left home because my parents are religious zealots and thought that being gay made me the spawn of Satan, they made it clear they no longer wanted me around. I made my way up here to Springfield, and was homeless until Travis took me in one night. He was so kind and caring at first, and even a little cute, but that changed over time."

"Why not just leave, then? Surely there's somewhere you can go?"

"Free drugs and booze, man. And I don't have to do anything, ever. He buys my cigarettes, pays for my phone, everything. It's awesome!" His voice sounds jubilant, but his face appears hollow and emotionless.

"Yeah," I nod, unconvinced. "It does sound interesting."

And weird and wrong and I should leave. But I don't. I am attracted to Mitch and he's wounded; Captain Save-A-Homo to the rescue!

"Does he hit you?"

Mitch laughs loudly. "No, nothing as dramatic as that. He's more into mind games and gaslighting. But he's kinda fried his brain with dope so it's easier to stay a step ahead of him."

"But you've never actually answered why I should be careful," I remind him.

Mitch sighs and turns his head up to the sky. Morning is blooming on the horizon.

"He wants to collect you, it's what he does. That's why there's always trouble and drama surrounding Travis, because he's collected so many gay boys. He'll feed you drugs and booze and throw orgies in your honor until he's got you. Anytime he asks someone to come over from Gropr, I know what he's up to."

A thought bubbles up through the sea of vodka.

"I set myself up without even knowing it, too. I wasn't on Gropr for sex. I was on Gropr for weed. I was literally sending out messages to everyone asking if they had any green beans. He immediately responded, asked for more pics, I sent them, and then he dropped a pin for his address. But wait, why are you telling me all of this if you're his star?"

Finally, he looks directly at me and his eyes are clear, all traces of weed have vanished; he is being sincere and I should heed his advice.

"Because I think you're really cute, and sweet, and I don't want to see you get caught up in this shit. And Travis, well, his habits are getting darker and for some reason, I feel like I need to shield you from him. I don't know why, really."

I blush and try not to smile; he thinks I'm cute.

"Well, thank you, then. I mean, I rarely mess around with hardcore drugs, so I don't think any of that would have happened, but thank you."

"You may not yet, but he'd get you sooner or later. One night, when you're drunk and he's had time to wear you down. It's how he got me."

"But where *are* all these other people? Don't they have lives and jobs?" I feel incredulous.

Mitch shrugs. "Some do, some don't. Sometimes they stay here, sometimes they're on the run or with their family, trying to get better. But once he traps you, he's pretty much got you for good. Who else will give you drugs for free?"

I shake my head, trying to poke holes. "Nothing is free in this world. Nobody gives something as magnificent as drugs for nothing. No weird sex acts? Or stealing or anything?"

He rises and walks around the hot tub edge, splashing water. I pass the vodka bottle to him and he takes a swig.

"He wants to play house, play gypsy family. Like we're all some hippie gang or something. As long as you're going with the flow and playing the game, you're fine, but as soon as you step out of line, boom!" he snaps his fingers, "the drugs and booze are cut off."

"Oh. So, this is a cult. You're in a drug cult."

As the words fall from my mouth, I decide it is time for me to leave. This space is not safe and I have made a terrible decision in coming here. Mitch must sense my urgency to get the hell out, for he beckons to a back gate with amusement in his eyes.

"A cult, oh that's funny! I'm gonna have to share that, I like that. Listen, the gate leads to a carport, where you can get to the street. That way you don't have to make up some shitty lie for Travis. And, Charlie, don't message people for drugs on Gropr. I mean, honestly, *you* should probably just stay off Gropr altogether."

I open the latch to the back gate and pause to give Mitch one last glance. His soul is lost, more so than mine, and I feel a pang of pity and compassion for him. The moment feels bigger than me, I see our futures laid out before us: he a drug addict and myself an alcoholic. We're seeking love in all the wrong places, and will pay dearly. I wince and look down at the ground.

"You should probably get out of here, too, Mitch. You seem broken and I don't even know you. Thank you for the heads up."

Mitch smiles softly, the morning sun shining on his dark hair. I close the gate and walk under the covered carport out to the sidewalk. Glancing briefly over my shoulder, I send positive vibes his way and turn left. I will walk for a bit and then call a taxi.

Cigarette smoke swirls upward to my ceiling fan. I lay flat on my back in the middle of my living room, an ashtray to my left and a pint to my right. It has been over twenty-four hours since I started drinking and I've yet to sleep. The experience of last night unsettled me so deeply, I am afraid of shutting my eyes or sobering up. Eventually, I'll drink the fear away.

A chill creeps down my spine as I reflect on my impulsivity and recklessness regarding Gropr. Any sense of caution or reason seems to elude me when signed in. I have now paid the price for that twice. Last night was not my first foray into drunken madness using the App. Several weeks ago, in a near blackout, I took a taxi to another individual's house, with the promise of Xanax and an orgy. Naturally, I went on the pretense of joining the festivities, but my hidden agenda was to smuggle some Xanies and disappear. Little did I know that I was about to be witness to a knife stand-off between two extremely naked, extremely drugged-up heathens.

It was a comical event until I realized they weren't play-acting and actually out for blood. I have no idea what started the fight, and didn't stick around to see who won; I was fortunate that night, as well, and left with an older man who dropped me off a few blocks from my apartment. He seemed innocent enough, but I figured it was best if he didn't know which complex I lived in.

"You might not be so lucky next time," I slur to myself and rise, flicking my cigarette and missing the ashtray. "Shit."

Smacking my lips, I decide to take a shower and wash away the filth of my life. Cringing, I think of who I have become: a lush, fluttering from one junkie's house to the next for drugs and sex. It won't be long before I contract a serious STI or end up missing. I am heading down a soul-crushing path, and the wise move would be to backtrack. To stop before the damage becomes too severe. It's too much to handle at once, though. I will delete the App and then shower, eat, and sleep, stuffing this away from my mind. I work tomorrow and can already taste the acidic hangover. Lovely.

# 5

# Tips From Trella

*July 2015*
*Springfield, Missouri*
*29 Years Old*

Stirring under my sheets, I feel my head throbbing and a knot of guilt in my stomach. I have done something dreadful, of which I cannot remember. Licking my dry lips, I turn and see Trella sleeping on my couch. Fractured memories flash in my mind, and I break out in a cold sweat.

It hits me: I called her in a drunken stupor yesterday afternoon, talking about failure and shame; I was on a rant about being too weak to control my alcoholism, and how I should do us all a favor and end it. I rub my eyes, blocking the tears before they can stream. How fucking selfish, Charlie! *How selfish*, that you would even think such a thing!

I retch, then move swiftly and silently to my bathroom, closing the door and turning on the vent fan. Spitting up bile, I watch as sweat drips off my nose. It falls with the beat of my heart, thumping in my temples. A cramp stabs my left foot and my legs are trembling. Another bender has left me malnourished and weak. Oh, how lovely, Charlie. Well done, chap, well done.

Sinking to the floor, I lean on the cool wall and massage the back of my neck. The bile was a reaction to my behavior, rather than the lingering effects of booze. My actions have been so appalling, I've made myself physically sick. My arms quiver and I inhale sharply, catching a whiff of myself. It is a strong odor of sweaty vodka, stale cigarettes, and shame. Pungent.

A drink would steady me. The thought crosses my mind and I am stunned. Stunned that vodka would show its face at a time like *this*. The audacity. However, it *would* steady me. And I bet I didn't tell Trella all my hidey-holes.

Sure enough, behind some bandages and peroxide under my bathroom sink, is a full half-pint. It will take me about six minutes to get this bottle down, and then I can wake Trella and begin to work through the disaster I've created.

Doing my usual trick of slowly chattering my teeth, the vodka goes down smoothly enough. I place the empty contents behind the bandages and stand, viewing myself in the mirror.

"You're pathetic," I seethe, sneering. "Had to get you another drink, didn't you? You're such a coward, you can't do anything without drinking! No, keep it up, Charlie. Keep it up, you're lame and predictable, at least."

Closing my eyes tightly, I open my bathroom door, walk a few paces, and kneel down beside the couch. Gently, I shake Trella's shoulder. Her eyes open and focus on me.

"Good morning," she says sleepily.

I scoot back and sit crisscrossed. "Good morning. So I don't remember much of last night, but I've noticed that my coffee table is broken and you're here, so I'm sure it wasn't good."

She sighs and raises herself up. "No, Bub, it wasn't. But it wasn't as bad as you probably think, either. You wanted me to sit and listen and I tried sitting on your coffee table, and it broke. We laughed about it."

My whole body ignites; I can't control the tears. "Trella, I'm so sorry! This is *nuts*! My life is fucking *nuts* and I hate that you're constantly dragged into it!"

Her face is sad and sympathetic. "Oh, honey, it's okay."

"No, it's not! It's not fair to *you* or *anyone* else. It's just, I wish my drinking didn't have such an impact on everyone! I wish that I could drink and it wouldn't matter, and even though I know that's not possible, I just keep drinking as though it is! I won't give it up, and it's taking us all down. Like, you know I was only *stupid drunk* last night and would never kill myself, but I just feel so angry and hopeless sometimes. I hate myself and I feel like everyone else should, too, and just leave me alone. I just wish everyone could *go on* with their lives."

I sigh and fall onto the floor, exasperated.

"And I know I say I don't remember the things I've said or done in a blackout, but sometimes I do. I know I've said the most hurtful, ugly things to all of you. I've abandoned the girls, and short-charged their troubles as less than because it's not on par with my alcoholism. Like, it's nuts. It's insane. I'm deranged and unreliable. I'm useless. Tay doesn't need that in her life. Brod doesn't, either. It's unfair for me to ignore them the way I do.

"It's unfair for me to make my Dad feel as though this is all his fault, when all he's done is try. I'm so lame! I'm such a disappointment for you all, and I'm so sorry you have to deal with my bullshit."

Trella shakes her head and I see tears glistening on her cheeks.

She stares at her lap and then lifts her head.

"You're too hard on yourself. That's such a problem of yours, you get so mad at yourself that you can't do or see anything else. And none of us are really that mad at you, we're just worried and tired, Bub. We're worried and tired."

For a moment, there are only the sounds of our sniffles.

"That almost makes it worse. I just wish I could disappear and drink. That's all I want."

"Well, that's never going to happen. That's another problem. You need to start living for yourself again, you need to find a reason to live other than to drink! And don't tell me you can't or it's too hard, Charlie Gray, because I *know* you. Nothing is too hard for you, *you* just have to *want* to do it. You know it and I know it."

I chew my lips. She has me pinned, she's known me since the day I was born; I am choosing this lifestyle, whether I want to acknowledge it or not.

"I just love drinking so much," I say meekly.

"I know you do," she answers softly. "But it doesn't love you back, Bub."

"No, it sure doesn't seem to, does it?"

"Your drinking reminds me of how my Dad, your Grandpa Joe, used to drink. And, Bub, when it eventually caught up with him, it was heartbreaking to see. Please don't make me watch you go through what he went through. Please don't make me go through that again." Her voice is pleading and it is heart-wrenching.

"What do you think I should do?"

"Go to meetings. Start small and go from there. I'll help you, I'll help hold you accountable. I feel like I've enabled you a bit, and I'd like a chance to correct that. And as for the girls, you need to worry about yourself before you worry about them, Bub. They're tough girls, and they need you to get healthy again. But first things first. I think you would feel much better if you took a shower and then we could go get something to eat, or I could grab some food and cook?"

I wince. "Yeah, I could most definitely use a shower. Also, you're speaking the lingo, saying 'enabled'—that family support meeting was good for you and Dad, huh?"

She nods and begins to pull her hair into a ponytail. "It really was. It was reassuring to see many other families are struggling with this right along with us, and it made me feel less alone. I think it helped give your Dad perspective, too. He really listened to what the other fathers were saying in the room, and he actually spoke. I was surprised, but impressed."

My mouth gapes open. "Dad spoke? What did he say?"

"Mainly he just said he was frustrated and tired and that he didn't know what he was doing wrong. He said it was relieving to know others felt that way, too. I think he got some validation that day, which he needed."

A chord is struck within me. I've treated my Dad with such cruelty; I've used him as my punching bag, piling all my problems on his shoulders because it *had to be* someone's fault, other than my own. Not I, the wounded victim. Not the kid who bore the brunt of adulthood far too early. Good God, Charlie, when will I give that up?

"What's going on over there?" Trella beckons me.

"Oh, I'm just sitting here thinking about how horrible I've been to my Dad for years on end. And for no apparent reason other than I didn't want to deal with my own shit."

She sighs, giving me a motherly smile.

"You're not wrong, but I don't think that's where your head

needs to be *right now*. Beating yourself up over how you treated your Dad, *right now*, will just give you another excuse to run back to the bottle. Go take a shower."

"I know, I smell," I pull at my shirt and cringe. "Thank you."

"You're welcome, Bub," she smiles.

As I round the corner, shower fresh, I notice Trella has kindly cleaned and tidied my apartment. The dishwasher is humming, and she's taken the blanket covering the windows down, cracking them open; it lays folded on the foot of my neatly made bed.

"I thought some light and air would do you good," she beams.

"It does smell better! And I feel better. I really do. I just hope it lasts," I say skeptically.

Trella tilts her head knowingly, putting her hands on her hips. "Let's go eat. We'll worry about that later."

"Yes. Food other than pickles and chips is probably a good idea," I say dramatically under my breath and we chuckle.

# 6

# A Minor Awakening

*October 2015*
*Springfield, Missouri*
*29 Years Old*

Birds chirp loudly outside of my bedroom window, and I snap open my eyes, realizing I passed out before turning on my fan. Blinking to moisten my dried contacts, I notice my light was left on as well. Shaking my head, I try to piece together the night, and am met with piercing pain. The red wine, Charlie. Why did you drink so much red wine?

As I roll over, my stomach gurgles sourly. Burping, I taste wine and whiskey. Whiskey? When the hell did I have whiskey? I know I finished my pint of vodka at my apartment, and walked over to the pizza pub for some wine, but I honestly don't remember much after that. My blood runs cold as I recognize yet *another* night lost.

"Oh, God. Where is my phone—did I send anything weird?" I scramble out of bed, searching, and feel woozy and nauseous. It was not a good idea to move so quickly.

Locating it on my nightstand, I scroll through the messages, my heartbeat pulsing in my ears. Everything appears tame until I get to a message sent to my cute, straight co-worker, Harley:

*"So why were you so handsy the other night? Tryna get into my pants, bro?"*

Closing my eyes, I swallow a lump in my throat and fight back tears. I will not allow myself to cry over my own embarrassing, drunken behavior; I'd be crying all the damn time. But I have to quit sending messages like this. I'm going to get myself killed or lose my job, and the few threads I have left of my dignity. It's an ugly reminder of my sexually deviant escapades in Oregon; this is a disgusting part of my alcoholism, and I'm not sure what it says about me as a person. I don't believe it wise to investigate that character defect alone, though, for fear of what may be found. It should probably be carefully handled by someone with letters behind their name.

Yet I don't need a therapist to tell me I need to stop drinking all the vodka in the world. I am able to ascertain that entirely on my own. I'm treading perilously close to how I was living before fleeing Kansas City a few years back, and I don't want to repeat that fiasco again. I have way too much going for me, just as I did last time, and highly doubt luck will lend me another chance.

Walking to the kitchen for a glass of water and aspirin, I wonder if I should go to an AA meeting? They will most likely advise me to stop drinking, and there's a slim chance of that happening. I simply need to lessen my drinking. Control it a bit more; I've been letting it run wild and need help reigning it in. Perhaps I could go and only listen? On nights when I attend a meeting, I will stay sober, thus decreasing the number of days I drink. Genius.

I gulp some water, and immediately regret my haste, for right back up it spews. All over my kitchen counter, microwave and floor. I cough and wheeze, sinking to the floor. Panting, I wipe the sweat from my brow and pluck the paper towels from beside the sink.

"Oh, your fucking ass is going to a meeting, Charlie! This is ridiculous!"

Troye Sivan plays as I shower and attempt to wash away my sins. I found another message, and thankfully, it was sent to an ex of mine, Alec. I told him I missed him, which isn't true, and that I hoped he was doing well, which is true. Clearly, I was in need of attention last night; it feels desperate and weak, causing me to shiver.

I remain still as the water runs over me, warm and constant. Alec and I were a very troubled couple, two drunks fueling each other's bad habits. It was messy, dangerous, and chaotic. Thinking back on him is like wading through a cloud of hazy smoke. Vodka, pills, and weed. At the time, I thought it was mild and nothing to worry about, however, it's now apparent that was the height of my love affair with the insanity of vodka. Oh, Charlie.

Drying myself off, I peer in the mirror. The shower helped, I'm regaining color and my eyes aren't as bleary.

"Okay, you're going to a meeting. And it feels weird and scary, but it's so necessary at this point, dude."

Giving myself a skeptic smile, I shut the light off and get dressed.

My heart flutters as I pull into the church parking lot. It's quaint and ornate, with a triangular design for the steeple. Twenty or so cars are parked in the lot, and I wonder how many are here for the meeting. From what I read online, it should only consist of ten to fifteen people, but it would be my luck to show up on a busy night. Maybe I'll blend in better that way.

I am seventeen minutes early and brace myself for awkward conversations. Opening the main door, I spot signs pointing me down a hallway, and trail down it to a large study, with tables and chairs arranged to form a square. The walls are covered with books and the space feels cramped but comfortable. Several people sit scattered around the table and smile invitingly.

Smiling in return, I take a seat at the edge of where two tables meet and remain mindful to keep my arms uncrossed. I want to appear friendly and approachable.

"Hello," an elderly lady with luscious silver hair says from across me. "My name is Eloise, how are you this evening?"

"Hi, I'm Charlie," I grin at her. "Honestly, I'm still fairly hungover. It's been a long, rough day."

She chuckles lightly. "You're in the right place, then."

"Much better than a bar or liquor store," a middle-aged man in the center of the table says gruffly. There are several-sized books, laminated sheets of paper, and a basket placed in front of him.

"This is true," I agree cheerfully.

"I'm John, an alcoholic, glad you're here tonight. Is this your first meeting?" he asks. His gray eyes match his bushy eyebrows.

"Kind of. I went to a few when I was in a rehab in Oregon a couple of years ago, but that was forced and I wasn't *truly* concerned about my drinking at the time. So this is the first time I've actually gone on my own. The first time I've felt the need to go."

Eloise beams at me. "Well, that's excellent!" she says, looking around the table at the others. "Should we do a First Step meeting? For Charlie?"

I see nods of agreement and my chest warms. I have no idea what I'm getting myself into, but I'm flattered these strangers are interested in helping me, validating I made the right choice in coming here.

John clears his throat. "I think that's a great idea, El. Do you know what a First Step meeting is, Charlie?"

I chew my top lip. "A meeting about the First Step?" I offer with a roguish smile.

"Basically," an older gentleman chortles at the end of the table. "Hi, I'm Dan, alcoholic. Once you get in 'The Big Book,' you'll start to work The Steps, and you'll become more familiar. The First Step says that we admitted to ourselves that we're drunks, that booze ran our lives, and that we needed something other than ourselves in order to put down the bottle. Can you agree with that?"

I take a breath. "I mean, I can't not agree with it."

"Good enough for now. Tonight, we'll share with you how we came to that conclusion, and what we did from there. You'll only have to listen."

"Oh, perfect. Wow, thank you, guys! This is very kind and I appreciate it—I was at a loss all day, and now I feel like I'm finally doing something right."

"That's what it's all about," Eloise says.

As the meeting commences, each member shares their experience with alcohol and sobriety. I am astounded by how vulnerable and candid they are, explaining in great detail their highs and lows with addiction. A clear resemblance to my life emerges, and I feel queasy. It is not from the hangover, but rather the discovery my affection for alcohol will most likely lead me down a devastating path.

My dependence on its soothing effects is ripped from behind its veil; I really might be an alcoholic. The thought has always been there, swirling in the back of my mind, but I've refused to tether myself to it. If I didn't assume it, it wouldn't consume me. Vodka seems to be winning, though. That much is fairly obvious.

My biggest plight remains whether or not I have the capability, or desire, to abstain entirely. Each member describes their life growing infinitely better once they released themselves from the bottle, but my circumstance is not as dire, as desolate. Yet. But why should I let it become that way? They weren't careful enough. They fell over the edge, but I simply need to stay near it. And I *must* stay near it, to keep my sanity. Navigating life without the aid of liquor is beyond my comprehension. It seems such a dull, uninspired existence.

After meeting wraps with a prayer, I find myself exhausted from listening, absorbing, and thinking. I rub the back of my neck as I file out behind Dan, and Eloise taps my shoulder.

"Wanna have a smoke?" she asks, her bracelets chiming against one another. There is a grace about her I find intriguing.

"Sure," I answer.

She leads the way outside, over to a designated smoking area, and lights up. I follow suit and wait for wisdom, but she surprises me.

"So, how long have you been drinking?"

I take a drag and think.

"I'd say it's been heavy since around twenty-three. I've had moments of sobriety, but they were usually short-lived. So that would make six years. Oh, wow."

Hearing myself say the number is startling, and I feel taken aback.

"It doesn't have to be any more time than that, if you don't let it. What is your drink of choice?"

"Vodka," I say flatly.

"I was a gin drinker, but it's all the same. Do you have a meeting planned for tomorrow night, or are you drinking?"

Her question catches me off guard; she is astute. But there's no need to lie to her, we barely know one another.

"I hadn't really decided, but probably drink. I was thinking I could drink on nights that I don't go to a meeting. Honestly, I really just want to cut down on my drinking. I'm not trying to completely quit."

She gives me a knowing gaze; Eloise understands and pities me at the same time.

"That really isn't how AA works, but I get your plan. And it's not a bad one, hun, you just won't find much support here for that type of plan. We're in it for the long haul, you know?"

"Yes, I figured that's what I would hear. And it's probably what I *need* to hear."

She sighs. "I'm going to give you my number, please call or text me if you need someone to talk to—I'm always available for a fellow alcoholic."

"Thank you!" I say earnestly. Her thoughtfulness for a complete stranger is touching and seems to be the spirit of AA thus far.

"And take care of yourself. You may not be ready to quit drinking yet, but you do have a problem and your life will be so much easier if you stop now. There, I've said my bit, I'm done. Call me if you need me, Charlie."

She smiles, disposes of her cigarette in the receptacle, and waves, heading off to her red SUV.

Driving home, I fight the urge to stop and grab a half-pint of vodka. If I can't stick to this, then I most certainly have a problem, and need to stop drinking entirely. But I don't want to stop, so I will be strong. I will rent a movie, smoke a bowl, and go to bed like a good boy.

"And then you can drink tomorrow. Or maybe you won't want to, and we can wait for the weekend?"

My eyes flicker to the rearview mirror and back to the road. "Don't push it, Charlie."

Pressing pause on *Avengers: Age of Ultron*, I step into my kitchen and start a cup of green tea. As the kettle boils, I stare out my balcony door. The wind blows gustily, rustling the limbs around my porch. It is peaceful, and I'm so grateful I chose to stay sober. I was too busy sailing in a vodka bottle to catch the latest Marvel flick, and I'd missed a captivating entry in the saga.

I will sleep like a lamb, and feel well-rested when waking. The vodka dragon of the morning won't pester me, I have fresh coffee and weed; it should make for a glorious morn.

"See, this is what normal people do, Charlie. They don't guzzle gallons of vodka every night and wage war with themselves in the morning!"

I give myself a hollow chuckle, aware of how ludicrous my life has grown. Yet again.

I am reminded of my conversation with Eloise. I didn't realize it at the time, but she hit a nerve when she said I had a problem. It wasn't that she called me out, but more that she was able to clearly see the battle raging within me. I've fooled so many for so long, I never assumed it was visible. Although, I'm rarely in a room full of fellow alcoholics.

"So you acknowledge it, then?" I say out loud, stunned. "You finally acknowledge that you're an alcoholic?"

My voice echoes in my head and the kettle flips off. I pour water over my tea and feel a tizzy creeping up. My Grandpa Joe was an alcoholic. I've been to rehab. I had to detox in the ICU. I was drunk when I crashed my car and fractured my neck. And when I ran a four-wheeler through a barbed-wire fence. I'm an alcoholic.

"Well, fuck!" I exclaim. "Damn it, Charlie! You took it too far—you've got to get a hold of it, man. You've got to."

I fumble for my cigarettes, stepping outside to smoke and collect myself. This is crazy. I shan't go down this road. I'll keep my drinking to the weekend so that I *can* keep it. I cannot give it away, I *will* not. This whole debacle has grown far too melodramatic and time-consuming; I will tone it down and find my balance. Vodka is my friend, vodka will not hurt me, I must master it. I love vodka and it's imperative I treat it more kindly.

# 7

# Chickenwire Foxtrot

*July 2016*
*Springfield, Missouri*
*30 Years Old*

Anxiously pacing my tiny studio apartment, I tap my phone to check Anne's location. As I'm waiting for my map to load, I glance hither and thither, ensuring everything is spic and span. Her pin pops up: she is four minutes away. Clapping my hands, I straighten the lid to the trashcan and lean against my wall, satisfied. I'm hosting a reunion for our old Drury gang and want my place to be as hospitable as possible. Wax warmers fill the air with a splendid masculine scent and I have my bong, Natasha Petrova, loaded and ready.

Anne and Bert will crash here with me, while Ransom stays with Keith in the country, at his Granny's old house. Keith and I are the only ones still located in Springfield. Bert attends grad school in St. Louis, Ransom moved up to Columbia, and Anne is making killer moves in Dallas. It's been a couple of years since the whole crew graced the same state, and I cannot wait for this weekend to begin.

Blunts on blunts on blunts. It shall be glorious! As they're all aware of my struggles with alcohol, weed will probably be the only substance we partake in. Keith may have other stimuli, one never knows with him. The others have tamed a bit, but Keith and I still rage. I sometimes wonder if he battles with alcohol as I do, yet we've never had that conversation; we've danced around it, but never addressed it full-on.

I drum on my countertop with excitement as Anne's dot arrives at my apartment complex. Rushing out the door and down the flight of stairs, I meet her as she climbs out of her gold car, Pussywillow. Or Pussy, for short.

"Lassie!" she calls, channeling Audrey Hepburn in her large black sunglasses.

"Oh, Lassie, you're absolutely lovely!" I fawn, hugging her tight.

"Lassie, you *smell* lovely!" she giggles.

"Oh shucks, thank you, I showered for you," I grin, helping unload her bags from Pussy.

As we walk into my apartment, Anne gasps at Natasha Petrova and turns to me.

"She's as beautiful as her picture, Lassie! Hello, Natasha Petrova, it is *most splendid* to make your acquaintance," she purrs in a throaty British lilt.

I chuckle as she assesses my home. I've gone with an Old World eclectic theme and I'm quite proud of my decor.

"Lassie, this is so sweet! And your kitchen is surprisingly spacious for a studio—are you still cooking?"

"I am," I answer, plucking Natasha Petrova off the counter and taking a seat on my red couch; it once belonged to Brod, but she left it to me when moving to Nashville last year.

"Oh yes, let's," Anne follows me and plops on the couch. I offer her Natasha Petrova and a gray lighter so that she may start the bowl with the greenest of hits. She winks at me, firing it up.

"So, how are you, Lassie?" she asks, holding the smoke in her lungs.

"Oh, I'm doing okay. I still struggle, but I've got a firmer grip on it now than I have in years, so that's good," I say and scratch my ear.

It's mostly the truth; I drink three or four nights a week and most Saturdays, and it takes all I have to remain sober on Sunday. On the odd Sunday I *do* stay sober, that is.

"I'm glad you're trying. I was really worried about you a few years ago when I visited Oregon. I know you said you weren't drinking on that trip, but I smelled it on you."

I bow my head, a bit crestfallen. "I knew that you knew, I just didn't want to acknowledge it at the time. I'm sorry. I was in such a fragile state then, and so embarrassed for you to see me, but so happy that you did. It was a trip of so many mixed emotions."

Anne nods and lays Natasha Petrova on my coffee table.

"I wondered if it was something like that. But I don't want you to *ever* feel that way around me, Charlie. We're Lassies, you know? That's part of the beautiful friendship you and I are so lucky to have. We're more than just college friends. There's a depth to our relationship, there's real meaning. I'm so thankful to have you in my life, and I know you feel the same way."

My throat is tight and my eyes sting. "Oh, Anne. You are so amazing. Really."

She winks again, plucking Natasha Petrova from the table.

AT LEAST I'M NOT THE FROG

Bert and Anne crawl into my car, Lucy, and we hit the highway toward Keith's.

"Lucy is very fine, but I do miss Martha," Anne sighs, causing Bert to giggle.

"Oh, Martha," he says.

"You guys, it was such a weird day, trading Martha in. I felt like I'd abandoned her! It felt cruel and wrong and it took me a while to get over it. It's like she was a part of me."

"Oh, but my Las, she was," Anne answers passionately.

"I know," I moan. "But I'm sure she has an amazing new owner and she's very happy. Maybe she got an elderly lady who barely drives her?" I hope.

"She's alright, she wrote me recently and said all was well. She was always a strong one, that Martha," Bert announces from the backseat, wizened and lofty. Anne and I cackle.

"Ope, Ransom just texted and said we should meet them at the cave," says Anne. "Yay! The cave!"

"Oh yeah, we haven't been there since college—that's an excellent idea!" Bert chortles.

"To the cave! Um. Where is the cave again?" I ask sheepishly.

Anne laughs. "Hop on James River Freeway and I can get us there."

"Your trusty co-captain!" Bert drums the headrest of Anne's seat.

The sky is cloudless, bright blue, and the air smells thick with flowers, fresh. I admire us, our motley gang, reuniting and it feels so good! Keith and Ransom brought a super blunt and intend for the five of us to smoke it in the cave, for old time's sake.

"So you just put two blunt wraps together? Why didn't we

think of that years ago?" I ask.

As we trek up the trail, I am greeted by a sense of nostalgia. It *is* just like old times, moving as a herd, the scent of marijuana in our wake. These are my people, through thick and thin, and I'm so thankful for their friendships.

Bert hikes up beside me and flashes a goofy grin. No matter how much older we grow, Bert remains the same: tall, lanky, and boyishly handsome.

"So what're you doing nowadays, chap?"

"I'm back in banking, and it's going well, but I'm kinda aching for a career change. How's the graduate degree going? What're you studying again?"

"It's kinda hard to explain, so I'll just say anthropology."

I turn to him, impressed. "That sounds fancy, dude!"

"I'm going in, bitches!" Keith calls from ahead and then disappears. Bert and I hasten our pace.

The entrance to the cave is on the side of a hill, about five feet tall with a similar width, and easy to fit through if hunched over. After walking four yards, it opens, and there is room to stand and comfortably pass a blunt. Bert enters before me and soon we're all crammed together in the dim light of the cave. Ransom strikes his lighter, and our faces are illuminated.

He holds the flame to the blunt and begins the sacred ritual. We snicker and cough, the cherry of the blunt casting shadows.

"It's been *so long* since I've hotboxed a cave," Anne says, exhaling a billow of smoke. "It was probably college, the last time."

"Me, too," Ransom says, holding in a hit. He's wearing his white-blonde hair shaggy around his ears, evoking a California surfer vibe. If there's any of us that would be a California surfer, it's Ransom. He is one of the most relaxed, accepting individuals

I have ever met.

Ranson, Bert, and Keith are the first guy friends I've had in my life. Moving to the Clinton School District in sixth grade, I wasn't exactly well-liked. I was new, cute, and gay. Which meant the girls took to me alright, but the boys wanted little to nothing to do with being my friend. I was never beaten up, but I was made fun of, called names, and constantly searching for excuses to get out of gym class. The psychological damage hurt worse than an actual punch. My lone guy friend in middle and high school was named Steve, and we still talk every so often.

It took an amount of courage I didn't know I possessed to rush my Freshman year of college; I assumed guys would see me as a girly gay boy and pass me over. Fortunately, I completely missed the mark on that and was invited to join Sigma Pi Fraternity, where I met Ransom, Bert, and Keith. They've never batted an eye at my sexuality; in fact, they have *developed* an eye for my type and we work as a team of wingmen.

My fraternity brothers helped me find my identity as a guy. I was able to relax around them, come out of my shell, and learn how to talk to other guys. They're my boys, friendships I never thought I'd have. They're also fiercely protective of me, and it is a source of pride.

Keith catches a whooping cough and pulls his phone out to see. As he turns on his flashlight, it shoots a beam at the ceiling, and we all shriek in horror. Hundreds of crawling bugs scatter, their many legs scrambling. I briefly glance at them before charging out, and they look like large centipedes with antennas. Freaky and disgusting!

Anne does a heebie-jeebie dance and scratches at her hair. "I feel like they're on me!"

"Me, too!" Keith brushes at his shoulders and back.

"They're probably more scared of us than we are of them," Ransom says, calm in the face of peril.

"Still, they're ugly little fuckers," I retort, shaking out my arms.

"The blunt's still burning, guys," Bert giggles from the mouth of the cave.

"Bert, get away from there with that! They might steal it!" Keith warns.

"Shall we walk the old trails, then?" Bert asks with an amused grin.

"Guys!" I exclaim. "We forgot about the *other* hill and the box of remembrances we found there in college—we should go check that!"

Their eyes widen with realization and excitement. Anne sings a high note of epiphany and we fall into line stepping carefully down the hill.

*****

Bert walks outside with me while I smoke a cigarette. It's early in the morning, Anne will sleep for another two or three hours, and we'll entertain ourselves until she wakes. It's a throwback to our Drury days and I'm digging it. Bert stretches and clears his throat.

"I wanted to go into more detail yesterday, but it wasn't the time. How are you *really* doing?"

His eyes meet mine, full of concern and love. We were roommates for two years in college, and developed a very close friendship.

"I'm okay. I'm not running around like the drunk maniac I was a few years ago, so that's an improvement."

He smiles softly. "True. But you're still struggling?"

"Yes."

"I feel like it's because you're not fulfilled, man. You're working for a bank, and there's nothing wrong with that, but it's so *not* Charlie. Climbing the corporate ladder?"

"You're right," I sigh. "You are. But it was a safe choice at the time, and now I feel stuck in it. Or stuck in the corporate game, that is. Like, just climb the ladder, there's job security *and* personal security there."

"But is there room for you in all that security, you know? Where do you get to thrive in the big picture?"

I cluck my tongue. "Oh, you're perceptive, aren't you? Sentient Bert."

He sticks to his guns. "You have no outlet for yourself, Charlie. You're not a monotonous person. You're airy and cheeky, a lightning bolt of charm, but that's all dimmed these last few years. Surely you feel that?"

I take a deep breath and stare into the distance. Bert has voiced what I could not, and it's overwhelming.

"I do feel different than I used to. It's hard to describe. Muted, I suppose. Or dimmed, that was a good way of putting it. It's just that I had this idea of how my life was going to play out, and it couldn't have gone more differently. So now I'm just like, what the fuck do I do with myself? I don't mean that to be whiny, I understand I'm super fortunate. But I just feel, well, lacking. And stagnant."

Bert puts his hand on my shoulder.

"You're losing yourself, Charlie. You've got to find your passion again, man. And maybe it's not acting—maybe it's something completely different. But you've got to find something before it just becomes vodka." He pats my cheek. "Take care of yourself, chap. I'm quite fond of you and would prefer it if you stuck around. The Girl would, too."

I grin sheepishly. "Oh, Bert. I'm so glad you're here right now."

The breeze whistles around us, and we stand still, enjoying the company of one another. He pats me on the back again as I finish my cigarette and we walk upstairs. I'm frightening those that I love most, and have the entirety of my family and friends worried about my mental and physical health. A sense of guilt pools in my stomach and I yearn to be more, to be better.

# 8

# Palm Beach Retreat

*July - August 2017*
*Springfield, Missouri*
*West Palm Beach, Florida*
*31 Years Old*

I awake from a drunken, vampiric coma and feel achy; my lower back is sore, probably a sign of early liver failure. Eluding the shower for the last four days, my hair is an oil slick and I might be flammable. Rolling out of bed, I stand in my apartment, straining to see in the dim light. Realizing I covered my window with a blanket in my stupor, I pull it back slightly, to assess the damage. Early morning sun streams over pizza boxes and empty vodka pints, scattered across every surface. Spotting an ashy, swampy glass, I notice that rather than stepping outside, I've used a broken glass as an ashtray, smoking indoors. I'm sure my apartment smells fragrantly of cigarettes, grease, and despair.

Walking the short distance to my bathroom, I flip on the light and inhale sharply through my teeth. A frighteningly pale man with bloodshot eyes and dark circles stares back at me.

Watching him, I think about avoiding my phone for as long as possible. I have far too many lies to spin, yet not enough mental energy. Exhaling slowly, I'm sure I can breathe fire with my dragon vodka breath.

Smacking my lips, I head to the freezer. Three more pints await me before I have to venture out for more. I pour a shot and stare at it, entranced, for a long while. This is terrible. This is insane. I'm so angry it has gotten to this point. I down some vodka and wait to see if my body tries to reject the alcohol. Sometimes I go too long in between doses and my stomach isn't prepared. After a few moments, my stomach settles, and I take a large swig from the bottle.

Taking a seat on my couch, I wait for the effect. Since it no longer matters, I light a cigarette and lean back as the heat of liquor begins to spread throughout my body. My mind is still racing, however. I'm at my limit of calling in at work and my family thinks I'm sober. Each day for the last several months has been a major battle to abstain from drinking, and I've lost more than I've won. As much as I dread it, the time for honesty has arrived.

While picking up my phone, a thought dawns on me: rehab. Surely that will soften the blow! I would have to find a legitimate facility, though. I shall not be duped again like I was in Oregon.

Panicking, I search Google and pound shots. After an hour of clicking and boozing, I have located the ideal treatment center: Palm Beach Retreat in West Palm Beach, Florida. The grounds are massive and calming, with tranquil landscaping and tasteful living quarters. Their website advertises a specialized, holistic approach, incorporating meditation, gardening, art, music, and equine therapy.

I push the number under Contact Us and my phone begins to dial. My mouth is dry, and I take another sip from the bottle, chasing it with pickle juice.

"Thank you for calling Retreat, this is Tasha, may I ask who I'm speaking with?"

Her voice is raspy, yet kind. I clear my throat.

"Hello, my name is Charlie."

"Hi, Charlie. How are you doing today?"

I give her a hollow laugh and blink, suffocated by guilt.

"Oh, not well, Tasha. Not well at all."

"I'm genuinely sorry to hear that, Charlie. Let's talk about it."

I pause and try to gather my thoughts. It is a futile effort, I am two and a half pints in and feeling wobbly. I grab another cigarette and perch on the edge of my bed.

"I don't even know how this works," my voice cracks and I inhale the smoke deeply, searching around for my weed pipe.

"That's okay. We can keep it simple: what made you call today?"

Locating my pipe on the window ledge, still mostly loaded, I take a big hit and cough.

"Sorry, I've been drinking. Like, a lot. And smoking. Not as much, though. But you didn't ask about that, you asked why I called. Sorry, I'm a bit out of sorts."

"It's okay, believe me, I've been right where you're at."

Swallowing hard, I focus. "I called because I'm at a loss as to what to do. I'm afraid to call work. I'm afraid to call my family. I'm just afraid. I know I need help, but this will blindside everyone and I'm freaking out. I figured if I already had a plan in place, it might help when I break the news."

"You've done right by calling, Charlie. And it's good that you're scared, it shows that you care. Let's keep talking, let me get some information from you, and we'll get you sorted out."

An hour later, I am frantically throwing clothes into my suitcase and finishing off the last of my vodka. A taxi will pick me up in forty-five minutes, and I still need to pack a few things and shower. I would like to sprint over to the liquor store and buy another half-pint, but I doubt there is time. I wonder, would the taxi driver make a pit stop? If nothing else I can always drink on the plane, as the treatment center was able to purchase a direct flight on my behalf. I'm not sure of the cost, nor do I care; it's all factored into my final bill, and I will deal with that at a later date. If all goes as planned, I should be touching down in West Palm Beach around 8:35 this evening.

Turning the water on, I sag against the wall and level with myself. I have not yet reached blackout, but I'm borderline. I should not get another half-pint. I should brush my teeth, wash my hair, and wait for my ride.

I admire the sunset from my window as the plane skids onto the runway. Turning my phone on, message notifications vibrate from my family and work. In the mad dash to the airport, I fired off several texts to my Dad, Brodie, Trella, my boss Haythem, and a few coworkers, explaining that I was admitting myself to rehab. I try to read their replies, realizing how incredibly drunk I am. Each message is long and mostly supportive, but I can't seem to comprehend its entirety. I put my phone in my pocket and decide to respond at another time.

Standing to deplane, I sway and catch myself on the seat in front of me. With my vision blurry and shirt sticking to my back, I long for a cigarette chased with a pickle.

Carefully, I exit the plane. I vaguely remember to keep an eye out for someone holding a name card bearing C. Gray. Scanning the terminal, I find him standing near the back of the crowd, sign in hand and smiling. He's taller than me, Latino, and rather attractive.

"I'm Charlie," I say and offer my hand.

"Hey, Charlie! I'm Bastian, how was your flight?"

"I drank the whole way!" I grin.

Bastian laughs. "Sure you did! Let's go get your bags."

After retrieving my belongings, Bastian leads me out of the airport to a parked SUV, sleek and black. He walks around to the driver's side as I open the passenger door and slide delicately into the seat. The world around me feels slippery.

"Bougie," I say, glancing over at him. He has shiny dark hair and wears a stylish watch on his left arm.

"Oh yeah, very fancy. It's one of Retreat's chauffeur vehicles. Do you want to listen to some music?"

"Can you play some San Holo?" I slur.

He grins. "Sure thing, man."

"Okay, thanks." The music beats. "Bastian, I'm drunk. Like, *drunk*, drunk."

"That's all right, are you going to be sick?"

"No," I answer quickly. "No, I just thought I should tell you. I mean, *you're taking me to a rehab*."

He drums the steering wheel. "You're good, Charlie. We've checked in a fair amount of drunk people."

"Oh, that's good to hear. It'll be easy, then."

Folding my hands in my lap, I lean against the window and watch the city whiz by, appreciating the new scenery. For the time being, my shame and anxiety are numb from the drink. I dread waking up tomorrow morning not only sober, but in a treatment center for an undetermined amount of time. I've made sure this isn't a repeat of my Oregon escapades, but I'm still apprehensive as to how it will play out. At the very least, I hope to stumble upon a few pieces of the Charlie I used to be.

*****

I sit in one of the many gazebos scattered across the grounds, holding a steaming cup of coffee and a lit cigarette. Palm Beach Retreat did not falsely advertise: their facility is breathtaking, straight out of a Sandra Bullock movie. It was nighttime during my admission, and with the rising sun, I have had a chance to explore.

The sprawling U-shaped compound is formed by three large, tan brick buildings. On the left side of the compound is their main facility, a crescent of windows three stories high, holding the living quarters, nursing area, admissions, and dining hall. Anchoring the middle of the U is the gym and indoor basketball court, separated from the main facility by a peaceful alcove with a coy pond. There is a massive garden stocked with vegetables, melons, and herbs between the fitness building and a squat round hall, completing the right side of the U. Music and art therapy are held on the eastern portion of the hall while the counselor offices and group spaces make up the western portion. Two ancient oak trees stand in the middle, providing shade for a pleasant and inviting communal space. Heavy wooden benches and oversized picnic tables are placed neatly amid flower boxes and a reflection pool. From here, rock paths twist through lush, manicured grass, connecting the myriad of buildings, gazebos, and serenity berms. Flowers and bushes grow in patches under large cypress and mahogany trees. If nothing else, I chose a peaceful setting for my collapse.

The grounds are still. I close my eyes and hear birds singing. Sleep evaded me last night, despite my first round of detox meds. I have been prescribed the usual cocktail for withdrawing alcoholics: phenobarbital, Keppra, Ativan, and Seroquel. They've also added loads of vitamin B, minerals, and Vistaril, an anti-anxiety med, for good measure. A chemical nap awaits me, far better than the usual nausea and shakes I experience when eliminating vodka.

I discard my cigarette in the receptacle and follow a trail back to the living quarters. My assigned room is on the second floor of the main building, facing away from the common area, with views of Florida's native trees. It is surprisingly spacious. Two full-sized beds are placed on opposite walls, each with its own dresser and nightstand. A shared desk sits between the doors for the entryway and bathroom, which holds a small sink, shower, and toilet. My roommate's name is Mark, a heroin addict. He arrived two days before me and must be detoxing hard, for I have yet to see him move unless sprinting to the porcelain throne.

I gently shut the door and crawl into bed, switching on my white noise machine. In a few hours, I shall rise and acclimate myself to this new environment.

The sun is setting on my first full day of rehab and I've spent it mostly asleep. I wander along a rock path to a stone bench near the gardens, rickety from my phenobarbital. Taking a seat on the bench, I smile over at a woman admiring the garden. She's slender and pretty, with bobbed caramel hair. She smiles back and begins to walk over.

"Hi, I'm Brenda," she says, waving slightly.

"Hi, Brenda. My name is Charlie," I say, with my own little

wave.

Brenda clears her throat. "I'm sorry, I just got here a few hours ago and you're the first person that's smiled at me. Can I bum a cigarette? I'm *so jittery* being here." She shakes her hands back and forth and laughs nervously.

"Sure," I hand her a cigarette and offer my lighter, which she waves away. She pulls out her own, which is green and yellow plaid.

"Oh, I've got one of these, just not any cigarettes."

"That's a fancy one," I say. "I just got here last night. You're the first person I've talked to other than my roommate and the staff."

"I haven't smoked since high school, but I figure it's all I've got left now," she says dramatically, taking a long drag.

"What's your vice?" I ask, suppressing a giggle at her tone.

"Alcohol," she answers, frowning. "And I didn't realize it was such a problem until recently."

"Me, too. Alcohol, that is. I've known it was a problem for a while now."

"Are you from around here?"

I grin. "No, I'm from Springfield, Missouri."

"Oh, wow, Missouri! I'm from Pennsylvania, not too far out of New York City."

Brenda stumbles a bit and catches herself on my shoulder.

"Oh, God! I promise I'm not drunk! I think it's the damn pills they gave me!"

I scoot over and she sits beside me on the bench. "I know, the pheno. It does it to me, too. I feel like I'm drunk, yet I'm here to quit drinking. It's all *very* confusing."

Brenda chuckles uncomfortably, her breath hitching, and grips her knees.

"It'll be alright," I say warmly, not knowing if I believe it myself but wanting to comfort her. "We came in at the same time, we'll stick together and it'll be over before we know it."

She smiles, her eyes watering.

"You're kind," she says matter-of-factly.

"You know, my mom's name was Brenda. I've always had a soft spot for women named Brenda."

"Was? Oh, I'm so sorry."

I shrug. "It was a long time ago."

"I hope you don't mind me asking, but how old are you, Charlie?"

"I'm thirty-one."

"I have a daughter, well two actually, but one is close to your age, in their late twenties. We will get along just fine! Now, I don't know about you but this medicine makes me hungry. Have you eaten dinner?"

"Not yet, wanna go?"

Brenda stands up and brushes off her pant legs. "I hope the food is good at this place."

Brenda and I carry our trays around the dining hall, deciding what to eat. It is on the first floor, down the hall from admissions. The setup is similar to a food court, with different stations serving various cuisines from around the world. There is a hefty fireplace in the middle of the room with sturdy wooden tables and chairs placed on either side; the windows provide sweeping views of the communal space.

As I walk over to the salad bar, I notice very few people dining. It is nearly six in the evening, and not long ago I heard an announcement about an upcoming AA meeting. While on detox status, I'm not required to attend any groups or meetings, and I plan to take advantage of this time. Doing what, I'm not sure. Decompressing, perhaps.

I find Brenda at a table near the fireplace with a plate full of chicken and vegetables.

"I wonder if these are from the garden," I say, nibbling at my greens.

"Yes, I think so. I know gardening is one of the groups here. I had a list of questions before coming. I was checking out a couple of places."

"Oh, wow, that makes me feel better. I looked around a bit, too. Also, my salad is really good, how's your food?"

Brenda nods and grins. "You know, maybe it's just the pills, but not bad."

I plod the trails with Brenda after dinner, shuffling along and sharing a pack of cigarettes. Our feet fall heavy from the pheno. We're candid, talking about fears of addiction and the moments leading up to treatment. She is calming and I recognize a kindred spirit. Keeping silent about my issues for months, it is refreshing to speak so openly with a "peer." I barely know Brenda, but our struggles are similar, and my feeling of loneliness is lighter.

Brenda tosses her cigarette butt in a trashcan and checks her watch.

"It's almost 7:45, I think we're supposed to go take meds," she says lazily. "Like I really *need* anymore, but I'll sleep well, I suppose."

"Sleep like a drunken baby," I say.

We turn toward the main facility, and the breeze picks up. We're near a serenity berm full of colored rocks emblazoned with inspirational quotes.

"I bet we make those in art therapy," I muse.

"I bet you're right," Brenda says as we walk by a group of smokers near the common area. "How many people do you think are here?"

"I'm not sure, sixty-something?"

"They told me it holds ninety-six but that they're rarely at full capacity."

"Damn," I say. "That's a lot of drunks and junkies to have in one location."

We arrive at our crescent home and split up, Brenda going to the third floor and me to the second.

"Catch you after meds for a smoke?" she calls, walking up the stairs.

"Sure thing," I call back, walking down the hall to the nurse.

*****

It has been six days since checking into rehab, and I'm beginning to find my pace. Due to the large population of Retreat, every patient is assigned a group based on their substance of choice and history. I have been placed in Journey, a group for individuals with acute trauma and an alcohol or opiate dependency. My conversation with Tasha is fuzzy, however, I'm assuming I spoke about walking in on Mom having her final stroke followed by the repercussions of my stepmothers. It's becoming more and more evident I haven't processed the pain of those moments. I feel I have made peace with the *loss* of Mom, but *not* with the circumstances. I accept that she is no longer here, although I must still harbor some emotional wreckage. Perhaps this is the root cause of my drinking?

Of the six groups, Journey is one of the smallest, and I am lucky to have Brenda in there as well. Our group meets twice a day for an hour, in the morning after breakfast, and in the evening after dinner. I spend the remainder of the day in art or music therapy, meditation, and educational groups. Retreat believes allowing a certain amount of freedom within their curriculum is vital for each patients' recovery. I am especially excited to add equine therapy and gardening once I'm cleared from detox. Horses have been a part of my life since before I can remember, and I anticipate their presence will do my soul well.

Mark, my roommate, keeps to himself and a couple of friends he made in his group, Clarity, which is designed for young opioid addicts. He is chill, thankfully, as the sheer number of patients makes for interesting entertainment. In my short time, I have witnessed several seizures, a bloody brawl, a meth psychosis, and a drunkard pass out in the entryway fountain. Meltdowns abound hourly, and with all the booze and drugs gone, the entire compound is spiraling.

All of this I have observed through my cloud of detox meds. The fuzziness is a welcome reprieve from the chaos. And, if I'm being honest, a crutch for the lack of weed or drink. My pill intoxication will not last indefinitely, though. Here shortly, the nurse will no longer see a need for my "comfort meds" and I'll truly be sober as a lark.

I spend most of my limited downtime with Brenda and her roommate, Claire. Claire is older than Brenda, with white-blonde hair and bright blue eyes. She is from New York City and absolutely hilarious. She arrived plastered, tricked by her family and friends into thinking she was headed to a girl's weekend. It was quite the spectacle, and for a petite woman, she made a helluva commotion. Staff chased her halfway down the drive, suitcases in tow, before persuading her to stay the night and reevaluate in the morning.

After making my bed, which is required, I leave my room for the dining hall. Grabbing some yogurt I find a table with a few others from Journey group.

"I'm not fucking dealing with her shit today," Melissa says with her arms crossed, teetering on the back legs of her chair. Melissa is a firecracker. She is tiny, with dark hair and eyes, and speaks in a nasally, Brooklyn accent. I enjoy her outbursts immensely.

She's referring to Joanna, a primary counselor and the leader of the majority of groups for Journey. Melissa does not appreciate Joanna's no-nonsense approach to sobriety and frequently challenges her authority. Joanna zings right back, though, and I believe it's because she sees a great deal of her younger self in Melissa, making it easier to bring specific behaviors to the surface.

"It's just because you know she's partially right," Caroline says evenly. Caroline is from Massachusetts, well educated, and loquacious. She is a junior in college studying journalism, and this is her fourth stint in rehab. According to her, she shouldn't be here at all, as she was taking her Adderall as prescribed. Apparently, there was a miscommunication between her therapist and psychiatrist. I'm not sure, it all sounds made up to me, but I don't question.

"Whatever, probably," Melissa spits back. She leans forward, letting the front legs of her chair hit the ground with a bang.

The counselor's wing is circular and painted dark blue. Potted plants and squishy armchairs line the walls between the office doors. I am here for my first session with my primary counselor, Andrew. I find his nameplate on the door and sit in the chair directly outside his office, which is open and vacant. From my seat, I can see a bonsai tree, and for some weird reason, it makes my palms sweaty.

The side doors open and I see a tall, slim, and bald Asian man walking toward me, beaming.

"You must be Charlie. I'm Andrew, very nice to meet you. Step inside," he says.

I enter his office and it smells pleasantly of cedarwood and eucalyptus. There is minimal furniture: a desk and chair, an organized bookshelf, a plush therapy chair, and the mini bonsai tree. Clean white curtains cover the window, allowing as much sun as possible, while still providing privacy. On the wall behind Andrew's desk is a striking picture of a stream in the valley of two mountains. I ease myself into his comfortable patient chair and fold my hands in my lap.

Andrew continues to beam at me for what feels like an unusual amount of time, but I go with it.

"How has your first week been?" he asks, entering data into his computer.

"Interesting. The compound is, wow. And the food is so good! I was pleasantly surprised by that. I'm very grateful my roommate doesn't snore. But, um. There's just a lot of people and a lot going on here. I mean, it's nice, I'm just trying to take it all in."

He nods at me, understanding my meaning.

"And I'm over my freak out from the other day, by the way. I'm sorry—I do *still think* someone took my cash during intake, but whatever. I'm sure they need it more than me, and honestly, it was probably just an excuse for me to focus on something else. So maybe that's something?" I hope.

"Yes, becoming self-aware is a very important step in the

process. The goal today is to acknowledge that this is an intense environment and plan your treatment accordingly. I've read over your intake and admission files, and I have a few ideas for us. This is your second treatment center, correct?"

"Yes," I answer, taking my hair down before twisting it back into a bun. "I went to rehab in Eugene, Oregon back in 2013, I think? Yeah, 2013."

"How long were you there?" Andrew begins typing on his computer.

"Thirty days. It wasn't like this place, though. It was only men, and we lived in this huge house, three or four to a room. I mean it was clean and legit, just very grim. I really just remember washing a lot of cars and watching old educational videos."

I shudder a bit at the memories. My first foray into rehabilitation was facilitated by my cousin, Marnie. She tried her best, but Calvin's House was no Retreat, that's for sure.

"Did you find the treatment there helpful?" Andrew asks.

"Well, no. I drank on one of the last few days I was there. They let you go on a pass during the day to look for jobs and instead I found vodka. I'm surprised I didn't smell like it when I came back. I was careful, though."

"So it's safe to assume you weren't ready to make any changes then?"

"No, I definitely wasn't concerned with changing my ways at that time. I had just broken up with my boyfriend and was much more concerned with that." I shake my head, remembering the stupidity of Alec and Oregon.

"Do you believe you're ready to make changes now?" Andrew's tone is serious.

I reflect before answering, truly contemplating his question. There *is* a desire within me to change my life for the better, but

I am also head over heels in love with vodka. Imagining my life without a bottle feels bleak. I am torn.

"I can't answer that right now," I say simply. "I'm here to figure that out."

"I'm glad you're being honest with yourself. Now, let's go over your treatment plan. You will have several one-on-one sessions with me and another therapist, Vanessa. She will specialize in trauma and triggers while I will help you identify patterns of behavior and develop new coping mechanisms. You and I will also explore your relationship with alcohol and marijuana. Joanna, your Journey counselor, will see you most often and Vanessa and I will touch base with her frequently. For the time being, I encourage you to engage in groups and activities. Go to meetings. Have you been to any meetings yet?"

I pull my legs up and sit crisscrossed in the chair. "I went to an AA meeting the other night. I've been to them before, and in a way, it felt comforting."

"That's excellent," Andrew grins. "Continue to attend meetings. Keep trying meditation. Bernard says you've been frequenting his groups, which is great! Talk with other patients, sometimes that is the best healing. I gathered from your information that you prefer written assignments and reading?"

"You know, I don't remember much of my intake or assessment, but I do enjoy reading."

He beams again and I am grateful for his joy.

"Perfect. I have two books I would like you to start with. I would also like for you to do a timeline of your life. From birth until entering treatment. Please be very detailed and thorough as this will help us understand what led you to treatment."

I widen my eyes. "Oh my, this all got very serious, very suddenly."

Andrew laughs and goes to his bookshelf, pulling one from the top shelf and one from the third down

"Here you go."

I take them from him. The top shelf book is *Anger: Wisdom for Cooling the Flames* by Thich Nhat Hanh, and the other is *The Velvet Rage* by Alan Downs.

I sigh. "Am I really that angry?"

"They're not strictly about anger, but more about cultivating our emotions. You see, anger and fear usually become our default emotional foundation. But with the right work, you can begin to change your emotional responses to something healthier, more rewarding."

"Can't argue with that. When would you like all this completed?" I untangle my legs and stretch.

"We will meet again in two days, how about then?" his eyes twinkle.

"Oh, okay," I answer, expecting at least a week. "I'll get to work, then."

I tuck his books under my arm and stand to go.

"And Charlie, please drink more water. The nurse told me your blood pressure is still very high."

"Will do," I say and exit Andrew's office.

I find my way to a serenity berm without noticing where I am going. My mind is racing. I am an angry person, I just never wanted to admit it. I'm ashamed of my anger so I have ignored it all these years. Have I felt justified somehow in being angry because my Mom died when I was young? And how are the counselors communicating so effectively? They know about my water intake? I shake my head and light a cigarette. This is much more difficult than I anticipated.

*****

I meet Claire while strolling the grounds and listening to music. Retreat provides mini MP3 players with chips of different genres, so I requested their version of EDM, and it's surprisingly impressive. Some of the songs are a bit on the nose, but they've sprinkled several gems throughout the playlist.

Claire is dressed in black athletic gear with her hair in a ponytail. On her shoulder, she carries a large, dark khaki tote, which is full of notebooks and Jolly Ranchers. Claire is not a smoker and has taken to eating hard candy to fill the void left by wine. She smiles and waves at me.

"Hey, Charlie! How did you sleep last night?" she asks, her voice chipper. Claire is most certainly a morning person.

"You know, the Seroquel really just knocks me the fuck out. It's great. As long as I pass out before I start eating, though. They give you a mighty case of the munchies. And then you're kind of messed up, in 'quilville,' they call it. Anyways, how did you sleep?"

"Brenda and I stayed up really late again, having one of our talks. She's having trouble processing a few things about her father and I'm just always a mess. Anyways, are you ready for another group? Who knows what it'll bring? Some of these fucking people, I tell you!"

I giggle. It is fun to hear Claire curse. She is so perky and fresh, you would never expect a sailor's mouth from her.

"Yeah, I'm ready, I like group, even when it is crazy. I wonder if we'll do it outside again this morning, it's kind of nice to be outdoors before the shade is gone."

"I think Bernard is doing a sunset meditation outside today or tomorrow," Claire says, digging in her bag for candy.

"Oh, that will be awesome!"

Meditation has *always* interested me. This is the first time I've had a suitable environment in which to practice. I still have trouble fully grasping the concept, but find the breathing exercises and the sound of the singing bowl relaxing. Bernard leads very calming guided meditations, and while I'm not having the emotional experiences I suspect some are faking, it is astoundingly soothing. My mind clears, and I am able to simply exist for a moment, without the worry of my past or future.

After a cigarette with Brenda, we make our way to the Journey group room. It is the furthest back and coldest of the group rooms; several of us bring along our blankets in the morning. Twenty large, cushioned gray chairs are placed in a semi-circle around the space. The floors are wooden and the walls have been painted a shade of ivory; it feels clean and safe.

I sit next to Brenda and Alejandro. He arrived last night and has introduced himself to me four times. I vaguely remember finding him on a couch when I woke up for water, but left him be. His eyes are puffy and sleepy, his lip curled in a constant smirk; he's on the good stuff, for sure. Melissa and Caroline are chatting with Pierce and Seth, another duo of Journey. Pierce is an older, rough alcoholic, and Seth is a middle-aged meth boozer with thinning ashen hair. I glance around at the others, names and faces I recognize but rarely see out of this room. I wonder: where do they disappear to when group is over?

Joanna bursts through the door, wearing a breezy white blouse and an infectious smile. She is a force. Much like Bernard, I have gravitated toward Joanna and listen attentively when she speaks. She has a clear message of making wiser decisions by implementing a change in thought patterns.

Joanna stands at the front of the room near the whiteboard.

"Good morning, everyone! I hope you're well-rested. Let's start group with a deep breath and a moment of silence for the still suffering addict or alcoholic."

She closes her eyes and inhales a long breath through her nose. Joanna begins and ends each group in this manner; her earthy, gypsy vibe inspires me.

"Very nice," she says contentedly. "Now, was anyone able to practice any CBT since we met last night?"

CBT, or cognitive behavioral therapy, is the main focus of Journey. In its simplest form, it is recognizing when to correct thoughts, lessen their power, and steer them in a more positive and productive direction.

"I almost left last night," a small girl from the corner says, wrapped in a blue and red flannel blanket. I think her name is Rachel and she usually keeps to herself. "It's not that I wanted to use, I just wanted to leave. But I worked on a thought record thing and decided I was doing more for myself here than at home."

"That's excellent, Rachel!" Joanna exclaims, throwing her arms wide. She is an animated talker, citing her roots in the Bronx as the reason. She retains a bit of her accent, but her years spent in Florida have mostly flattened it out.

"I remember, way before I knew what CBT was, or sobriety for that matter, I had the same moment in one of my first AA meetings. I was shaking like a leaf and convinced I had addled my brain from drugs and alcohol. I thought, 'Joanna, you should just go out there and snort and drink up everything under the sun and go out with a bang!' And then, miraculously, I was able to see that thought for what it was, and I chose to stay. Of course, a few days earlier I had chosen to sniff coke and get in a high-speed chase with the cops, which may have helped motivate me. But the important thing is I chose to stay."

"Joanna, you have the most exciting stories!" Brenda says, her eyes wide.

"So fucking exciting!" Seth echoes. "What is the craziest thing you've done?"

"It's fun now, to laugh and talk about the insane things we did, isn't it? But it wasn't always fun and games at the time, was it? I didn't enjoy coming out of a drug stupor, walking the downtown streets of Chicago with no recollection of how I got there. I came to, peering up at tall buildings and I had to ask where I was. At the time, I was living here in Florida. I didn't enjoy having to send my son abroad when he was younger to protect him from the depravity of my lifestyle. I don't enjoy the fact that if I show my face in certain parts of Pennsylvania, I'm a dead woman. Seriously, and believe me, they'll never find me. I don't enjoy that after three bouts of sobriety, each followed by worsening relapses, my family can't help but view me with a hint of skepticism," she pauses, surveying the group. "Addiction is a cruel, dark, lonely life partner."

Joanna's words hang in the air. The room is still, each of us absorbed in our own thoughts. She has a way of doing this, highlighting the gravity of our decisions.

I drift in and out the rest of group, half listening. Joanna has stirred something within me. My life *feels* very dark and lonely, and I am cruel to myself because of my shame. It is wretched. This is not who I was supposed to become. This is not who *anyone* is supposed to become.

As group wraps up, I dart for the door. The walls are closing in on me and I need to be outside where I can breathe. I can feel my body shaking and my ears are ringing. My arms are growing tight and tingly. Am I having a panic attack?

The sun is setting and I hear noises of commotion around me. The air feels hot on my skin. I try to focus on these things as my heart bursts out of my chest. I wasn't aware, I didn't know there was so much damage in my life. It's jarring.

Melissa walks up to me and gently puts her hand on my shoulder.

"You good, man?" she asks. "I could see it on your face in there, something got to you."

"I'll shake it off, it just blindsided me."

"Maybe that's your problem," she says earnestly, "you should quit shaking it off."

"Maybe." I feel weak and unsteady.

*****

"There you are, Charlie! I've been searching for you everywhere."

I open my eyes and see Vanessa, my trauma therapist. She is stunning, to say the least. She reminds me of an Olympic volleyball player, with her long limbs and straight blonde hair. Her fashion choices are excellent, as well. Today she is wearing fitted white pants with gray sandals and a flattering blue top.

"I was working on meditating, but I have too many intrusive thoughts."

She laughs. "I see you've picked up on the lingo. I have mail for you."

"Oh?" I say, hearing a hint of my old affected British accent. I am more relaxed than I thought.

"Open it, I think I have an idea what it is."

I take the large yellow envelope and glance up at her, confused.

"Why would you have an idea," I start, tearing it open and seeing my wallet. "Oh! Is this what you thought it was?"

"Yes, actually. You may not remember this but during your admission, you mentioned something about thinking you left your wallet in the taxi. You were right."

"Oh shit, I remember now! That's what started the whole lost cash ordeal! She's sent a letter, too!" I exclaim.

I read the letter out loud.

"Charlie, I noticed your wallet in my backseat too late. But I remembered you said you were going to a retreat rehab in Palm Beach, Florida. I hope I've found the right one! Keep trying your hardest, as I said that day, I think what you're doing is very brave! Here is my number, when you get back maybe we can go to lunch or something? Take care!"

There is a lump in my throat when I meet Vanessa's eye. Her smile is radiant.

"Isn't that nice?" she asks.

"It's more than nice," I say, astonished. "That was so kind, so meaningful. For no reason other than one conversation on the way to the airport."

"Maybe she saw more in you than you see in yourself."

"Hmm. Maybe."


We unload from the "druggie buggy," which is a large white passenger van. Vanessa and Joanna decided Journey needed an escape to the beach. And spectacular as the grounds are at Retreat, I am thankful to get out for a bit. The sun blazes mightily, the roar of the ocean and seagulls a soothing embrace. I breathe the salty air deeply into my chest and glance around. The sands are surprisingly empty, save for a few scattered sunbathers.

Brenda, Claire, and I spread out towels and sit crisscrossed.

"You know," Claire says, pulling out a nail file, "the last time I was at the beach, I threw my husband's car keys in the ocean."

"Well, you can't stop there," Brenda says eagerly.

Claire smiles and lifts her designer sunglasses on top of her head.

"We were at some function in The Hamptons, I can't remember which, and I was having a marvelous time drinking and dancing. He made a stink about wanting to go and I wasn't having it, so I threw his keys in the ocean. He called me all sorts of names, told me that I was a dumbass since it was my ride home, too. I told him, 'no it's not. I'll call a fucking taxi when *I'm* ready to leave.' Anyways, he left in a huff and I *continued* to have a marvelous time until the early morning hours!" she says, cackling.

"This is why I like you, Claire." I grin and stand, shaking the sand off my legs. "I think I'll take a walk."

Brenda relaxes on her towel. "Enjoy, I'm gonna soak up some sun from here."

I head toward the water, where the sand is denser. Practicing mindfulness, I focus on how it feels beneath my feet: cool and coarse. It is an attempt to stave off my thoughts, which are uncomfortable to be with when I'm alone and sober.

I suppose a part of me has known for quite some time I am dissatisfied with my life, with myself. That knowledge has been smothered by vodka for so long, though, it was easy to ignore. Now, with clarity, I can see myself for who I am, and fighting past the disappointment and shame is all-encompassing. I barely have anything left to spend on growth. Perhaps this is all part of the growth. And I know I'm fortunate, I do understand my problems are a luxury compared to those of others. However, I do not feel that should discount their value. Having to contend with self-disappointment, regardless of one's lot in life, is exhausting.

I walk further than I intended and turn around to head back to the group. Halfway there, I see Vanessa sauntering in my direction, looking out over the ocean.

I pause and wait for her.

"Having a nice walk?" she asks, approaching me.

"Yeah, just thinking and trying to sort things out."

Vanessa gives me a beat.

"Let's process."

I sigh. Processing is a necessary component of recovery. A draining, vexing, dehydrating one.

"It's just that I feel so guilty about being mad or sad or anything, really. I honestly *do* know how lucky I am, but at the same time, I can't believe I've let my life come to this! No offense, but it's *ridiculous* that I had to come to rehab to try and get my shit together. All I have to do is fucking *stop drinking* and I can't even do that. And I don't even know if it's *'can't,'* or *'won't!'* It's like I'm dealing with this other person that I don't know and he's fucking insane! There's no pleasing him. He's a little bitch—and he's *me!*"

I pull at my bun. "I don't know what I want or what to do, and I'm scared."

"There!" Vanessa snaps her fingers. "There it is! You're scared. Fear underpins so many emotions. It's a natural, evolutionary response. You just need help in manipulating how it manifests."

"I don't even know what that means," I whine.

"Yes, you do. You're exceptionally bright and self-aware, Charlie. You can't play that card with me. It would be helpful if you could view yourself without judgment. I have a feeling you're much harder on yourself than you are on others *and* you have a tendency to devalue your emotions and demean yourself. This isn't helpful."

We stand in the breeze, watching the waves crash on the shore. I shut my eyes for a moment, taking full, steady breaths in an attempt to level with myself.

"I know what I don't want, and that's a start."

"What is it that you don't want?" she asks, beginning the trek back to our group.

"I know I *don't* want to be fortunate enough to live a long life and remember none of it because I was blackout drunk. I know I don't want to get up one day and feel like I wasted my life by getting wasted. I want meaning in my life and I don't want to engage in behavior that robs me of the chance to find it."

"You're at a turning point, Charlie. I remember when I was first getting sober, I felt very similar to how you feel now. I wanted to find purpose, it was extremely important to me. But just know that wrangling your inner demons is, itself, quite meaningful. And it's where the healing begins."

Her wisdom hangs between us and I give it time to fully absorb into my thoughts.

"Thank you," I say genuinely. "For bringing us here today and for talking with me. I appreciate it."

Vanessa gives me a disarming smile. "You're very welcome! I am always happy to talk with you, you've got a spark that I admire."

"That's kind of you to say."

"It's the truth."

"Vanessa?" I ask as we near the huddle of Journey. "Was it hard for you, getting sober?"

She turns toward me and raises her eyebrows. "It was one of the hardest things I have ever done in my life. And it took a couple of years and many attempts, but it was worth every moment, good and bad. I wouldn't be who I am today were I not an alcoholic."

On the ride home, I listen to instrumental music and gaze out the window. I have a sinking feeling sobriety is not an overnight sensation, but rather, if cultivated, grows slowly and surely. It is frightening to imagine living another two years on this hamster wheel.

*****

The morning sunlight feels soft and fresh on my face. I am sitting in my favorite spot on the compound, a horseshoe of gnarly flower bushes with a bench in the center. It's like a massive compression blanket, safe and enclosed. I smoke a cigarette and sip oolong tea, balancing the yin and yang of my health. Craving space, I am relieved to be alone and reflect over the last two weeks.

After overcoming the first-week jitters, I have started to notice just how sick I am. With the guidance of Retreat's daily structure, I have had a chance to view my life objectively and gather some takeaways. Until vodka was removed from my daily routine, I was not able to do this and did not realize the power and weight it held in my life. Honestly, it was an embarrassing realization. Andrew assured me this is a normal response, however very little feels normal right now, especially in my surroundings.

I am in an oasis of chaos, and it has shown me how sheltered of a life I've lived. I knew treatment would be unnerving but never considered dealing with overdoses and seizures on a regular basis. I was stunned by my first experience, but now it has become commonplace. Emotional breakdowns are another constant of Retreat. I'm never entirely sure if they're real, or a bid for the facility's go-to anxiety med, Vistaril. Lord knows I've played up one or seven for some of the green and white pills.

I stretch and snuff out my cig, in need of breakfast before my first equine therapy group. Andrew has agreed to allow me more sessions than normal and for that I am grateful. After learning of my youth spent showing horses, he and Vanessa felt it would be an extraordinarily rewarding therapy experience.

I am daydreaming about the arena when I see Seth jogging toward me.

"Hey, Charlie," he says out of breath. "You should head up to the third floor, they're kicking Dina out right now."

I groan. "Seriously? Why?"

"She flew off the handle again and swung at staff!"

"Sounds about right," I say.

Dina is another member of Journey who suffers from trauma and alcoholism. I believe her main and most sensitive issue is rage. A few days ago, she suffered a fit, and I had never before witnessed a person become so furious that their physicality changed. Her neck grew thin and long, and her eyebrows rose an inch. Luckily, I was not at the receiving end of her wrath, as it was mighty. She is only one in a sea of *dozens*, though. Treatment is full of volatile, fragile individuals frequently lashing out. I do my best to give them space.

"But for real, I think I'll skip that. Give her my best," I holler over my shoulder as I follow the stone path toward the dining hall.

135

In my first few days, I noticed Retreat held an assortment of temperamental personalities, and that it would be important for me to navigate wisely. As such, I have chosen to remain rather quiet and aloof. Operating as though behind a pane of glass has made it easier to practice meditation and try my hand at journaling, hoping a more personalized outlet will provide relief.

I enter the dining hall and grab some yogurt and an apple. Scanning the room I find Claire and Jack sitting near the patio doors. Jack is a Retreat repeat on his third stay. He arrived a little over a week ago, strung out and singing. In his early twenties, he's having trouble shaking off a heroin addiction from his late teens.

"So Dina's out?" I ask, settling in a chair and opening my yogurt.

"Oh, what a shit show!" Claire says. "I had to leave, she lost her damn mind. But we were just talking about equine. Are you excited?"

"I am!"

Jack drums his hands on the table.

"Well, you'll have to do the hard work then, cowboy. Those things are fucking huge! I've only gone once in all my time here, I usually get out of it, but they've caught on."

I laugh. "Will do."

Group is held in the arena and I am thrilled. The smell of horses and hay makes me nostalgic for my childhood as memories of lessons with my trainer, Suezetta, rush back. I move around the space, feeling at home.

Our therapist, Callie, explains basic etiquette regarding the horses and ponies. I pay little attention to this, more interested in assessing their equipment. Several halters and lunge ropes are hung on the wall above ten or so white barrels. It must serve as a training arena when not being used for therapy. The ceiling is high with exposed beams and wide windows are placed every fifteen feet. I am very impressed with their facility.

Tuning back in, I hear Callie finishing up.

"So, most importantly, just enjoy the experience! Let's divide into groups of three and bring out some horses!" she beams.

"Yo, Charlie! I call you!" Jack yells, walking over to me.

"Me, too!" Brenda says and Claire groans.

"Damn it!"

It is small, but gives me a rush of pride. Our group knows of my history with horses, and on our trip to the arena, they were full of questions. I was surprised to learn so many people had never ridden nor been near a horse in their lives.

"Do you have experience with horses, Charlie?" Callie asks, sliding open a door to reveal the massive stables. My jaw drops. From where I am standing, I can see eight square stables, polished and expensive.

"Whoa, this is so nice!" I gush, then remember to answer. "Yes, I grew up riding them around our farm and then showed in APHA when I was a teenager."

"Paint horses, huh?"

"Oh good job, yup, I showed for almost three years. We traveled and did trail rides, too."

"Oh excellent, you'll be a good hand! I always enjoy having patients with equine experience!"

I grin as three horses are brought out, one for each group. Leading the way is an absolutely stunning black Destrier, a giant of a horse that looks as though it stepped off a movie set. After admiring its beauty for a moment, I take notice of the others, Quarter horses: one a deep chestnut and the other with Palomino coloring. They all appear docile and well-groomed, making my spirits lift.

"This is Prince," Callie says, indicating the Destrier, "the brown one is named Sandy and the Palomino is Lancelot."

I stand eagerly with Brenda and Jack as Lancelot is brought to us by a stable hand. He is roughly sixteen hands tall and handsome, with a nicely maintained mane and tail. I reach my hand out for him to smell, and then stroke his neck from head to shoulder. He snorts and Jack steps back quickly.

"I don't think he likes that, bro!"

Callie chuckles from the group next to us, who are busy admiring Sandy.

"He's just saying hello," she calls.

Brenda steps near me and rubs his neck. She smiles over at me.

"Can I walk him around?" I ask.

"Sure, if anyone feels comfortable enough to walk with the horses the rest of us will set up our activity," Callie claps her hands and starts arranging the barrels.

Taking Lancelot's lead rope from his wrangler, I walk toward the far end of the arena. I feel his heat beside me and place my hand on top of his neck. His scent is comforting, like an old, worn hoodie

"Just another day at the office, huh, Lancelot?"

Glancing around, I notice no one else is taking advantage of free time with the horses. The rest of the group stands around the arena door watching Callie and the other stable hands build a course of barrels, poles, and exercise balls.

I make a wide turn with Lancelot and massage his neck muscles. His presence is rejuvenating me, I can feel my own muscles softening as I work on his. My soul needed this moment; it feels pure, a return to something I had lost. We stop a few paces short of the group and I see Callie smirking. She winks at me.

"Alright, the goal is to navigate your therapy horse through the obstacle course we have assembled. I will have Prince's group go first. You will need to work as a team to effectively communicate with him. Once each group has completed the course, we will discuss and process."

I cluck at the word process.

Twisting my hair up, I walk outside to the common area and spot a large portion of Journey, smoking and laughing at Pierce. I take a seat between Jack and Rachel, lighting a cigarette.

"But I thought I heard something funny behind one of the serenity gardens," Pierce says, his eyes wide, "and as I got closer I realized it was two people just going at it, man!"

The group explodes with laughter.

"Seriously?" Melissa squeals.

"I shit you not!" Pierce yells. "I don't know who it was, I got out of there as quick as I could. I'm telling you, this place is like reality TV!"

"You know," Jack begins, "it would be highly illegal, but super entertaining if they put hidden cameras all around here. I mean, just think about all of the drama!"

I grin. "It *is* like a soap opera! I never imagined there would be so many rehab romances. It sort of defeats the purpose, but I love it!"

"It's all the damn teenagers," Claire says, "they fuck like rabbits!"

I giggle along with everyone else, my rehab friends. It's

unexpected, I also never would have imagined I could become so close to strangers in such a short amount of time. Treatment is an environment where trauma bonding is rampant, but if used properly, can be quite healing. I feel lucky to have met my newfound friends. I am able to be a more authentic version of myself around them and it is freeing. Not since college have I felt this, not since I handed my life over to a bottle, and it is encouraging.

*****

"*Blackbird*, please, Bernard!" Caroline begs beside me, curled up like a kitten on her yoga mat.

We are in music therapy with Bernard. He is an older man, nearing his mid-sixties, and the epitome of sage wisdom and grace. Bernard has a way of relaxing the atmosphere of a room by simply being there. He sits upfront, on a weathered, wooden stool, while the rest of group is scattered around the room on chairs and yoga mats. He begins each therapy session by taking requests, giving us time to decompress.

Bernard strums the opening notes and I close my eyes. I have stacked four yoga mats on top of one another, building a squishy zen pallet. It is in these moments I find the most peace and hope. I am embracing a new outlook on life, one involving perspective, gratitude, and awareness; it is foreign and exciting, allowing me small glimpses of clarity. Even though I am still struggling with the processing and understanding of my grief and anger, I feel more solid. Learning to view myself objectively has led to a great deal of forgiveness.

From beside me, I can hear Brenda humming along with Bernard. She is sitting in her chair straight-backed, with her feet planted firmly on the ground and hands laid neatly on her thighs. This is her favorite meditation position. I prefer to lay on my back, but to each their own. She has fully embraced meditation as well, and we have spent many quiet evenings in this room, navigating our own journey in the company of one another. I will miss her very much when we part ways.

"*Fast Car*, please," I say as Bernard finishes *Blackbird*.

"Yes!" whispers Jack from the back of the room.

Jack is another lost soul with whom I feel a connection. It was quick and unexpected, happening a week or so back while watching *Logan* during recreation. He made a comment about being afraid to be alone in his head, "it's a dangerous town I shouldn't visit by myself" were his exact words. His meaning resonated. I often find the narrative in my head to be quite demeaning and cruel. Recently, however, I've realized pausing that monologue suits me very well. Jack is having trouble silencing his inner monologue, which explains his risky behavior. After hearing about his childhood, I wonder how he's able to silence it at all.

Jack's tragic youth is one of textbook childhood neglect and trauma. To have someone who survived extreme physical, mental, and emotional abuse throughout their most formative years sit face-to-face and walk me through their trauma was a raw and humbling experience. It was a visceral moment for Jack as well. We were both quiet for a long time afterward, a bit dazed from his vulnerability. Strangely, these moments have been more healing than any group or CBT course offered. Hearing others speak about the depravity of their addiction helps me wrap my head around my own past. I am beginning to understand the phrase "path to forgiveness."

I inhale through my nose and listen as Bernard plays the

last notes of my favorite Tracy Chapman song. The scent of lemongrass drifts through the air and I focus on relaxing my muscles. My index finger tingles, relieved from the pressure of my neck. Fracturing it a few years back did a number on me, and I am continuously grateful I did not walk away with more damage. Foolishly, though, after a couple of months' rest, I was back in the bottle, and my neck never had the time to heal properly. Alcohol has numbed the pain for years and I'm finding it difficult to manage the discomfort.

Calming my mind, I let my thoughts drift as if they were floating down a stream. I can hear the air conditioning blowing through the vents and the muffled sounds of group members. I try to remain in the present, paying attention to my senses. I'm hoping meditation, along with strengthening muscles in my neck, will alleviate my neck tension. The air feels mild around me and I sustain my breathing. Laying very still, I let my mind go.

Bernard chimes the singing bowl. I snap my eyes open, pulled back to reality. I wasn't sleeping, but I wasn't awake, either. Sitting up, I look around the dim room and see others moving slowly. As usual, Bernard's music therapy has relaxed us to the point of sloth.

*****

"Hello, Charlie," Andrew says, leaning against his office door and smiling.

I stand, slinging my knapsack over my shoulder. I am meeting him for my sixth individual session, I believe. Between Vanessa, Andrew, *and* Joanne I am beginning to lose count.

His office is bright and smells of oranges and lavender today.

I take a seat and cross my legs, waiting for his move. I can't help but wonder if I'm nearing the end of treatment, as my last couple of sessions have felt more final, regarding the future and relapse prevention.

Andrew turns on low, soothing music and studies his notes.

"I'm happy to see your blood pressure has been stable for the past week or so. The alcohol has finally worked its way out. How do you feel?"

"I'm *feeling* stable. I'm calmer, which is nice. I was so ashamed and emotional when I first got here, it's all a blur."

"Yes, it was a rough first week for you, but that's not uncommon. I almost find it helps, a good shock to the system."

I grin. "It was a *trip*, bro! I'm actually enjoying my days now, though. I haven't had fun, sober, in a long time."

I think, in particular, of a few evenings ago, playing Cards Against Humanity with a load of people from different groups. We slid a few tables together in the common area and played for almost two hours, smoking and laughing the whole time.

"Yes, it will be important and difficult to find pleasure in everyday, mundane activities for the first year or so. Did you have a chance to read the article I put outside your door that explained re-regulating your hedonic set level?"

"I did, and it was very interesting! I never even knew that could be a thing, but it makes sense. It was daunting information, but I suppose I'm happy I know about it upfront."

Around mid-way through my second week, Andrew left an article on the door to my room explaining the damage alcohol inflicts on the brain and the science behind its healing. I had a vague knowledge of how vodka was pickling my brain and liver, however, I never considered how difficult it would be to bounce back from such abuse. My brain will need to rewire itself to form new, healthy pathways. It will also take time for my dopamine and serotonin levels to settle back down to a normal, functioning level. I have spent the last several years blasting them out, causing my hedonic levels to rise abnormally high. It will be as though I am walking in a fog for a couple of months while I wait for my brain to find its proper baseline. According to the article, this is when I will be most susceptible to relapse. I feel like I'm always susceptible to relapse, but I suppose that's beside the point.

"Understanding that sobriety is hard, constant work is crucial. If it were easy, there wouldn't be treatment or AA or other support groups. Addiction is more than trauma or socio-economics or exposure, it can be hereditary as well, I believe."

"I agree. And honestly, that is refreshing. I mean, I know I've had my fair share of trauma, and that my coping skills are shitty. But I also know that I just love being drunk! It feels *fucking great* and makes me happy. So there's got to be something there, biologically, or genetically, right? I mean I could trace it back to my Grandpa Joe on my Mom's side, and I'm pretty sure my Great Grandpa on my Dad's side was an alcoholic."

"You're most certainly onto something there, Charlie, but I don't believe it is the best rabbit hole to fall down. You're intuitive and can analyze with the best of them, although I think that will be more of a hindrance for you. Bright people often have the most trouble *staying* sober. You may end up rationalizing yourself right into a bottle."

I sigh and watch the vapor rise from Andrew's gray diffuser.

"It is because you're bright that I've given you so many articles and reading assignments. I do not mean to overwhelm you with information, but rather help you understand the disease of addiction. You're getting very good at finding the root cause of your actions and behaviors, and I think this knowledge will benefit you. You have a tough road ahead of you, Charlie."

His gaze is piercing and serious. Gathering my focus, I clear my throat.

"I want to say something, and I know it will sound petty and childish, but it's how I'm feeling."

Andrew shakes his head disapprovingly. "Charlie, you've got to quit discrediting your emotions, we've talked about this! And I know Vanessa has covered this with you in a couple of sessions as well. It is so detrimental to your recovery and happiness!"

I raise my hands in defense. "I know, I know, it's bad and I shouldn't do it. I know! But what I wanted to say is that I'm going to be so *bored* without drinking. Other people don't *love it* like I do, so they don't understand how lonely I'll be. I mean, it just makes everything better!"

Andrew gives me a slight grin and raises his eyebrows.

"Better, eh? Shall we count the ways?"

"You know what I mean," I say and chuckle self-consciously. "Life feels better with a little drink. Everything flows better, it's easier."

"Yes, it is easy and feels good to escape and numb our problems with substances. However, it makes for an underwhelming, groggy existence. My life now, a sober life, is immensely better than the fucked up, drug-fueled days of my past."

I almost gasp. Andrew has never disclosed his drug use with me and rarely curses.

"How long have you been sober, Andrew?" I ask boldly.

He gives me a strange smile and there is a twinkle in his eye.

"I usually refrain from sharing much of my personal experience. Many other therapists use that approach, and while I respect it, it is not my style. That said, I am willing to make an exception today, with you. Let me take you back to a different time, the '90s, when I was punk rock with a green mohawk."

"A mohawk, huh?" I giggle.

He grins. "Once upon a time I had a full head of hair much like yours. I still miss it sometimes. But in all seriousness, I remember the moment I realized drugs were my best friend, and that in order for me to get better, I had to lose them. It was a moment of profound grief. Anyone who hasn't struggled with addiction may have a hard time grasping that concept, but I have a feeling you understand."

"Yes, I do." I nod, a bit stunned by the depth of what Andrew has said. Mourning the loss of alcohol had not yet crossed my mind.

"I had a fortunate upbringing, my parents were both professors and we lived very comfortably. I graduated high school with honors and went to Tulane in New Orleans right after. During my sophomore year, I discovered substances. And then in my junior year, I started to really enjoy pills, specifically. I would drink occasionally, but I mainly wanted pills, any and all kinds. I was able to graduate with a degree in philosophy and anthropology and started applying for grad schools, but my drug habit soon overcame me. Opting out of grad school, I ran away to San Francisco and became a hardcore junkie.

"By this time, I only wanted to get high by shooting up, I wasn't worried about my hygiene, and I was having unprotected sex with both men and women for drugs on a regular basis. It was the lowest point of my life. I lost contact with all my family and friends and lived on the streets for nearly six months. I finally washed up in an ER in LA, and my family was contacted. My Mom agreed to pay for my flight back, as long as I checked in to a long-term rehab and vowed to change my life.

"There was an earnest effort for nearly a year to walk the straight and narrow, until the day I came across a bottle of Xanax and went out for around eight months. In that time, I stole from my Dad and ruined Thanksgiving during a blackout. I sobered up the day after in my parent's basement, covered in bruises and blood. I found out later that I had fallen down the stairs after destroying our dining room. My parents checked to make sure I was breathing, then went upstairs while I slept it off. I woke up the next morning and bolted from the house. I couldn't meet their eyes before I walked out the door.

"It took five months before I was able to have lunch with my family and apologize for my behavior. It took a year and a half before they began to trust me again. It has now been thirteen years, and my family, along with myself, have learned to be grateful for my troubled years. It has allowed me the opportunity to guide others away from a dangerous and dark path. It is my hope for you."

He leans back in his chair and gives me a kind, lopsided grin.

"Thanks," I say, my voice hoarse. "I appreciate you sharing that with me, Andrew. It helps me understand that *time* really is what it's all about. It just takes time. I can relate to you slipping with the Xanax, too. A part of me knows I'm going to drink again, and it makes me really sad and really happy, at the same time. It's dizzying."

"That is totally understandable, Charlie. Just remember to be gentle with yourself. For some, relapse is a part of recovery. It's nothing to be ashamed of. But don't run with it, either. You have a history to contend with, and chronic relapse could very well be your greatest struggle."

"Well, that sounds highly inspiring and motivational. I can't wait to run with that."

Andrew laughs softly. "Keep pace with yourself, don't rush or set unattainable goals too early. I have a strong feeling you're going to turn out alright, Charlie. Keep your spirit about you, too. You're kind and gentle. It's why people feel comfortable opening up to you. For as hard as you judge yourself, you're very forgiving of others. And I think there's much to be said of that quality."

I smile, touched by this compliment. "Any assignments for me?"

"You've finished your relapse prevention plan, which is great. You can always revise that, but I would encourage reading 'The Big Book' and journaling."

"Will do," I grumble.

*****

I am rinsing the shampoo from my hair when a strange feeling settles over me. Today is the day I leave Retreat. No one has given me any indication this is my last day, I just feel it in my soul, and know I'm right. Surprisingly, I'm more excited than nervous. I've experienced a great deal of self-growth these last few weeks and I'm ready to test the waters of sobriety. I will miss the friends and relationships I've fostered, and vow to stay in contact.

Making my way to morning group, I search for Brenda and Jack. The news will be hardest for them, and I would like to soften the blow in person, yet both are nowhere to be found. I sigh and press on.

Sitting nervously in the Journey group room, I keep my eye on the door for my friends, but it is Vanessa I see first. She smiles at me sadly.

"Hey, Charlie," she asks sweetly, "can you come with me?"

I bow my head and stand to leave, disarmed it's happening so abruptly.

"And so the adventure comes to a close," I say.

Vanessa glances over her shoulder at me with a surprised expression. "Intuitive, aren't we?"

"I had a feeling."

She leads me to her office, which I prefer over Andrew's. Vanessa's space has an offbeat feel. She uses tall, antique lamps to provide soft lighting, and her walls are adorned with paintings of fruit and contemporary art. I take a seat in her exceptionally comfortable, high-backed patient chair, my throat tightening.

"I'll miss this cozy space."

Vanessa is quiet for a moment and we hold steady eye contact.

"You will be missed as well, Charlie. You've been an unusual patient and I have grown quite fond of treating you. It's rare for a person to be as self-aware as you are without prior intensive treatment. It's just not common. This is why I believe I can tell you this: you're not ready to stop drinking. You know it, I know it. Andrew and Bernard are living on hope, and it's sweet, but it's not practical."

Vanessa gives me a beat and I remain silent. She is right, I still want to drink without the consequences.

"I just wish there weren't such dire side effects," I sigh.

"That being said, don't give up, Charlie. You will get it, one day, but I think it's more important you prepare to weather the storm. Get a plan in place for when you relapse. Has anyone talked to you about harm reduction?"

I listen to the sound of rain from her white noise machine

and focus my thoughts.

"I appreciate you being candid, I really do, because these thoughts have been swirling around my mind for a while now. I have not read into harm reduction too much, but I'm familiar with the theory. It's basically just trying to minimize the damage when I drink, right?"

"In a nutshell, yes, I suppose it is."

"I don't know when it will happen, but I know it will. And I don't feel weak, I feel annoyed at how stubborn I know my future self will be!"

I exhale audibly, a bit dramatically, and pull my hair out of its bun. Vanessa chuckles.

"Just be safe, Charlie. If you're going to do it, stay home. And then call someone the next day, get up and get out of it. If you fester in it, it'll suck you right back in. I did that for years and it's a serious waste of time."

Jitters begin to peck at me. "On that note, should I go and start packing?"

She swallows. "Yes. I think that would work best, group should be out by the time you're done, and then we can all say our goodbyes."

"Right," I say and stand.


Several hours later, I am departing from Palm Beach International on my flight back to Springfield. I stare out my window, a bit dazed. My last hours of treatment felt frenzied. Deep down, I know I am not ready to be leaving, but I am at the mercy of my insurance company. It is surreal, to spend four and half weeks in complete self-assessment and reflection, then turn around and re-enter normal, functioning society. I should be back at work in two days and the suddenness of it all is a bit off-putting.

I think of Brenda and smile. Word had spread before the group ended, and she rounded the corner to my room as soon as she heard.

"Don't think for a *second* that we're not calling or texting or emailing weekly!" she exclaimed and then burst into tears, entering my room and throwing her arms around me, breaking several rules.

My friendship with her is truly unique and responsible for much of the healing I experienced at Retreat. Between our conversations and meditations with Bernard, I *was* able to find a few pieces of my old self, and for that I am grateful.

Vanessa was quite astute, and I shudder a bit thinking of vodka. I could order a glass now, on the plane, but I don't feel compelled to partake. Yet. How long will I last, I wonder? Is it inevitable that I will end up right back where I started? Am I meant to be an alcoholic, and nothing more?

I take a steadying breath and rest my head on the seat. I suppose, for now, I will take it one day at a time.

# 9

## Reflections

*February - March 2018*
*Salt Lake City, Utah*
*31 Years Old*

I sit alone in the massive, windowed group room of Reflections Recovery Center, my hands trembling and my stomach sour. For once, it is not due to withdrawal. I'm spiraling out of control, mentally and emotionally. Locking eyes with myself in the window, I inhale sharply and attempt to wrangle my thoughts. This is my third rehab in six months; I left my last one only twenty-two days ago. On my sixth day out, I ran back to the bottle and made up for the lost time.

Standing, I begin to pace. I've run away again, this time to Salt Lake City, Utah, of all fucking places. After drunkenly sending a group text saying I would return better in a few weeks, I shut my phone off and cried. It wasn't in despair, but a full-on tantrum. I wanted to beat myself within an inch of my life.

"Everything okay, Charlie?" asks the sweet, elderly nurse as I pass her station. I met with her less than thirty minutes ago yet cannot remember her name.

"Yeah, just super anxious. I'm trying to process being *back* in treatment, and it's putting me on edge, sorry."

"Oh, hun. Your medicine should kick in soon, and then everyone will be back from meeting in an hour or so. That should help distract you. Until then, would you like to talk with me? You were awfully quiet during your intake."

Her sincerity touches me, and I falter.

"I'm so angry," I whisper, my voice cracking. "I used to be sad and confused, but now it's just rage. Rage at myself, rage at my life, rage at my family. It doesn't even make sense, but I can't help feeling it."

"You're disappointed in yourself, huh?"

I nod my agreement.

"That's tough, hun. It sure is. But that's just part of it, you know. Part of addiction."

"Yeah. So how many people are here?" I ask, wanting to change the subject. I'm not keen on falling to pieces quite yet.

"I believe you make nine but let me check," she says, turning to her computer. "Yes, nine. We usually have anywhere from ten to fourteen. We can't hold much more than that."

"Nine, huh? That'll be nice. Um, not to be rude, but I'm gonna keep pacing. I feel antsy."

"I understand, hun," she says, and I continue my circle of the room.

Reflections is an extremely large and luxurious residential home that has been converted into a treatment facility. Part of intake included a tour of the house, an enormous three-story manor. Two capacious group rooms, the nurse station, and an epic kitchen with a charming dining area occupy the first floor, while the upstairs has been divided into living quarters for women and men. The basement was finished as office spaces and another kitchen; a covered porch holding a fire pit and two ping-pong tables complete the suburban motif.

Guilt pierces me and I sink to the floor. My poor family, this is unfair. It has not been my intention to drag them down this twisted, battering road but I've done it nonetheless. I am apoplectic with myself. I'm pathetic. I must have severe psychological issues and probably need to be placed somewhere. There has to be something fractured within my core. Otherwise, why would I continue on this cycle? I sleep, drink, and then go to rehab. Am I seeking attention? That makes me feel lame and childish. Am I lame and childish? Sure I am, or I wouldn't be here.

My body trembles and I shut my eyes tightly. This is ridiculous; I have finally lost my fucking mind.

Headlights shine through the windows, and I bring my attention up from the floor. The other vagrants have returned, perhaps providing a reprieve from my mind. My heart quickens as I wait.

Chatter and laughter fill the kitchen as each patient wanders in, politely introducing themselves. So far I have met McKinley, Dakota, Jordyn, Moses, Katie, and Keeton. Their excitement and joy is overwhelming, but I try to keep up appearances. I'm not drunk and have no excuse for an awkward first impression.

"So where are you from, Charlie?" Moses asks, leaning against the base of the staircase, giving scale to his tall height. He has thick, wavy black hair and dark eyes; he is Latino, which drives me wild.

"Springfield, Missouri," I answer with a smile.

"Missouri, scary," he chuckles.

"Uh, yeah, sure," I agree quizzically.

The noise settles as the final few trickle in, taking their seats. I glance around, assessing. It is an eclectic group of young adults; I reckon no one here is over forty.

A lanky man stands near the nurse station with a clipboard and clears his throat.

"All right, let's go around the room and do our nightly check-in. We've got a new guy, Charlie. You can go last, bud, so you get familiar with the format. I'm Jake, by the way. It's nice to meet you."

He grins, and I nod my agreement again.

"Katie, addict," an Asian girl across the room starts.

"Hey, Katie!" the group calls back.

"Today was a very productive day for me. I finished my second draft of my relapse prevention plan, and I feel like I've got a really good plan to leave here with. I still haven't talked to my Mom, but I did text her. For us, that's huge. I'm going to focus on staying positive and motivated these last few days. I'm really gonna miss it here, and I'm gonna stop now so I don't cry."

"Thanks, Katie!"

"Hey, I'm Tyler, alcoholic," says a plump, pleasant bald guy with smiling eyes.

"Tyler!" the group catcalls at him.

I tune in and out over the next twenty minutes as each member recounts their day. My detox medication, Ativan, is taking effect, and I feel sleepy. As my turn nears, I grin and scratch my ear nervously.

"Hi, my name is Charlie, and I'm an alcoholic."

"Hello, Charlie! Good morning, Charlie!"

"'Good morning, Charlie.' Clever. I think I can get pretty

close to doing this right. Today was fucking crazy, dude. I'm in treatment. Again, which is nuts. I literally left treatment twenty-two days ago. I'm super angry, so that's cool. Um, nice to meet everyone, I'm gonna focus on not being angry. I'm tired and a little fucked up."

Jake laughs and leads the group in the Serenity Prayer.

"God, grant me the serenity to accept the things I cannot change, the courage to change the things I can, and the wisdom to know the difference. Amen. All right, guys. Night meds," he says, opening the door to the nurse station.

Seeing everyone line up, I head upstairs to my room. I long for sleep, eager to draw a curtain on my boiling wrath. As I'm walking, I marvel at Reflections; it really is a damn mansion, with its wide curved staircase and spacious rooms. I share my room with two other guys, McKinley and Matt, I recently learned, but there's plenty of space for all. We don't even share a closet.

*****

My eyes open and find the gleaming red clock—4:26 in the morning. I listen to the dull hum of the fan and Matt's snores. My mouth feels dry as I gaze at the shadows on the carpet, tree limbs twisting back and forth in the street lamp. I'll need to lay here until at least 4:55, when they turn off the alarm between the stairs and the loft railing. It's their way of keeping the boys and girls from sneaking into each other's wings. What they do about boys who like boys or girls who like girls, I have no idea. It's an often overlooked detail that usually plays to my advantage.

I roll over and sigh. My anger is still asleep, for all I feel is sadness. I am now the weird, drunk, rehab boy. I've cut contact with most of my family and friends, jumping from vodka bottle to rehab. I wonder, how far off is jail or permanent lockup of some sort?

Tears fill my eyes. I am a selfish, entitled, demanding brat of a man child. There is no reason for my deplorable behavior. My life has presented me with nothing but amazing opportunities and privileges, yet I've mocked and whined about each of them. Anything apart from acting has been deemed unworthy and treated with contempt. A tear falls onto my pillow.

Oh, this is terrible. I must do something about my life. Rolling flat on my back, I close my eyes, shifting focus to my senses. I've found that breathing and becoming aware of my surroundings helps me collect myself. Slowly, I settle.

Hearing others stir in the hall, I fling the covers off and reach for my hoodie. I'm not sure if Salt Lake City is actually colder than Springfield, but it sure feels that way.

"Good morning, Charlie," Moses says quietly, winking.

I grin and wink back, making my way to the staircase. The hall is wide and lofted over the entryway, providing a beautiful view of the chandelier and floor-to-ceiling windows.

The strumming of a guitar greets me as I step into the windowed group room. Dakota shrugs politely and continues to play. She is very young, maybe twenty-two, with purple and red hair and several earrings. Neo-punk.

She sings a bit while playing, and her voice sounds raspy and textured. I suspect she is quite the singer. We sit this way for a while, her playing on the guitar while I listen. It is comforting.

Others begin to drift through the group room and kitchen. The smell of coffee is wafting and livening up the house. Dakota puts the guitar away and wanders off to the girl's wing without a word. I want to thank her, but settle for finding a seat at the kitchen table to watch the sunrise. Cigarettes are not permitted at this facility, and I miss them dearly.

"How's it going?" McKinley asks, taking a seat next to me in the windowed group room. It is shortly after lunch, and I'm having trouble controlling my body temperature. I wasn't out long enough to need serious detox, but it's still an uncomfortable process.

"I've been worse," I say and smile. "How are you?"

"Well, I've been better. I got in about four days before you and I'm detoxing hard, man."

"What's your DOC?"

"Heroin," he says.

"Oh yeah? I had a roommate at another treatment center who was a heroin addict. Are you cold all the time? He was."

"Sometimes. Really, though, I just ache all the time," he grimaces.

"Sounds horrible."

There is a beat of silence.

"So, everyone seems fairly young here, except our other roommate, I can't remember his name."

"Matt," he answers. "No, he's only like thirty-five, he just really liked eating pills and it shows."

"Oh wow, but he walks with a cane!"

McKinley laughs. "Yeah, I think he had a leg injury or something and relapsed while he was healing. I'm not sure, he's been here before with my older brother. So, you've been to another treatment center, eh? How many?"

He looks over at me. He has a boyish face, with light brown hair and hazel eyes. He wears glasses and a lopsided grin.

158

I chuckle and scratch my ear. "Oh man, I've become that guy. This will be my fourth."

"Nah, it's no big deal. We're a very accepting group. And you don't top Jordyn, he's been to eleven."

I nod. "You know, I've wondered if we get addicted to rehab."

"I dunno, but I could see that. This is my first time. And my last, I hope. No offense," he says, nudging me with his shoulder.

"It's all good."

"So how old are you?"

"Thirty-one," I answer.

"Sweet, me too! There's a couple of us here that're thirty-one. Well, um, to be real, I'm not feeling so well. I'm going to lay down before group, but it was nice talking with you, Charlie."

"You too, McKinley," I say as he walks toward the staircase. Despite detoxing like hell, he is surprisingly chipper and positive. It's cute; I remember when I felt that way in my early rehab days.

I find myself growing increasingly bitter as each hour passes. Sighing, I rub my temples and think. It's important to find some semblance of neutrality in my current circumstance. Flailing from one emotion to another will offer me little comfort. As much as I know this, though, I cannot force it through my head. I'm an emotional live wire.

I want to scream. Or break something. Or do something super dramatic and unnecessary. My skin is itchy and hot; my neck feels tight, sending a dull throb down my right arm. I walk toward the French doors in the dining area, intending to step outside and cool off for a moment; I'm caught by a man with tightly curled brown hair and a beard. He has an uncanny resemblance to the actor John C. Reilly.

"Hi, Charlie! I'm Jerry, I'll be your therapist while you're here.

Lucky I ran across you, I was just about to begin roaming the halls. Let me grab some water, then let's head downstairs and chat for a bit? That sound good?"

"Oh, fuck. I mean, hello—sorry!" I extend my hand to him. "Sure, yes, that would be fine. I mean, I'm just spiraling into the abyss over here." I smile to let him know I'm only partially kidding.

Jerry laughs. "Oh, you're gonna be fun, huh?"

I chuckle and scratch my ear. "Buckle up, bud."

*****

Tucking my hoodie into a cubbyhole, I take in the full scope of the gym. Two long rows of treadmills sit behind a gleaming line of exercise bikes, all surrounded by weight machines. Massive TVs hang every twenty feet and music thumps from scattered speakers. It's 9:15 in the morning and a ghost town. I watch as the others break off to their favorite equipment. Having spent very little time in a gym, I walk around cautiously, deciding where to start. Settling on an exercise bike, I choose a three-mile course.

Five minutes in, my legs and lungs are burning like the fires of hell. Sweat pours down my face and back, and I can hear myself wheezing. So glamorous, so appealing. But I keep pushing as if the bike will fly off its holster and allow me to escape. From what, I'm not sure. Myself? I feel raw, wounded, and stuck. I feel alone.

Making our way back to the van in the cold, Jordyn throws his arm around me. He's taller than me, and I pat him on the back.

"How are you doing, man?" he asks.

"You know, it's not my first rodeo. I'm hanging in there." I say and grin at him, hoping to seem somewhat "okay."

"You know, it's not mine either. When you're ready to talk, I'm here, man."

I reflect on his words on the van ride back. I can't even fool someone who barely knows me; I'm broken, and it shows.

Snow falls dreamily outside the entryway windows as I lay on the lofted floor. The day has passed in a blur after the gym. Without noticing, I have begun to withdraw into myself and shut down. It is my way of becoming numb without the aid of substances.

I hear footsteps behind me and turn to see Jordyn. He is gaunt, with wavy blonde hair and light blue eyes. He stretches out beside me and sighs exaggeratedly.

"Fucking treatment, eh?"

I laugh. "Yeah, what is this, your tenth or something?"

"Eleventh, bro!"

"Oh, yes, my bad. Eleventh."

"McKinley said it's your fourth, and you're an alcoholic. My name is Jordyn, and I'm a heroin addict. I feel like I know where you're at right now, mentally. Certainly, our situations are different, but I can empathize with that specific feeling of disgust at being back in fucking rehab."

I turn my head toward him and our eyes meet.

"I never knew I could have this kind of contempt for myself. I didn't know it could get this bad, that I could think of myself with such...such *loathing*, that I could *despise* myself. I mean, sure, I've heard other people tell their stories and how awful it got for *them*, but I never thought *I'd* get here. I thought I was different, somehow. Hmm. Don't we all."

161

"Yes, yes we do. Well, let me tell you my shitty saga and maybe you'll feel a bit better."

I chuckle and roll onto my back. "Please tell me your shitty life story, Jordyn."

He raises up and rests on his knees.

"I was born on a harsh winter night, in the middle of the deadliest storm in a decade. Not really, but it would explain a lot, because honestly, my youth was pretty ideal. Good parents, fun brothers and sisters, and solid home life. I was active in school and had plenty of friends, I was happy. It's not like I was seeking an escape from abuse or trauma. Maybe I was just bored, I'm not sure. But I started taking pills and smoking weed when I was twelve. Nothing major, just a peach or blue Xanax and some reggie. But by the time I was fourteen, I'd say, I was popping Oxy and rolling blunts. My very religious, very sweet parents discovered this and sent me to my first juvenile rehab. It was intense, an eight-month program full of manual labor, sort of break you down to build you up.

"I stayed clean for about five months after getting home, but forcing someone into sobriety never works. My parents and I played that game several times until I was eighteen and on my own. Which is when it got really messy. I started using needles. Up until then, I had only ever smoked or snorted pills and never fucked with heroin.

"And it's almost like it was fate because once I shot up heroin for the first time, I *knew* in my *soul* that I was never getting high another way again. I had found my nirvana. I met a girl who felt the same way, and it was like living in a hazy, druggy dream. We had a beautiful, twisted, toxic relationship that lasted for a couple of years before she overdosed one night. I woke up to find her cold and blue. It didn't seem real. It still doesn't,

162

honestly.

"After she died, I decided I wanted to clean up for her, become a better man for her memory. And noble as that may sound, it still didn't work. I went to about five rehabs in a row, basically spending a year and ten months in different treatment centers. Constantly trying to hide from the pain, from drugs, from sobriety. I'd leave one, relapse, and then enter another. Eventually, I think I got tired of the grind so I stayed sober for a year and a half. I got a decent job in construction, started dating again, and felt really content."

Jordyn pauses as McKinley walks out of our bedroom and sits crisscross near the railing.

"Don't mind me," he says. "I was reading and heard you guys talking."

Jordyn smiles. "I forgot you hadn't heard this part. Apparently, though, I still had some lingering issues because I relapsed hard. It started with alcohol, oddly enough, on a family cruise. And what a glorious fucking disaster it was. We had docked for a bit and I left the ship feeling good, not even really thinking about drinking. Thirty minutes later, though, I'm drunk and searching for drugs. Which I found and did before miraculously re-boarding the ship in time. I, um, don't remember doing any of that, though. It's just what my family and I have pieced together. Long story short, I destroyed both of our cabins, got in a fight with the staff, and my entire family was told to clear the ship at the next port.

"I begged and pleaded for forgiveness but they were done. My Dad said they would always love me, but didn't want me to hurt them anymore. He said they'd been waiting for 'the call' for a couple of years now and that some of my family had stopped asking about me. I've never hated myself more than at that moment.

"So, here I am. In rehab, or treatment, or whatever you want to call it, for the eleventh time. That shame you feel, that disgust and contempt, I feel it too. As I'm sure McKinley does," he says, motioning toward McKinley.

"For sure," McKinley mumbles.

"It's natural," says Jordyn. "It means you actually care and you actually do want to get help. It's just hard to see that from the outside looking in. And we sure don't make it easy on our family."

"No," I say, my voice a bit hoarse. "No, I sure do not."

"You know," McKinley starts, "why couldn't this be it, guys? Like why stay on this hamster wheel of rehabs? Don't take this the wrong way, but we're all thirty-one, shouldn't we have moved on from this?"

"Oh, if it were only that easy," I chuckle. "But yes, you're right, McKinley. You are, we should have."

Jordyn raises his arms and claps in agreement.

McKinley clears his throat. "What if we make a pact that while we're here together, we'll hold one another accountable and do our best to really focus on recovery and progress? The thirty-one pact. We can do better and be better if we help each other."

"I'm game for anything at this point," Jordyn says.

"Sure, why not?" I say, sitting up. "Maybe the fourth time's the charm. Or the eleventh."

*****

Seeking refuge, I silently close the French doors to the kitchen and drift toward the ping-pong tables. A patient's intake process has spilled into the windowed group room and is causing quite the commotion. The last thing I heard before exiting was heated yelling about cigarettes and coming down. Rather than perch and peer, I opted for some space.

Taking a steadying breath, I enjoy the crisp night air. Reflections is surrounded by buttes and the view is breathtaking at night. It reminds me of the Ducks Unlimited paintings my Granny and Dad hung on our walls. I can feel my guilt softening; last night's conversation with Jordyn and McKinley helped break down my shame and lifted a weight from my shoulders. I'm floundering, struggling to find a path forward, and I know I need to make some headway.

The doors burst open, and I step closer to the wall, watching as the intake walks to the end of the porch, hugging himself tightly around the shoulders. He screams at the moon and begins to cry.

I give him a moment and then clear my throat. He spins quickly, meets my eye, grimaces, and then bows his head.

"Fuck," he whispers.

"I'll go back in through the side door and give you your space, man." I begin to walk away but he speaks, his voice strained.

"No, please stay."

"Okay," I say, unsure of what to do.

"Is it alright here? Is it chill?" he asks abruptly.

"It's a rehab, of course it isn't chill. But yes, it's alright. There's definitely worse places to be."

"Yeah, it's this or jail for me."

"I would think that's a fairly easy decision, then," I say, continuing to the side door.

"I'm just not ready to stop," he pleads.

As lame and whiny as he sounds, I immediately empathize

and understand.

"Then don't. Or do. Just stay here until you figure your shit out, dude. No one chooses jail over rehab."

He rubs his eyes and exhales loudly.

"Fuck, you're right. Thanks. I'm Jayce, by the way."

"Hi, Jayce. I'm Charlie." I offer my hand, and we shake, smiling and sizing up one another. He is taller than me, with light brown skin and sparkling, straight teeth.

The door creaks and breaks our gaze. It is Jake, our usual night tech.

"Do you want to come back inside and finish intake, Jayce? Or are we gonna have to call the Po-Po?"

"No, I'll stay," he says and follows Jake into the kitchen. "Can Charlie be my roommate?"

Shaking my head, I turn back to the night sky. "What. The. Fuck."


"Charlie!"

I hear my name called from outside of my bedroom and sigh. I had just eased my mind, and was blissfully without thought, vibing on the Ativan.

"Charlie, what's up?"

It's Jayce. He leans in my doorway and crosses his arms.

"What's up, man?" I say.

"Do you play chess?" he asks, not at all what I was expecting.

"Nope, sorry."

"Do you wanna learn?"

I blink. "You know, why not?"

He beams. "Right on, man! I found a chess set downstairs."

I roll off the bed and follow him to the vacant dining table. Other patients are scattered throughout the house, talking, reading, or working on assignments. We sit across from one another, and he begins placing the pieces on the board.

"So do you know anything about chess?"

"Not really. I know there's a Queen and a King and something about a Knight. And it's not like Checkers."

Jayce laughs. "No, it's not like Checkers."

He is definitely younger than me, in his mid-twenties. Tattoos snake around his arms and neck, which are toned and muscular. I can't decide if I'm attracted to him, but he feels magnetic. As he teaches me the rules of chess, we talk about our lives, and I am reminded of my conversations with Brenda. She knows I have relapsed, and I'd love a chance to chat with her. Maybe if I'd done that more often, I wouldn't have strayed quite as quickly.

"You don't want to make that move," Jayce says, his eyes twinkling.

"Why? I think it's a good move," I say and study the board. "Oh, I see. Shit, this game is tricky!"

He laughs. "It's strategy."

"Clearly something I know very little about, or I wouldn't be here."

I glance up at him as Jake rounds the corner holding sheet of paper.

"New chores list, guys! Charlie, you're on breakfast duty after the gym, and Jayce you've got the bathroom near the main entrance."

We both groan.

*****

Rain patters on the high window of Jerry's basement office.

It is a small and homey space, much more cluttered and used than Andrew's immaculate "zen den." He has stepped away to the kitchen for water, and I take this time to try and organize my thoughts. Rather than focus on the loss of my Mom or the trauma of my teenage years, I would like to understand why I cannot let go of the bottle.

Jerry rounds the corner with two mugs of water and a smile.

"Now, where did we leave off last time? I believe we were up to your late twenties, yes?"

"Yes, but there's not much else to cover. By then I was mainly drinking alone, working and scraping together two or three days sober at a time. Finally, I started going to rehabs as a last resort, but now I feel like I'm on a new cycle, and it's no better. Do you think I have some sick fascination with being the struggling victim? That I need to feel important, somehow? Unique? I'm not sure what that says about me. It's frightening."

"It's just kinda coming to me, but I'm wondering if you've developed a bit of a grandiosity complex as a defense mechanism?"

"I'm not sure I'm following," I say, folding my legs up into the chair.

"This isn't the first time I've heard you express a feeling of being different from others. I understand you don't feel this way because you're gay, that it goes deeper for you than that. I'm wondering if you needed to bolster yourself in some way in order to cope with the passing of your Mother and subsequent trauma. Our young selves can create a protective cocoon without our ever knowing. As you grew, this emotional response could very well have grown with you. This is not to say you view yourself as better than others, merely different. Maybe you feel life was unfairly thrust upon you at a young age, which sets you apart from the majority of people. In your created identity, that is."

Silence hangs in the air. My mind is reeling. Much of what Jerry stumbled across is resonating within me, and I feel on the verge of an epiphany.

"You really opened my eyes there. I was crying out for help, but I needed it validated. I needed it to be more than your average bout of alcoholism or depression. I just couldn't realize that's what I was doing. I wasn't able to accept and work through life, I was working against it without ever knowing. Wow. Shit. Damn it! It took all of *that* to understand *this*? That's insane."

Jerry grins at me.

"I would call that a light bulb moment! This is good work! Now, how is your biography coming? Do you think you'll be ready to share it next week?"

"I think so. I did a timeline once before, so it's going pretty smoothly. I haven't gotten to the darker parts yet, though."

He nods thoughtfully, his hands folded.

"Tell me a little about the darker parts."

I exhale audibly. "Oh, why not? These last few years have been the darkest of my life. I've been so lonely. And so drunk. And it hasn't been fun for years, I don't know why I do it. I mean, I know why I do it, I really do. I guess the better thing to say is I don't know why I haven't fixed it. Because that's why I remain lonely and drunk—and I *know* this! Which makes me feel shameful. And then I think of my sister, and I feel terrible."

My face begins to warm and my throat feels raw and tight. Talking about Brodie is the only topic where I struggle to maintain composure. Ever since our Mom passed away, I have felt a profound sense of responsibility for her, something I have squandered these last three or four years. I couldn't get my ass out of a vodka bottle during a most crucial and devastating time in her early twenties, and it has left me deflated.

"What do you think is the cause for these feelings?" Jerry asks calmly, noticing my loss of control.

"Because I love her so much and I feel like I abandoned her!" I burst, fighting to keep myself at bay. "I never meant for my behavior to hurt her so badly. It goes beyond feeling angry or disappointed in myself—it freaks me the fuck out! That I am capable of that *brutality*."

He fixes me with a stern gaze.

"Charlie, I want you to really think about something. While you may feel that in your last treatment center you forgave yourself, I am not seeing it. Bits, maybe, but you're just chipping away at the tip of the iceberg. I think you're just now realizing the amount of damage and wreckage you created in your alcoholism, and that is fueling much of your anger. I'm so glad you decided to seek help again, because I think we really need to work on your relationship with yourself. Once you begin to heal that, your relationship with your sister will start to mend itself. Do you think you can give that a try?"

"Yes, I will try."

*****

Watching the drops of lavender fall into the diffuser, I enjoy a few moments of quiet in the group room before our morning meeting. After breakfast, we have an hour or so to ourselves before congregating in the largest group room. Originally a three-car garage, it has been repurposed into a welcoming space with plenty of light. Moses has already completed his chore of setting up the chairs and I take a seat near the furthest window.

It is surreal, living this intimately with other addicts and alcoholics; it feels much more personal than my previous rehabs. I sometimes feel like I'm on *The Real World: Rehab*, and it helps me find humor in my circumstance. My other experiences with treatment have been vastly different and this alternative approach is welcome. The shared dynamics of the house may provide me with a more solid foundation, or at least I hope.

"Doing alright, Charlie?" Don, the head therapist, asks as he enters the room. He is, without a doubt, one of the most jovial individuals I have ever met. He seems perennially cheerful, which is ironic considering his struggle with drugs and alcohol. I see him rarely, usually during morning groups, and have come to admire him.

"So good so far," I say breezily.

"Good to hear! You're much healthier—I noticed you haven't missed a day at the gym since getting off detox status."

I laugh. "Yeah, I thought, what the hell? Let's try this whole exercise thing. Honestly, I'm really enjoying it. It gives me time to think and sort through stuff. Or something like that."

"Certainly, certainly," Don says, taking his seat at the head of the group. "Exercise is great for the body *and* mind."

"Yes, I'm learning that," I say, stretching.

Dakota and Tyler walk in, both sleepy-eyed and delayed. We are joined shortly by the rest of the house, and Don calls the group to order.

"Good morning, everyone. I hope you all had a restful night. Before we begin our activity today, I wanted to open up the group and see if anyone had any thoughts or concerns they wanted to process."

A moment of silence rings.

"Tyler, alcoholic."

"Morning, Tyler!" we echo.

"This is kinda hard for me. I wasn't brought up talking about my feelings, and it still feels weird, but I'm working on it.

"Last night, I had a family session and it helped me realize a lot of things about myself. And I guess the main thing I realized is that I don't want to keep bottling everything up and pretending like I'm only ever happy or pissed off. I'm a lot more than that. I know this comes from how I was raised and it's no one's fault.

"But last night, my Mom and I were having a really emotional talk and we were both hugging and crying, and my Dad was just so embarrassed; he kept asking us to pull ourselves together. It hurt my feelings *so much* because I just wanted him to hug and cry with us, but he was so distant.

"I don't want to be like that. Stoic, I think that's what you said, Jordyn?"

Jordyn dips his head softly. "Yup."

"Yeah, I don't think stoic is so cool, guys. At least not for me. It's like there's this whole idea of how a man is supposed to be, but it makes no sense. And I've idealized this, blindly. Because of it, I've caused so much more trouble by not dealing with my emotions than if I'd just worked through them. I know I'm simple, but I feel like it's not a hard concept to grasp."

"You're not simple at all, Tyler," McKinley says forcefully. "And you shouldn't think you are. That's huge, what you just figured out!"

"Yeah," Dakota agrees. "I've watched you grow so much while you've been here, Tyler, simple is not the word to describe you."

"I feel the same way, man," Jayce says, leaning back in his chair. "I was on and off the streets most of my life, so I had to present myself a certain way, to protect myself. But inside, I was never that hard. I don't think many people are. Everything is just a front, an act."

There are several nods.

"And you're able to come here and feel safe and explore those feelings. But what happens when you're out again, on your own?" Don asks.

"Oh fuck, bro, I haven't made it that far yet!" Tyler jokes, and we burst into laughter.

"Maybe not yet, but you're well on your way. And it's very nice to see the support this group has for one another. It's always a toss-up as to what the house vibe will be, but right now we have a very solid group. Lean on one another in these times, it will prove very helpful when you're outside of these walls."

"Just no rehab romances, right?" Moses giggles and his eyes flicker to me.

"I would highly recommend refraining from relationships of that sort for at least a year, however, that is just my opinion," Don says, waving his hands in the air.

I spend the remainder of group trying to participate in the activity on cognitive dissonance, yet my mind wanders. Being stuck in the waiting room that is rehab has begun to take its toll on me. While I know it's catastrophic thinking, I wonder if I'm becoming institutionalized. As though I prefer to function in the safety and structure of a facility. Images of shuffling down hospital hallways flash before me and I cringe.

As we clear out of group, I tap Jayce's shoulder.

"Hey, I'm gonna go lay down for a bit, I don't feel so well. If anyone asks, will you let them know?"

"Sure you don't want me to come snuggle with you?" he grins, handsome and mischievous.

Heat spreads throughout my chest, and I laugh nervously.

"You're too much," I say and dart up the stairs.

Shaking my arms out, I work on keeping myself in check. Cute boys have a tendency to make me lose my head, which is the last spiral I need added to my life.

Wrapping my blanket tighter around myself, I shuffle to the pantry in the kitchen. It's nearing lights out and my Seroquel is giving me the munchies. Slicing an apple, I hear muffled sobbing in the corner of the dining area. Why do I find everyone crying? I make eye contact over my shoulder and smile sympathetically.

She's new to Reflections, the lady I'm smiling at, for I haven't seen her before. Her short brown hair is tangled and she is wearing fluffy, pink pajamas. She hiccups and gives me a gloomy shrug.

"Sorry, don't mind me. I'm just a mess, I apologize," she says, wiping her nose.

"Oh it's alright, we're all a mess here. Did you just get in?"

"Earlier today, around noon. I think everyone was gone somewhere and I was so drunk, they gave me some water and sent me upstairs. I fell asleep and woke up, and forgot where I was for a moment."

At this, she laughs, hiccups, and then continues to weep.

"I'm so sorry, it's just—I don't belong here. I was forced, but I can't leave or my family will never speak to me again! So I'm stuck here, in this hellhole with all these—these people I don't know! Oh my God, I don't know what to do!" she cries frantically.

I stare at her and blink.

"Why not try taking a deep breath and relaxing your muscles,"

174

I say, trying to keep any annoyance from my voice. A few statements have put me off, however much of her disdain could be from shock of the situation and lingering booze.

"Yeah, I don't think that will help! What I need is to get out of this prison camp before something terrible happens to me!" she snaps loudly.

I line up my apple pieces and sprinkle a bit of salt over each slice.

"Hmm," I say, "my name is Charlie. May I ask your name?"

"Ashley," she answers sulkily.

"Well, Ashley. I would recommend getting a tighter grip on reality. The only terrible thing currently happening to you is that you're disillusioned. Good night."

Sweeping up the apple slices, I leave the kitchen, my anger flaring. Projecting is never a healthy coping technique, although it is satisfying. It would be bigger of me to approach Ashley with more sympathy and understanding, but I'm hesitant to co-sign on her need to be pampered.

Indulging my temper is becoming more and more alluring. It feels like a natural response to the lifestyle I have chosen. I tried being sad at my alcoholism, which ultimately led me back to the bottle. Perhaps sheer, boiling rage will distill me.

*****

"So fuck the new girl," Dakota says, coloring in one of her many books.

Moses giggles beside her.

"Why's that?" asks Jordyn from the kitchen island.

A few of the patients have gathered by happenstance in the kitchen and dining area after breakfast. I sit anxiously in the far corner, paging through *The Book of Mormon*. I must admit, I am curious as to Dakota's assessment of Ashley.

"I was trying to be friendly last night and talking with her, and she was so above it all. And when I told her I'm a heroin addict, she was like, 'Oh my God, you're a drug addict?' Like dude, you're in rehab, what the hell?"

"Oh you remember how it is when you first get here," Tyler says cheerfully, always in an attempt to lighten the mood.

"Yeah, but I wasn't walking around judging people," Dakota mutters.

"Anyone excited for CA tonight?" Keeton interjects, changing the subject.

"They're still going to Cocaine Anonymous at Soleil? Right on!" Matt says, buried underneath his hoodie. He's having trouble shaking off the chills from detox and spends most of his time bundled up and shivering.

"They don't have them very often, but we usually go. Jake takes us," Moses replies.

"Do we ever do anything just for fun?" Jayce asks, rocking his chair back and forth.

"We'll go to the movies sometimes, or laser tag. Stuff like that. We're so obvious that we're in rehab when we go out, though, it's kinda embarrassing," Keeton answers, grinning.

"I wish they'd take us hiking," Jordyn says.

"I'm not sure about hiking, but a leisurely walk in these buttes you guys speak of would be nice," I retort.

"Ah, you're ready for a hike, Charlie. You've been killing it at the gym!" McKinley walks over and pats me on the back. "Speaking of the gym, shouldn't we all change, it's about time?"

Stepping outside, I spot Ashley sitting near the ping-pong tables.

She is still wearing the fluffy pink PJ's but has added a pair of large glasses and a luxurious cream robe. She turns her head toward me.

"Hello, Ashley," I say stiffly.

She whimpers, wounded and lost. It is not within me to be cruel, and guilt smacks me across the face.

"How are you?" I ask much more gently.

"Sad. And scared," she answers meekly. "I feel like I'm not supposed to be here."

"Oh, it's not so bad, really. And I once heard someone say something very similar to that, and the reply they received was that if they felt they shouldn't be in rehab, then most likely, that's exactly where they needed to be. Believe me, this is a very nice facility, with very mild patients."

Ashley is quiet, peering intensely down at her lap. This is a jarring change for her, and I suppose that should be respected. Comparing life struggles is shallow, and only devalues a person's story. I place my hands in my pockets and wait to see if she would like to chat further.

"My family has been threatening me for months, but I never thought they'd actually go through with it," she whispers. "I wish they'd at least picked somewhere on the coast."

"Oh, I've been to those, on both sides, and yet here I am." I grin over at her. "Can I ask why you think you shouldn't be here?"

"I just don't belong here. I'm not that far gone that I need to be put away somewhere! I like to drink, who cares? I don't drive. I don't cause scenes. I'm fine." She takes quick, sharp breaths and leans forward. "Great, now I'm going to have an anxiety attack!"

I watch her as she leans forward and trembles, yet I don't

quite buy what she's selling. I've faked my fair share of panic attacks and seizures, and there are usually tell-tale signs of a charade. She flings back in her chair dramatically and breathes loudly through her nose.

"Better?" I ask after a moment, suppressing a cheeky grin.

"Not really."

"I'm sorry to hear that. So the only reason you're staying here is to appease your family?"

"Basically."

"Hmm, well why don't you treat it as a vacation, then? If you've decided you're staying to make your family happy, why not try and make the best of it? I'll be your friend if you promise to tone it down a bit."

Her eyes narrow, and I brace myself for a scathing.

"Oh my God, I have been acting bratty, haven't I?"

"Oh you've just demeaned everyone here several times, but we get it. You're lashing out because you're scared and lonely and probably want to drink."

She laughs. "You have no idea! And I'd turn tricks for a cigarette right now!"

I giggle with her.

"Me too, girl! Well, I'm glad we got all that settled. Heads up, you may want to smooth things over with Dakota."

Ashley grimaces. "I figured I'd done something last night when she slammed the door, but at the time I honestly didn't care."

"Yeah, maybe don't react so harshly to others' addictions. Not the coolest thing to do in rehab."

She touches my arm and gives me an earnest, imploring gaze.

"Can you teach me the rehab rules, Charlie?"

I guffaw; it is the funniest thing I have heard in months.

"Yes, Ashley, I can teach you the rehab rules. I suppose I *am* a bit of an expert at this point."

\*\*\*\*\*

Grabbing an apple from the kitchen, I rush to the group room in the garage. It is Keeton's last day and we're about to begin the farewell process. It will be my first time experiencing this, as none of my previous treatment centers had a specific group for completion of their program.

There is a pleasant buzz of chatter as I take a seat next to Jayce. He lays his head on my shoulder.

"I want a blunt," he whines.

"Don't we all," I say, patting his back.

His head springs up.

"Hey, since Keeton's leaving, do you wanna ask if we can be roommates? It's stupid that your room is full, and now I'll be the only one in mine. And you're like the only person I feel comfortable with."

"Yeah, for sure, I'll go talk with Jerry after this."

I swallow. I'm not sure what is happening between Jayce and me. He knows I'm gay, and claims to be straight, but there is a dynamic developing, something I've never encountered before. I scratch my ear and feel a bit archaic, as I know sexuality isn't always rigid. Perhaps I'm afraid of catching feelings for him. Perhaps I should focus on catching feelings for myself.

Don clears his throat from the front of the room, and the group falls silent.

"Hello, I'm Don and a drug addict."

"Hi, Don!"

"This morning we will be celebrating Keeton and his many

179

successes at Reflections."

There is some whooping and playful trash talking. Marina, his therapist, is especially jubilant.

"Keeton came to us in January, and slept for how many days?"

"Five," Keeton chuckles. "I only woke up for food and the bathroom."

"Oh God, I remember, you stinky man!" Tyler teases.

"But once you woke up, you really did begin to blossom. It has been a privilege to watch your growth, Keeton. I have chosen a very specific coin for you, The Camel Coin. And I would like to push patience into this coin. Patience with yourself and those around you."

Don holds the coin in his palm for a moment, then passes it to his right, to Dakota. She places it in her palm, thinking.

"Keeton, you have been so sweet to me. I love your sassy hair advice, and I really do think you have a gift with styling! I'm going to miss you so much, but I know I'll be seeing you all the time once I leave here. It's only goodbye for a short time. Into your coin, I push love. I hope you can come to love yourself as much as I love you."

Keeton smiles, his eyes shining. "Oh shit, this is gonna be harder than I thought!"

As Dakota passes the coin to her right, I understand the pattern. While listening to the others provide Keeton with encouraging words, I am grateful for the inclusivity of this group. I glance around the room, at each of us in our various stages of detox and recovery. A sense of belonging settles over me, and it is relieving. Despite our differing backgrounds, we are united by a common goal, and it is a welcome binding of friendship.

I take the coin from Jayce and grin at Keeton.

"We didn't spend much time together, but from what I've heard, you're a very respected, admired guy. I would recommend using that support once you're on your own again. Into this coin, I push resilience. I wish you the best, Keeton!"

Once the coin has made its round, it is given to Keeton. He thanks everyone for their kind words, tears up, and we end with a big group hug. It is cheesy, straight out of a Hallmark rehab story, but the feeling of connection is nice after being alone for so long.

*****

Jayce rolls my suitcase into our room as I make up my new bed.

"Dude, this room has a balcony!" I say.

"Yeah, it's locked 'cause suicide, but still cool."

"Oh, morbid. You can put that in the closet, please."

After Keeton's send-off, Jayce and I spoke with our respective therapists and Don, and I was given permission to switch rooms. I've decided to remain optimistically cautious regarding our new arrangement; I'm not eager to make a fool of myself over a boy and hopeful that Jayce and I can create a bond outside of sexual tension.

Jayce flings himself on his bed and sighs.

"Bro, I'm so thankful that you're my roommate. I don't really trust people, or like sleeping in the same room as them, or having my back to people I don't know. They're a threat. But I don't feel that way with *you*. You're definitely *not* a threat."

I laugh and dust my filthy nightstand. Keeton was not a tidy tenant.

"No, I'm just a stick boy. Actually, I've never even been in a fight. I wouldn't know what to do."

"I didn't mean it that way, Charlie. I meant you're not aggressive or twisted. You're a kind, gentle guy. I like that about you."

"Oh, shucks. Well, I'm a nasty, mouthy drunk, though. Which is ugly."

"Yeah, but that's not you. That's your addiction."

I turn my head toward him.

"It's a part of me, though. Don't you think? I mean, shouldn't we take responsibility for our actions when we're blacked out, even *if* it isn't us in the moment?"

"True. Most of the time, though, I was just trying to survive, you know? I was always running. Running for drugs, running the streets, running from people. Just running, all the time. It was fucking exhausting." He raises up and leans against the wall. "But you just drank, didn't you?"

I smirk and cluck my tongue. "'Just drank.' And drank, and drank, and drank. But I mean in a way, I was running, too. Running from reality. Life was easier for me when I was wasted. Which is just what I thought at the time because saying it out loud, sounds ludicrous, but that's honestly how I felt."

"Nah, I get it, man. I really do."

The light is fading in our new room. It is smaller than the one I shared with McKinley and Matt, with two beds pushed against the far wall and a long, dark wooden dresser opposite the balcony doors. There is a small walk-in closet and two nightstands. It smells strongly of Axe body spray, but I suppose that's better than farts and feet.

I arrange the clock and desk fan, then straighten my blankets.

"So, when you say you were on the streets, were you in a gang or something?"

His eyes darken and he gives me a hard gaze, which slowly

182

melts into amusement.

"You're clueless, huh? It's kinda nice, actually. Refreshing, I think you'd say," he chuckles.

"I know you're making fun of me, only I'm not sure what about," I say, shaking my head.

"The way you say it, 'in a gang or something.' It's not like the movies, and yes, I was in a gang. But it's not something I usually talk about."

"I can understand that. Is that when you started using?"

"No, I've been doing drugs for a minute. I was into drugs before all that shit, but it sure didn't help."

"What do you think you'll do when you leave here? Do you still feel like you're not ready to stop?"

Jayce grabs a fidget spinner from his nightstand drawer. As he watches it glide, his eyes are miles away from where we sit.

"I wish I could go somewhere and start over. That's the only way I'd stop. But that probably won't happen, so I'd say I'll go right back to what I was doing."

"What is it they say, though, 'wherever I go, there I am?' Something like that."

"Yeah, but at least it'd just be me, I could probably handle that. It's everyone else."

"The people you don't like to talk about?" I ask seriously.

He gives me a soft smile. "Yeah."

"Hmm. Don't give up just yet, Jayce. Talk to your therapist about moving. If there's one thing I've learned bouncing around from state to state and facility to facility, it's that there are dozens of programs out there, you just have to ask properly."

"Ask properly?" he mimics and laughs. "Oh, you're a trip, dude."

"Shut up," I say, laughing along with him.

Tyler pokes his head through the door, a candy cigarette hanging from his lips.

"Hey, we're about to head to CA," he says and then disappears.

We drive through the gates of Soleil and my jaw drops in awe. Up the drive, an enormous Montana ranch house sits majestically. I know it's actually another treatment center, but it has the appearance of a celebrity vacation home, which helps explain the high population of famous entertainers. I wonder: did I call here in my blackout? Surely I wasn't that pretentious.

Entering a fancy door on the side, we file through a marbled hallway that opens into a large, sumptuous square room. The dusty-colored marble continues into this room along with nearly two hundred black, cushioned chairs arranged neatly, facing a podium. Jake leads us to a section on the right and we take up part of a row. I peer around at the walls and ceiling, impressed by the detail. We're early; I cross my legs and wait for people to watch. I wish I would have thought to bring snacks.

As the meeting progresses, I listen silently and with rapt attention. While the format is the same as traditional Alcoholics Anonymous meetings, the culture is much more rambunctious and lively; I find it infectious. Most conversations and testimonials mainly concern cocaine and other drugs, but I am able to identify with each story shared. Regardless of the substance, addiction rears destruction in all who tread its path.

I am particularly moved by an older lady, sharing that she had twenty-eight years clean and then recently relapsed. It was not the actual use of drugs that boggles her, but that she fell so easily into an old routine. It has her questioning if she ever truly knew herself or if her disease played a masterful trick. Her anguish is palpable, and I mourn with her.

My thoughts swirl as we ride back to Reflections. Recovery seems so random. Some take to it like a duck to water and others, like myself, can barely tread. I suppose I've never really put in the work, though. True, I've read "The Big Book," a couple of times, but managed to steer clear of working past Step Four. I've done the homework assigned to me in treatment, but on a surface level. Reflecting back, I can see that I wanted to be fixed, but I didn't want to do the work involved. A pill, a couple of sessions, and send me on my way, Doc; I should be good.

I chuckle softly to myself as we circle around to the back of the house.

"What?" Moses asks from behind me.

"I think I just had a 'come to Jesus' moment," I say and slide out the van door, stretching and stopping by the ping-pong tables to gather my thoughts.

As I walk up the stairs, I call out for McKinley, who saunters out of my old room.

"What's up, bud?"

"So about that pact, I need you to hold me accountable for working The Steps. Otherwise, I'll just fluff my way around it like I do everything else."

He beams at me.

"Charlie, this is great! I just started Step Three the other day, for sure I'll hold you accountable!"

"Thanks, McKinley," I say and walk to my new room, *my* step a bit lighter.

*****

Morning sunlight spills through the windows of the garage group room. It is still, and I am alone. Jerry is requiring my

185

story to be shared on Tuesday, two days from now, and I'm determined to provide a thorough, accurate depiction of my life. I will not let my grandiose complex bind me any further; what has worked for others will surely work for me, if only I complete the necessary tasks.

Closing my eyes, I focus on being mindful. The heat from the sun, the ring of silence, the smell of lemongrass and tea tree oil from the diffuser. I linger on each sense, inhaling slowly through my nose and exhaling through my mouth. My thoughts scatter, and I let them roam about, like pinpricks of light behind my eyelids.

A bird chirp brings me back, and I clutch my pen. It's time to engage previously ignored thoughts and issues. To be honest and objective, to create transparency.

I groan. "Pretty sure this is why you drank, bro."

After several hours of toiling away, I walk to the kitchen for provisions. Ashley meets me in the pantry.

"Where have you been all day?" she asks brightly.

"I'm doing my life story thing for Tuesday," I say, pilfering through the granola snacks.

"Oh, that's right! How's it going?"

"Super intense, but I guess that's the point."

"Oh! So I guess you haven't heard about the new girl, Faye?" Her brown eyes are alight with excitement.

"No, but I can tell you've got something interesting to say."

"Well, she used to run the streets with your boy, Jayce, and he's flipping the fuck out that she's here!"

A chill of dread passes over me.

"Where is he?"

"Down with Marina."

"Hmm," I say. "Well, I'm sure I'll hear about it sooner or later."

"Let me tell you, she's a feisty little bitch! She went ape shit when she saw Jayce, too. I kinda like her," Ashley chortles.

"You like the madness of it all, let's be real." I grin sardonically at her, settling on a chocolate chip granola bar.

"Caught," she holds up her hands. "I love it!"

"Embracing flaws with honesty, Ashley, right on!"

"Oh go finish your sappy life story," she teases and leaves the pantry.

I am propped against my bed, reading a story from the back of "The Big Book," when Jayce walks in, closes our door, and slides to the ground. He rubs the back of his neck and stares up at the ceiling. Deciding to give him space, I go back to reading.

"Thanks, man," he whispers a few minutes later.

"Yup," I say and close "The Big Book." "So, are you all talked out about it? Or—"

"I know Faye from forever ago—we ran the streets together, with my best friend Riley. She's his girl, or was. I don't even know now. The first thing she screamed when she saw me was 'he's dead,' but I don't know if I can believe her. She's always been a liar and a thief, even when we were tight. And she was fucked up, but who knows? Maybe she is telling the truth. And if she is I—I—." He takes quick, short breaths, and tears fall down his cheeks.

He lays down on the floor, and his body shakes with sobs. He doesn't make a sound, and I wonder if that is a learned survival skill, to grieve and rage noiselessly. To keep any trace of emotion contained. I remain still, gazing out the window. It is unspoken, but I know he doesn't want to be alone, yet he doesn't want to be coddled, either.

"Oh my fuck," he says breathlessly, rising up from the floor. "I just need to sleep. Will you let Jake and Marina know? I don't wanna see her yet. I'm not gonna do *evening fucking check-in*. You're cool to stay. I just don't wanna deal with anyone else right now."

"I'm gonna chill here for a bit and read, but I'll let them know when I go down, bud." I give him a small smile and reach for "The Big Book."

"You're so cute," he says and crawls under a San Francisco 49ers blanket.

"You're not well right now," I say with a laugh, trying to ignore the rush of emotions those three simple words release within me. I'm weak for the attention of boys, even when they're in distress. I sigh, acknowledging my shallow and misdirected use of energy. Oh, boys. Oh, Charlie.

Jordyn and I stand near the kettle in the kitchen, making sleepy tea. I lean toward him.

"Hey, I don't wanna turn around, but I think Faye keeps trying to make eye contact and get my attention. Try to be discreet. Is she looking at me now?" I whisper.

He feigns reaching for a paper towel.

"Oh for sure, dude."

"Shit. It's because she knows I'm Jayce's roommate."

"Yeah, how's all that mess going?"

"I mean, I have no idea what's going on. I honestly try to stay out of things but I'm too nice and somehow get roped into them," I explain, a bit exasperated.

Jordyn sighs and pats my back. "But you like it, Charlie. You're a fixer."

I shake my head. "Am I? How convenient."

He smiles and heads to the pantry for honey. I glance over to Faye but she is gone. Taking my chance, I dash for the staircase, only to come face-to-face with her in the windowed group room. She is waiting for me near the staircase.

"Hey, Charlie," she says, her voice husky and low. "Can I talk to you for a minute please?"

A strange sensation spills over me.

"Sure."

"It's just, I know you're Jayce's roommate, and Dakota said you two were kinda close. Can you ask him to come down and talk to me? Tell him it's about Riley."

And it hits me: jealousy. I tense my body to avoid shivering. Why am I reacting with jealousy? It's weird. I'm weird. This situation is weird, and I don't want any more of it.

"Yeah, I'll let him know. Night." And with that, I scurry upstairs, spilled tea be damned.

As I open the door, light from the hall pools on Jayce's bed. He's on his side and appears to be sleeping. I switch on the fan and decide to relay Faye's message in the morning. It would be rude to wake him; after all, he did say he wanted to sleep.

I kneel beside my bed, pulled there, and say a silent prayer for myself. It bubbles up from where I do not know and is simple: please help.

*****

Tapping my feet in an anxious rhythm, I twist my hair into a tight bun. I arrived early to morning group, in anticipation of sharing my story. My nerves are not from speaking in front of others, but rather being vulnerable and candid. Glossing over my tattered parts is a forte of mine, and reversing the process is proving to be a challenge. I've concluded I'm a master at lying by omission.

Jayce walks through the door, his 49ers blanket wrapped around him. Faye was telling the truth: Riley did overdose, and the funeral is early next week. It was a poignant moment, watching the bitterness between them melt away into a need for comfort. They are by no means friendly, but able to tolerate the company of one another.

He lays down on the ground near me.

"I'm just gonna listen from here, that cool?"

"Yeah," I say and stretch. "I think you've heard most of it when we've played chess."

Jerry's laughter echoes from the kitchen and my palms start to sweat. He rounds the corner with a warm smile.

"All ready then, Charlie?"

I attempt to mirror his sunshine. "Yup, ready to go."

Pulling my legs up into the chair, I flick Jayce's fidget spinner and wait for Jerry to begin group.

McKinley takes a seat next to me and rubs my shoulders.

"I felt freer and lighter after sharing my story. Get it all out, bud. No one's gonna judge."

"We're all here to support you," Matt says. He's recovered quite well, and appears much more his age, especially without his cane.

"Shucks, thanks," I say, soothed by their thoughtful comments.

Jerry claps his hands and peers around the group, a sparkle in his eye.

"We're all quite healthy and bright. I'm very happy to see you all today. Please, everyone, get comfortable as we'll be spending the majority of group sharing Charlie's story, followed by a quick process."

190

"Charlie bit me," Dakota mutters in a British accent, after the YouTube video. A few in the group giggle, and I smile over at her.

"As usual," Jerry says, "please be mindful and courteous while Charlie is sharing. Charlie, are you ready to begin?"

I glance around the group and swallow.

"Hi. Charlie. Alcoholic, but then you know that."

"Good morning, Charlie," they respond in unison.

I laugh loudly, touched by their planning.

"You know, I worked really hard on an outline the other day, but I think I'm just gonna lay that down here and wing it. It was a good springboard.

"Okay, so to start. I was born in Texas, but when I was three we moved to Clinton, Missouri. My Granny and my Step-Grandpa, on my Dad's side, had built a fishing resort on Truman Lake, called Bucksaw. My parents and I moved to take over the business since Granny and Grandpa wanted to travel and do other things.

"And it was amazing, really, growing up there. It was massive, with an actual marina floating on the lake. We lived in an apartment above the restaurant and tackle shop in the marina, so my house floated on the water. There was a pool, a huge pavilion, a lodge, and cabins. It was the most elaborate playground and I have such fond memories of growing up there. My aunts and uncles from both sides came to work there, and it was like this crazy, fun family business.

"We lived there until I was twelve, and then moved into town. Which was super small, like 9,000 people, but huge to me after living in the country. I had switched schools, too, from a smaller, rural elementary school to the Clinton School District. It was rough, guys. I had never been called 'gay' before and these new kids picked up on it quickly. Honestly, they weren't too hard on me, compared to what most endured.

"We'd lived in town for almost a year when my Mom died suddenly. It all started one afternoon in June, shortly after my thirteenth birthday. She told me she had a bad headache and went to lay down. My Dad came home and went to their bedroom just as she was having a seizure. He yelled for me to call 911, and there was clear panic in his voice. What I remember most vividly is hanging up the phone with 911 and then walking outside and standing underneath our upper deck. I had an eerie feeling that I couldn't quite grasp, and I kept saying to myself that she was gonna be okay.

"She was moved to Kansas City fairly quickly, and they had trouble figuring out what was causing her seizures. She was coherent for the first few days, and then my Dad and sister and I went to see a movie, *Big Daddy*, and when we came back she was having a stroke.

"I remember walking ahead of my Dad and Brodie, and when I opened the door she was convulsing and foaming at the mouth. My first reaction was to keep Brodie from seeing, so I turned around and started yelling for a doctor until Dad held Brodie back. After that, everything is a bit of a blur. I know I ran down to the main desk, frantic, and then I think we were all taken into a room somewhere. I'm not sure, but I have a clear memory of being in some kind of waiting room with Dad and Brodie. They were both crying so hard, and I didn't know what to do. Looking back, I think I was in shock.

"After that, we were told that she would need to be on life support permanently and had no brain waves. We were able to see her in the ICU, but she was gone. She was lost, and that image haunted me for years.

"It was important for me to speak at the funeral, and I wanted to be a part of the planning. I was trying to be strong for my Dad and my sister. I thought it was the best way to show respect for my Mom.

"That fueled me for a while, the need to be strong and reliable. I took on Mom's duties as a coping mechanism. I cooked, and it was terrible but they ate it without complaint. I cleaned and did laundry as best I could, but usually my Aunt Trella and Granny had to sort out the mess I would make. Anything to stave off my grief.

"Soon, though, I needed something more to distract me. And it came in the form of a girl who lived down the street, Penelope. Now, I want to be very clear in that I understand it was me who chose to drink, smoke, vandalize, and have sex. Penelope did not force me, but she was a welcome influence. I was embracing my dark teenage angst and it felt exciting and wrong, all the better to avert my attention from Mom.

"I carried on like this for a couple of months, until I saw the way my sister started looking at me. She wasn't mad; she wasn't scared. She was alone. It knocked the wind out of me and made my knees weak."

I pause as my eyes begin to sting, and I feel a lump in my throat. It's happening again: my guilt is overwhelming me, and I am nauseous. I swallow and try to lick my lips, but my mouth is dry. Slowly, I shake my head.

"I'm sorry, guys, I thought I was ready to do this, but I'm not. I appreciate everyone's support, but I don't want to talk about this anymore."

Silence fills the room.

"I understand it's difficult, Charlie, but it's important to let these things out," Jerry says coaxingly.

193

Rage explodes within me.

"Is it? Or does it just make *your* job easier by *me* doing all the work?"

I storm out of the group room and stomp up the stairs, fuming. It takes a moment for me to realize that I'm fuming at myself; I'm disappointed in myself. It has nothing to do with Jerry, and everything to do with me.

I punch my pillow and fall back on my bed.

"Yeah, just keep rehearsing that anger there, bud," I say scathingly.

I awake to Jayce poking my cheek.

"Wake up, handsome, it's almost two," he says happily.

"I fell asleep," I say, confused.

"Yeah, I told everyone to leave you alone for a while."

"Was Jerry pissed?" I ask, dazed by an emotional hangover.

"No, he understood. We talked for like a minute, and then he let us go."

I sigh. "Why is life *so* fucking *hard*, dude? And why am I such a whiny asshole?"

"Come on, you're not a whiny asshole, bro! You're a sassy gay drunk!"

I am engulfed by a fit of laughter. "Thank you, I needed that."

McKinley gives me a bear hug as I slice an apple in the kitchen.

"You're so good at establishing boundaries, man! I wish you would have shared, but it was also cool to see you stand up for yourself."

"I'm not sure that's what it was, but thanks for the positive spin."

He drums his hands on the counter.

"So, you wanna go for a hike with Jordyn and me in the buttes? Don said it was cool for the three of us to go with Jake as a chaperone."

I clap my hands. "Yes! Awesome, I'd love to! When?"

"Later this afternoon. You need some shoes to wear?"

"Yes, actually, thanks." My head spins a bit from the day. "Well, at least there's this."


"Alright, guys, meet back here in an hour or so, yeah? Be good," Jake says with a grin and wink.

I look at McKinley and Jordyn, each of us ecstatic to be on the outside and alone for an entire hour.

"I'm gonna turn on some tunes and explore. Peace, guys!"

I flip on Halsey and begin my nature trek. The day is surprisingly warm, hovering in the low fifties, with clear skies and sunshine. I take a deep breath and enjoy the scent of the outdoors, earthy and wooden. The sun feels pleasant on my back as I follow a winding path.

It leads me to a copse where I stop walking and stand very still before sitting on a small rock. A faint breeze carries in snowflakes, and I gasp. I did not expect snow, but it dawns on me that I'm at a higher altitude. I giggle like a child and hold out my tongue, catching a few.

"Thank you," I say to the sky and wander on. From a distance, I can see Jordyn climbing a steep rock wall. I watch him and am inspired to climb, as well.

Steadying my grip, I glance down at my progress. I'm nearing the top and amazed my breathing isn't more labored. Those hours in the gym are paying off. With a last heave, I pull myself onto a ledge.

It is a spectacular view. I can see Salt Lake City in the distance,

195

like a tiny Christmas village. The wind is a bit stronger up here, and I close my eyes as it flows over me.

It happens organically, as though something within me has been waiting for this.

"I'm sorry!" I scream to the wind. "I'm sorry! Thank you, and please help! Please help!"

My throat is raw, and tears stream down my face, yet there is a sense of buoyancy that wasn't there before.

"Well, that was awfully dramatic, Charlie. But I do feel better," I say, assessing the best way to climb down. It becomes clear the ascent was the easier portion.

As I walk toward the van, I take in the sunset, its dark purples behind the buttes reminding me of a mystical painting. I wish I could take a picture.

McKinley is waiting with Jake, who hands me a water bottle.

"Thanks," I say. "Jordyn wasn't far behind me."

"There he is," McKinley points.

We roll the windows down on the drive back and enjoy the evening air. For a moment, we're just four guys taking a cruise. For a moment.

*****

I make my way to Jerry's office, my stomach in knots. This is our first session since my melodramatic exit from group. I find him sitting at his computer, his glasses slipping down the bridge of his nose.

"Hi, Charlie," he says in a friendly tone.

"Hi, Jerry. Listen, before we begin, I want to apologize for group the other day, I could have handled that better."

He swivels his chair to face me.

"Thank you for the apology, but you're not the first patient to snap at me. Do you want to talk about Brodie today?"

"Sure," I say meekly. "I don't, but probably should."

"When was the last time you talked with your sister?"

"I called her a day or so after I got in, to let her know I was here and safe."

Jerry nods and makes a note. "How long did you two talk?"

I exhale loudly. "Oh, probably five minutes, at most."

"What is it that you feel when you're talking about Brodie?"

I take a moment and sort my thoughts, attempting to tease out specific emotions.

"A month or so after my Mom died, my family and I were on a pontoon on the lake, and Brodie and some other kids were swimming near the front. A speed boat passed and threw off waves, which scared the kids, and they scrambled for the ladder to get back on the boat. Brodie was further out so she couldn't get to it as fast, and I remember seeing the fear on her face as she was bobbing up and down. It was like something took over me, and I felt very protective, in a way I hadn't felt before. It was surreal, and I remember recognizing the feeling in that moment and knowing something within me had changed when it came to Brodie. I scooped her up into the boat and held her while we headed back to Bucksaw.

"It is the only way I can think of to explain that I feel like more than a big brother with Brodie, almost like a third parent. I think that, subconsciously, I wanted to spare her any of the pain I was feeling, and I thought that in order to achieve this, I would need to take on a more parental role.

"Which was great, before I was a raging alcoholic. Now, though, I'm the cause of so much pain in her life, but does it stop me? No! Which is why I become so emotional, too many feelings hit me at once when I think about what she's been through, and the part I play in that.

"And she's a lot like Dad: she gets very angry and blows up. I don't respond well to that, so I shut down and let them yell, and then nothing is resolved. But I understand why they react that way, I do. I know it's coming from a place of love and that I have pushed them to the breaking point. But I feel like nobody's ever heard, and there's so much love there, but we're not putting it to use in the right way. I'm afraid I'm going to lose them, that they'll need to move on with their lives, and I get it. A part of me almost wants that to happen, so I can drink freely. But I'm sure you'd say that was the disease talking." I lean back in the chair, crestfallen.

"Yes, but everything before was entirely you, and very insightful. Would you like to do a family therapy session? I can be a mediator, so you have a neutral party."

I tilt my head, thinking. "I'm gonna say no on that, I don't think any of us are ready. It's too soon. Or maybe I'm just not ready."

"I say this with sympathy and understanding, but that feeling of 'being ready' is elusive, it's best to rip off the bandage and start the healing process."

"For now, I'm going to let time work its magic. Maybe when I'm back home we can set up a time to talk."

Jerry gives me a skeptical eyebrow raise but doesn't push the topic any further.

"You mentioned shutting down, is that why you left group? Not only to shut down the conversation but to shut down yourself?"

"I hadn't thought about it that way, but yes, you're right. I went upstairs, brooded, and fell asleep."

"And you were angry when you left, correct?"

"Yes, I was angry," I answer evenly, wondering where he's going with this.

"Do you ever blow up, Charlie?"

"Sometimes. When I was younger, I was always blowing up, but I learned to control that after puberty. Now, though, if I blow up, it's usually because I'm drunk. Sober Charlie is pretty tame, honestly."

He studies me for a moment, and I feel exposed.

"Is it possible you replaced blowing up with shutting down?"

Surprising myself, I chuckle. "I see where you're going. And you're right. I don't process my emotions, for many reasons, but the fact remains that I handle them incorrectly and it's killing me. Literally, I'm poisoning my body because of it."

I stretch my neck back and exhale loudly. "Well shit, Jerry. That's not good news, is it?"

He laughs softly. "It's not so bad, really. Tell you what, why don't you do some of those automatic thought records you enjoy so much, only in retrospect."

I perk up slightly. "Oh? That could be useful, huh?"

"I think you'll begin to see a pattern, which you can work with."

"Aren't you clever?" I jest.

"Let's hope so," he grins, and I rise from my seat.

"Thanks, Jerry. Until next time."

We shake hands, and I make my way back upstairs, hoping Jayce is down for a game of chess. I was able to say "checkmate" for the first time yesterday, and it felt like I'd won an Olympic Medal.

*****

"Oh, how nice," I sigh to myself, laying down on a mat in the large group room for a much-needed meditation.

Lanie, one of Reflections more holistic therapists, has lent me a CD of singing bowls and yoga music. I've filled the air with lavender and closed the blinds; it feels secluded and warm.

An hour passes quickly, and Moses opens the door.

"Is someone—oh, hey, Charlie. Sorry, were you doing your meditation thing?"

I spread my arms out, stretch, and roll up to a sitting position.

"Yup, but I think I'm done now. What's up?" I ask, relaxed and serene.

He shrugs. "Oh, just killing time and wandering the house before we go to Hill Aerospace."

"That's right! I forgot about that today!"

"Yup, should be pretty cool."

I begin to roll up my mat and tidy the room.

"So, are you nervous about leaving next week?"

"Yes and no. I'm going to sober living, which is a huge relief. I heard McKinley talking about it and Marina and I were able to find a gay-friendly house."

"A sober house for gay boys?" I exclaim.

He laughs. "Not just gay boys, silly. It's an accepting house that does have some gay guys."

"Can you imagine? I feel like it'd be all drama or all sex." I clasp my hand to my mouth. "I can't believe I said that—I'm sorry, we're so much more than that, my bad."

Moses laughs harder than before. "I'll let it slide, but I'd say you're pretty close to the mark, though."

"I'm just saying, it'd probably be a dream," I quip.

The sun soothes my skin as I stand open-armed outside of the van, waiting for the others to load up. I prefer to sit in the single-seat nearest the sliding door, my princess seat, aptly named by Jordyn and Matt. Faye and Tyler will stay back to meet with the doctor, and it should be a fairly comfortable ride with only eight.

Lainie rounds the corner, and I beam.

"Are you chaperoning us?"

"I sure am!"

"Right on!"

Dakota, McKinley, Moses, and Jayce follow behind her. Jordyn leads Matt through the French doors, and we wait for Ashley.

"She's probably changing clothes for the fourth time," Dakota chortles. Since Ashley's simmering down, they have developed quite a bond.

Ashley sprints from the side door.

"I'm sorry—I couldn't find anything to wear! I've lost weight!" she shrieks, her voice surprised and awe-struck. "I guess I didn't realize since I've just been wearing PJ's, but my jeans barely fit!"

Lainie snaps her fingers rhythmically from the driver's seat before starting the ignition. "See! One of the many benefits of a healthy diet and exercise versus that dang wine bottle!"

The weather is mild as we make the journey to Hill Aerospace Museum. From what Jake explained, it has more than seventy aircraft on display as well as historical artifacts from the Air Force. My inner history nerd is stoked.

"You guys," Jordyn says seriously from the back of the van, "I just saw a construction sign that said 'road rehab.' I bet its DOC was crack," he finishes ominously.

There is a staccato of silence and then raucous laughter.

"Who says treatment can't be fun?" Laine asks jovially as we quiet down.

Dakota turns from the front seat, radiant with the light behind her, and I notice she has added in a few freckles with her make-up.

"They tried to make me go to rehab and I said," she sings beautifully, "I don't have insurance. And that was the end of that."

Hilarity ensues again. A thought crosses my mind while caught up in the merriment, that I could keep this network of support and friends by moving to Utah. Sure, it's scary, but it could be what saves me from the damned bottle.

Ashley lays back on the wooden picnic table seat outside of the Hill Aerospace Museum. We are lounging while the others explore in the field, which houses a large helicopter from the '90s.

"Oh I want a nap," she yawns. "Getting sober is so tiring."

"But you're doing it so well," I say.

"Well, I had a good teacher," she teases. "But seriously, you're so easy to talk to, I hope you don't ghost me when we leave rehab."

I mock being affronted, "I would never!" and decide to be candid with her.

"I was thinking, what if I just stay in Salt Lake? I could live in a sober house, I've got some money saved up. I don't think getting a job will be a problem. I've seen a few companies I could work for."

She rises and takes my hand. "Oh, Charlie, I think that's such a good idea! Honestly, I do! I'm sure Jayce and Jordyn and McKinley will be supportive—you guys should all live together!"

"That'd be a trip," I agree and trace the patterns of the wood.

"It's just that, I think unless I keep myself in some sort of contained environment, I'm going to slip again. I mean, flying home and living in my apartment, alone, probably isn't a good idea."

"Oh, totally," Ashley agrees. "I don't know if I'm strong enough for sober living, but I'm sure it's what I need. And I'm so thankful to live in this area, I'm going to keep going to CA at Soleil."

"See, that's what I'm noticing. I fly off to all these great cities and make all these deep connections and then leave after thirty or forty days. It makes no sense, but I keep doing it!"

"Then just stay, Charlie," she says encouragingly.

We smile at one another. I want to say I will, but something pulls at me. I'm not sure if it's my family, my job, or just the capability to drink once I'm airborne. Knowing and doing are two very different actions.

*****

Dakota sings and plucks the guitar while McKinley beats on a bongo drum he found downstairs. They are creating silly, amusing songs while I continue my pursuit through *The Book of Mormon*.

Tyler strolls down the staircase behind me and leans on a chair.

"How you liking our Book?" he asks playfully.

"I, um, don't really know. Let's just leave it at thought-provoking."

He chuckles. "Good answer. So you decide if you're gonna stay in Salt Lake?"

Dakota and McKinley stop their rehearsal to listen.

I sit upright in the chair and scratch my ear.

"I've decided that I'm going back to Missouri. My job is too good to walk away from and I need to get ahead of my alcoholism, regardless of where I live."

Dakota stares out the window and McKinley sits his bongo drum on the floor. I did not say what they wanted to hear. I turn to Tyler, and for once his face isn't gleeful.

"That makes me really sad, Charlie. But I get not wanting to walk away from a good job. I'm so lucky that mine was willing to work with me—*I* wouldn't want to either. I just hope you're careful, man. You've gotta stop relapsing."

"I know, I know. You're right, and I think this time out I'm so much more educated and have developed so many more roadblocks, that I have hope I can stay sober."

"I hope so, too," Dakota says, giving me a soft smile. "But if not, you can always come back."

"Yeah," McKinley pipes up. "Fifth hair don't care!"

It is the lighthearted spin we all needed.

"So you're going back to Missouri?" Jayce asks softly as we lay in the dark.

The news spread, culminating in a session with Jerry in which I was forced to explain that as a grown man I can decide where I would like to live, and I choose Springfield. I was able to fend off becoming hostile, but I was certainly agitated and it showed.

"I have to, man," I answer.

"Yeah. I just wish you didn't. So we could stay together or something after this. But you have to, so that's that."

He is upset, I am as well, but I can't see another way.

"I can come visit you. And we can text, it's not like we're not allowed to talk again," I offer.

"I know, we will. It just sucks."

"It'll be alright, buddy."

We're quiet after that, neither of us asleep, lost in our thoughts. Separate, but together. I will miss this about Jayce.

\*\*\*\*\*

Three days later I stare blankly out the windshield of the van. Jerry is driving me to the airport for my flight back to Springfield. It is early afternoon, and I should touch down in Missouri around seven this evening, local time. From there I will take a taxi back to my apartment. I feel sluggish.

"What is your plan when you get home?" Jerry asks.

"Find a meeting, clean up my apartment, unpack, go to bed. I'll head back to work in a few days, but until then I'll just go to meetings and get phone numbers."

"And you have an appointment with an addiction counselor in two days. Make sure you let them know you're interested in doing SMART Recovery."

"Yup, I think that will definitely be helpful."

As we pull near the curb of my terminal, Jerry gives me a kind smile.

"Be strong, Charlie. And be happy. If you should need any of us, please call—you know we answer any time of the day."

I shake my head, agreeing. "Will do, Jerry. And thank you, you've been really great with me, and I truly appreciate you."

Unloading my suitcase from the van, I enter the terminal doors.

Gazing out of my taxi window in Springfield, I am overcome with an urge.

205

"Can I add a stop?" I ask, a bit breathlessly.

"Sure, where to?"

"Awesome, I need to stop by a gas station."

I see my reflection in the car window. My eyes narrow. A pint should be enough for tonight: any more and I'll be super hungover in the morning. And pickles, I need to get some pickles.

# 10

# The Welcome Foundation

*March 2019*
*Kansas City, Missouri*
*32 Years Old*

The meeting room is filling up and I scoot closer to the table, allowing others to pass sleepily behind me. It's a morning meeting, and they're always packed; addicts and alchys getting their daily dose of AA before heading off to work.

My phone vibrates in my pocket; it's Dad calling. This isn't good, it's not even eight in the morning. Granny has passed away: it hits me and I know it in my bones. I swiftly exit the meeting room and find a vacant office down the hall. Bracing myself, I answer my Dad's phone call.

"Hey," I say flatly.

"It's me and Brod. Granny went to Heaven this morning," he says, his voice strained and shaky.

I exhale a long breath. "Oh, you guys, I'm so sorry! I had a feeling that's why you were calling. How are you guys?"

As when Mom died, I have an instinct to stay strong and

supportive for them, to keep myself together so they may fall apart.

"Not good," Dad says and I hear Brodie sniffle.

"I just wish I wasn't so far away," she says through tears.

"Brod and Dillon are gonna head this way in a bit. When do you think you can come home, Bub?"

I chew my bottom lip. I'm still in the first week at my new sober house, The Welcome Foundation, and on restriction; I am only allowed to leave the premises for work and AA meetings, and they provide the transportation for the meetings. I weigh my options, confident previous residents have used every excuse in the book to leave and relapse. These are the consequences of *my* actions, though, and should not apply to my family.

"I'll head out shortly, I'll just need to touch base with my house manager."

"Do you think they'll let you leave?" Dad asks, more knowledgeable than I thought.

"I'm sure they'll understand once I explain what's happened," I say.

A half-hour later, I am speeding down Highway 71 on my way to Clinton. After locating Jared, the house manager, and earnestly explaining my situation, I was given a two-day pass contingent on a clean piss test and breathalyzer. Which I *will pass* since I refuse to insult the memory of my Granny with some bullshit relapse. I am stronger than that, at least.

The Welcome Foundation is my third attempt at sober living in the last year. Unable to handle another rehab and without much trust in myself to live alone and abstain from vodka, I moved into sober living. It does have its advantages, although, in my case, they are few. My current palace houses around eighty men, on four floors. I believe it was a rest home for the elderly before being taken over by those in recovery.

While it does offer an outstanding program, it is extremely difficult for me to adhere to rules set by others. I understand their purpose, to aid those requiring more structure, but I'm constantly testing the waters. Curfews, for example, astound me as a grown man. Nonetheless, I have relegated myself to this lifestyle and must make the best of it.

I have one roommate, in a tiny room with a single closet, and he's easy enough to share the space with. Honestly, most of the tenants are stand-up men who have simply fallen on hard times. While I do not believe I'm fostering life-long friendships, I appreciate the connections I've made these last few months. There is a brotherhood that is both refreshing and reassuring, a camaraderie.

When I first moved in, I bunked in a room in the basement with seven other men. Surprisingly, it wasn't as disgusting as one would think, yet there was a definite odor of musk. And chips, weirdly. Stale chips. On this level, there was another room housing six guys, and a final room that held four. The eighteen of us shared two toilets, two showers, and one sink. My aversion to grimy living conditions has had to take a back seat, and it's vexing, to say the least.

The kitchen and mess hall occupies the basement as well, and the mixture of smells can be nauseating. None of this is to imply I am not thankful, however. I realize how amazing it is that programs such as this exist and do not take for granted their offerings. While education regarding addiction and recovery is broadening, misconceptions still run rampant and we're in need of more facilities like The Welcome Foundation.

Choosing this lifestyle has been a constant reminder of my previous poor decisions, and while it may be drastic, I do believe it is necessary. I have proven, time and time again, that I cannot stay sober unless the situation is dire. My affliction with alcohol baffles, frightens, and enrages me. I've dealt with it for nearly a decade and I'm growing so damn tired. Yet I'm beginning to fear there really is no way out, other than forced communal living and regular meeting attendance. Without the mandate of recovery, I am not capable of keeping the bottle at bay.

Clinging to this identity, of a washed-up drunk who needs constant surveillance, is defeating. It's a bad image and one I'm growing bored with. I don't know who I am, but I do know I *can't* be this guy. A recovered alcoholic mortgage banker living in a sober house with eighty other men? No, thank you. Sounds sketch.

*****

As I drive back to Kansas City, I reflect on my Granny. After Mom passed away, Brodie and I were so fortunate to have her as a surrogate mother. She formed part of a trifecta, along with my Aunts Trella and Dena. While we may have lost our Mom, we were given the gift of three maternal and loving women who thought of us as their own.

This is not the life she would want me living. Before dementia overtook her, she was acutely aware of my alcoholism and in full support of my recovery. A part of me is glad she was spared the torture of my last few years. She was a born worrier and I was a constant source of inspiration; I would have worried her into the grave.

Another part of me feels I'm destined to be a lifelong alcoholic;

I don't think I can even use the term 'chronic relapser' to define myself any longer. How can it be a relapse if I never really stopped in the first place? The urge has been building in me for a while, and deep down I know it's only a matter of time before I drink again. I've already started searching for an apartment, and it's heartbreaking how I lie to myself: *I'll start fresh this time, I can feel it.* But I know the clock will strike one fateful evening, and I'll slip to a gas station and buy a bag of chips and a pint. I'll fret and pontificate, but ultimately I'll slam that pint down like the alcoholic I am. It doesn't stand a chance and neither do I.

"I'm sorry," I whisper, catching my eyes in the rearview mirror.

For now, I have the safety net of my sober house. Once the strings are cut, however, I anticipate a free fall like no other. Heat rises from my chest and I swallow hard.

"What the fuck is your deal, bro? Like, what are you doing with your life?" I roar for the thousandth time in the last few years. I am unraveling; I am beginning to rip myself apart. I can feel my rage seething, and take calming breaths, relaxing my shoulders and lengthening my neck.

"Shh, now. Settle down and take it easy. You probably won't drink for a while longer, and we'll deal with that mess when it gets here."

I nod my head and wonder if I have, indeed, cracked up.

# 11

# Es-Cop-A

*Early January 2020*
*Albuquerque, New Mexico*
*33 Years Old*

"Whoa, dude, what happened to you?"

I glance to my right and focus on the source of the question. A grungy, albeit handsome man, wearing stained and torn clothing leers up at me, his greasy brown hair covered by a frayed tweed hat.

I chuckle and hiccup. "I fell off a Greyhound bus."

He is referring to the gash over my left eye, the swollen scab on my left cheek, and a missing chunk of my chin. I am a fright and have bruised all the soft tissue in my left shoulder, but between the pain meds and vodka, I feel fucking excellent.

"Damn," he says, his mouth gaping. "Looks like it hurts!"

"Nah, I'm pretty medicated. And speaking of medication, do you know where I could find some weed?" I ask the question without fear or shame.

"I mean, what you got? Maybe we could make a trade," he

counters slyly.

"For sure," I giggle. "I've got some Percocet."

"I'll smoke a blunt with you for four," he smiles.

"Two," I answer boldly and sit down beside him. "Fire it up and I'll get you some."

He stares at me a moment, his eyes intense, and I stare right back. It's broad daylight, beside a busy street. Let him try something. I'm no fighter, but I can create a hot mess of a scene real fucking quick in this state of mind. Perhaps it's all in my head, because he doesn't push any further and lights the blunt. As he passes it to me, I rummage in my plastic hospital bag for the pills.

"Here you go," I say politely and press two Percocet into his hand.

A few hits and I am smashed; it's been a while since I've smoked and I was hammered before starting. My stomach growls and I feel sleepy.

"So, but, do you know where there's a homeless shelter or something?" I am profiling, but don't know what else to do at this point.

He laughs. "Yeah, man, there's a place a couple of miles from here. It's massive and called Fresh Start or something gay like that."

"Yeah, that's super gay," I say flatly, smacking my lips; my mouth is dry from the sands of time and I have no water. Cars whiz by and I stand shakily.

"Which direction?"

He points left. "I don't know the street, but just ask around, everyone knows it 'cause it's so big."

"Right on, thanks," I answer, making my departure. The sun is shining and I am in a chemical-induced state of bliss.

The further I walk, though, the more aware of my destitution I become. Despite being in New Mexico, I'm not in unfamiliar territory, and that's the problem. It's almost as if I feel more at home operating under a depraved sense of reality. I've conditioned myself to be content with less than. Just as I begin to engage in a great bout of self-pity and wallow, a memory from a couple of years ago in Clinton flashes before me; at the time I had thought it was the lowest I could fall. Little did I know.

*Morning sun spills on our feet as Trella and I sit on my front stone steps. I stretch, gazing across the yard as Trella's friend, Heather, crawls out of her car.*

*"Hey, guys!" she waves, walking toward us.*

*"Hi," Trella and I answer, a bit subdued. Heather catches this and gives us a sympathetic look.*

*"Oh, Charlie. So what happened, exactly?" she asks.*

*I offer a hollow chuckle. "What didn't happen is a better question."*

*Heather takes a seat on the step beside us and lights a cigarette. Her long, dark hair wisps in the air.*

*"From what I can remember, I was on my way to Springfield, to enter a detox facility, when I got into a fender bender and was arrested. I vaguely remember waking up in a jail cell and was like 'well, I can't be here,' so I faked a seizure and they rushed me to the ER, where I said I was suicidal. I spent a few days in a psych ward, which was intense, and then got my car out of impound and drove home. It's just a fucking mess. I can't eat or sleep. I've gotten a third DUI now, I'll probably have to go to prison. And, it's like, I can't even be mad, I'm just like 'fuck, this is gonna require so much clean up!' I don't know why I do this shit to myself."*

*Heather gapes at me, shocked but not judgmental. "Wow."*

*"Oh, yeah," I answer, bemused myself.*

*Trella leans forward. "It'll be alright, Bub—oh, look at that snake under your car!" she exclaims, pointing to a black snake near my front tire. I peer at it closer.*

*"Holy shit, it's eating a frog!" I gasp.*

*We watch as the snake coils around the frog and opens its mouth wide to eat it whole.*

*"Well, at least I'm not the frog," I observe and they cackle.*

"Yes, boy. At least I'm not the frog," I repeat.

*****

*Late January 2020*
*Wichita, Kansas*
*33 Years Old*

The smell of disinfectant and body odor lingers in the air. A noise machine throws the sound of waves from the nurse station, and the lights are turned low. I hug myself tightly and lay uncomfortably in the reclining bed/chair thing each patient is assigned. My breath catches and I stare blankly at the ceiling.

This is my fourth psychiatric ward in four weeks, which means I'm averaging one a week. I have truly and wholly lost myself, spiraling in a most unexpected direction. Leaving California in early January, I was supposed to take a Greyhound back to Missouri, although my trip has included several un-planned stops. Vodka is to blame for each. Well, myself and vodka. But mainly vodka.

Unable to get back to the bus in time, or sometimes because I didn't care, I have graced wards in Los Angeles, Albuquerque, and Amarillo. Now, I will add Wichita to the esteemed list. Too many A's, I needed one at the end of the alphabet, I suppose.

Surely that's the answer, for it cannot be that I am broken, ashamed, and at a loss. I curl into a ball and close my eyes, hopeful sleep will leave me in its wake.

*I dream of a strange house, missing parts of its walls and decorated with miniature furniture. There is a kitchen from the 1800's, connected to a bedroom with a mattress covered in a red and blue quilt. I flip the eggs on the stove and then scurry to the mattress before the shooting starts. A drug deal is transpiring outside in the outhouse, and a black SUV rolls up raining bullets.*

*Once the coast is clear, I run to the outhouse and scoop up bags of meth, then hide them in the missing parts of the walls. After watching them safely disappear, I open the refrigerator door and debouch into the backyard, crouching and hiding behind a fig bush.*

Faint mumbling wakes me and I roll over in the chair. What the hell was I dreaming about? I rub my eyes and put on my glasses. Focusing my view, I see four people sitting at a set of tables in the center of the room. We are in the basement of the behavioral health center, where they house overflow patients until they're placed in a wing upstairs. The room is bleak and square, its cinder blocks painted a light blue that fades to white near the top. I count seven patients, three nurses, and glance at the clock—6:42 in the morning.

Late last night, I was wheeled over from the ER. It felt a bit silly, but due to my high dose of liquid Ativan, I wasn't allowed to make the trek on foot. Everything before that is foggy. I vaguely remember waking up in a hotel room and using the phone to call 911, then being placed on the gurney. I know I was on a bed in the hallway of the ER, where they gave me medicine, but after that my memories are fuzzy.

Shaking my head, I hit the lever to shift the chair into a sitting position. My eyes catch a nurse sitting at the table and she smiles warmly, the soft light refracting on her sparkly glasses. No one would answer how long I'll stay in this basement *or* the psychiatric ward. I have a sinking feeling that is a grave sign. What did I say when I called 911? I wish I could remember, it would give me some indication of what to expect. It is sad to say, but I have become quite versed in the world of psychiatric wards.

These last few years, especially, are wrought with visits. Perhaps it is a throwback to my time in Oregon; a learned, pampered survival technique. Rather than take to the streets, I seek a roof, bedding, and scheduled meals. With scheduled drugs. Once my money is gone, off to the psych ward I run, in need of some pill intoxication. I have become a common cliché and it stings. Clenching my fists, I recognize my grandiosity complex rearing its head.

Standing, I walk to the men's bathroom across the room. A women's and men's facility, with toilet, sink, and shower, occupies the entirety of one wall. The nurse station and entrance are perpendicular to the restrooms. We are rats in a cage.

"What in the actual fuck," I whisper, latching the lock and catching my reflection in the mirror. I move closer.

My appearance is terrible, and it makes me shiver, taken aback at my scraggly beard, grimy hair, pale skin, and hollow eyes. A ghost of Charlie, as if I've given up. It's despair, my light is barely a flicker. Grabbing a paper towel, I wet it and wash off my face and neck. A memory bubbles up as I do this, from a couple of months ago. It is from the beginning of my stay at Simple Recovery, an intensive outpatient program that also provides sober living in Newport Beach, California.

*Rain overflows the courtyard's fountain as I smoke a cigarette. Leaning on the railing of the second-story balcony, I watch drops fall languidly to puddles below. Group was scattered and grating; it felt stuffy and I breathe the fresh air to steady myself. The patio door creaks behind me and I turn to see Poppy stepping out.*

*"Sorry, I didn't mean to skip out on group, I just needed a moment."*

*She gives me her knowing, comforting smile. "It's okay."*

*"It's just—I'm scared, Poppy."*

*She folds her arms and stands with her back against the railing. "What is it you're scared of?"*

*"Falling back into the same patterns once I leave Simple."*

*"That's fair, I understand that concern. So let's say you do relapse when you leave Simple. Tell me how you think that will transpire."*

*"I'll probably hide it for like a day, or maybe two, if I'm lucky. But inevitably, I'll end up drunk somewhere and probably be too ashamed to call Simple, so I'll call 911. Whatever happens, it will be a cluster fuck because that's how I do it. I run to the hospital in a drunk, gay tizzy yelling about my heart hurting. It's so messed up. I mean, I now understand the reason behind the pattern, but it's still so messed up."*

*Poppy gives me a wry smirk. "So where do you go from the hospital?"*

*"Well," I say, rubbing my temples, "the psych ward, of course.*

*Because who doesn't love taking frequent vacations to a psychiatric ward?"*

*"And there's no way to throw a wrench in this system?"*

*"It works, so I won't. Or at least, drunk Charlie won't. In the moment, his needs are met, so that's as far as he thinks."*

*Poppy steps closer to me and pats my shoulder. "You're drunk Charlie, Charlie. You have to come to understand and accept that. You are the only one in control of processing your thoughts, which lead to your actions. And while learning restraint is difficult, you're the only one who can do it."*

"I need a better processing system," I whisper, taking a final glance at my appearance and exiting the bathroom.

The lights are ablaze and most of the patients are seated around the table eating breakfast.

"You hungry, Charlie?" a nurse asks, indicating a tray for me.

"No, thank you. Um, I know everyone says this and there's lots of protocol, but I need to speak with my doctor and case manager about leaving. I was drunk, I'm not suicidal. I'm selfishly occupying a space that someone needs, believe me, and it's best to discharge me."

Her smile never falters.

"I understand, Charlie. We'll need to wait until you're assigned a doctor, and the case managers aren't quite in yet."

I nod.

"Very good, when do you suppose their ETA is?"

"Later this morning, but it's Sunday, so it'll probably be tomorrow before you're assigned a permanent doctor. They will need to meet with your case manager and approve your discharge plan."

"So another day, at least. Okay, alright. Well, that'll have to do, then."

I blink around the sparse room.

"But you did this, Charlie," I say quietly. "Okay, I should make some phone calls. And do you have any books?"

Wrapping the thin hospital blanket tighter around myself, I rub my neck and watch the food trolley wheel in. I skipped breakfast and lunch, having no appetite, but it's important for me to eat dinner. They're probably monitoring my food intake, and right now it could be perceived I'm practicing restrictive eating. Shit.

I nibble at the hospital dinner, attempting to keep my mind blank. Too much has happened while I've run amuck. My Aunt Judye passed away, my Dad spent two separate nights waiting for me at the Greyhound Station in Kansas City to no avail, and no one knew whether or not I was safe for days on end. My antics are longer tolerated.

Which I understand completely. I no longer want to tolerate my antics. The news of Aunt Judye's passing pierced my heart but I kept quiet. I didn't think my pain and grief, no matter how pure or honest, would be appreciated at that moment. It stings, knowing I created this rift. It was certainly unintentional, but pain, anger, and fear are capable of concocting a deadly cocktail for clouding vision.

As I hand my tray over to the night nurse, he tilts his head toward a set of cabinets on the back wall.

"I unlocked the book cabinet if you'd like to check it out."

"Yes, please. Thank you."

Any book will do as a distraction from reality. Books have been a welcome reprieve at nearly every facility I've attended, whether it be a psych ward, rehab, or detox. Strangely, as if my

Mom is somehow with me, I've read so many of her favorite author's novels, John Grisham, while in captivity. More than once I have found great comfort in finding one of his books tucked in a corner shelf or cupboard. Breadcrumbs from the universe, I wonder?

Scanning their limited stock, I settle on a book without a cover yet bearing an intriguing title: *Nine Perfect Strangers* by Liane Moriarty. The villain in *Casper* was played by an actress with the same last name, I muse, and decide it is the pick for me. I close the cabinet and walk the short distance back to my chair/bed.

Flipping to the back, I see a smaller font and a page number of 464. Hallelujah, I'm saved for a little while.

\*\*\*\*\*

*The sun is moments from setting as we drive down the PCH in the evening haze. My head sways back and forth with the music as I watch the waves crash in the distance. This is amazing. Is this really where I will start over? In this beautiful, oceanside town full of gorgeous people? Newport Beach is booming with recovery, why not stay?*

*Kellan flicks his fingers on the steering wheel to the beat.*

*"Your fingers are gonna hurt again," I warn him.*

*"I know but I can't stop! It's like it hurts, but I like it."*

*"Kinda strange, but you do you," I say evenly.*

*"So are you getting me frozen yogurt since I'm going to your gay boy meeting with you?" Kellan teases, grinning playfully.*

*"You like it, you know you do. Besides, your boyfriend will be so happy to see you!"*

*"He called me again last night and we talked for like twenty*

221

*minutes. I don't think he has many friends."*

*"Ah, Kellan. You should make it clear to him that you're an ally. It's very kind of you to be nice to him, but don't get the poor boy's hopes up."*

*"I know, but it just feels awkward to have that conversation with him."*

*"Well, not really. Just say 'I'd like to be your friend and that's all, I prefer to date females,' or something like that. Trust me, it'll save him a lot of time and energy if you're honest with him."*

*"But then who's gonna call me?"*

*"You mean chase you? Probably one of your trap hoes back home."*

*He gasps in mock horror. "Charlie, how dare you?"*

*I laugh and scan the beach. Kellan turns down the music and clears his throat.*

*"But in all seriousness, Charlie, I think we're doing really well. And I think it's living at Viva House, you know? Like, we're given just enough freedom to really grow in our recovery."*

*I turn to him, impressed.*

*"That's really insightful, man! I agree, too. I like that we're held accountable and there's a night tech and everything, but I also think that since we're not micro-managed, we're not angry at living in a sober house. Sometimes it feels like living back in the frat house, really. Just a lot of sports and guys."*

*"I bet that's really hard for you," he says with mock sympathy and then erupts in laughter. "Get it?"*

*"Stupid," I laugh.*

A patient's breakdown snaps me back to attention. I have no idea how it started, but he's currently walking tight circles and raging, flailing his arms and scratching his face violently. He calls himself names and punches at his chest.

My heart aches. I've now spent enough time in these spaces to gain a grasp of severe mental illness. I am by no means a doctor or therapist, but I have begun to recognize the behaviors of particular illnesses. Most likely, he's been on the streets without proper medication, and his affliction has run rampant. No doubt he has had to self-medicate, as well, and severely tipped the scales. I hope for him. I hope for him to find help.

"Oh, he knows not what he does," I whisper and stay very still, bowing my head.

After the nurse settles him, I crack open my book and lose myself in the fascinating story taking place in Australia. An hour later, I am tapped on the shoulder by a tall, Black man in khakis and a blue button-up. Ah, the case manager. Lovely.

"Oh, I am happy to see you," I say and stand.

"Right on! My name is Damian and I will be your case manager. Would you like to step into the side room?"

"Sure," I say, following him into the small, locked room next to the nurse station.

We sit on opposite sides of the tiny table, the fluorescent light glaring on its sanitized surface.

Damian opens my file. "How are you doing, Charles?"

"I'm fine, really. Now, what I need to know is what I said during intake. I was blackout drunk, I'm sure I'd eaten Ativan and Seroquel, so I remember absolutely nothing. Once I know what sort of nonsensical story I've spun, I can unravel it for you. You see, this is a bad reaction to alcohol that I've developed."

He smiles and maintains eye contact. "You know, Charles, you told us you were going to say that. Listen, I understand that you're most likely not going to hurt yourself or others, but you were very specific about your plan and we have to take that seriously."

"Hmm. Well, what did I say?"

"Your plan was to step into oncoming traffic," he answers directly.

Irritation and fury with myself would be an understatement.

"Was it, now? Well, that was a foolish thing for me to say. Please understand that I do not take the subject of suicide lightly, nor do I mean any offense to those impacted by it. But suicide is not my issue, alcohol is. And when I'm in a blackout, I become, well, ruthless and selfish. In the moment, I will say or do anything that I feel is necessary to maintain the blackout. It's twisted and dark, and I've spent so much time and money trying to sort it out.

"I haven't yet, but what I have learned is that me crying suicide is an attempt to find temporary safety so that I can sober up and figure out my next move. Which is usually how to get money and vodka, but that's another matter entirely.

"I will be compliant while all the paperwork and assessments are completed, but it is probably in everyone's best interest that I am discharged as swiftly as possible. Is it a seventy-two-hour hold? I've done at least twenty-four already. This is not the facility for someone like me, I'm in the way of someone who truly needs to be here. Surely you all must see that?"

Damian folds his arms and leans on the gleaming table.

"I can see that you're very aware of your situation, and while I definitely believe you're in need of help, I will agree with you that this is not the most ideal facility. However, we are here and happy to help as best we can. Now, as to the seventy-two-hour hold, that's not necessarily the case. It's usually seen more as a minimum. Please have patience and be honest with the nurses, doctors, and me. Once we all feel you're safe to be discharged, we'll discuss your next steps."

I sigh. "You've just answered everything I needed to know. Is there a script somewhere you guys use? You all sound the same. But, I understand."

"Is there anything you'd like to talk about? Do you feel safe here?"

I fold my hands in my lap.

"Yes, I feel safe. I have no thoughts of harming myself or others. My body feels regular and I am not experiencing audible or visual hallucinations. There is nothing further I need to discuss, thank you for your time and information, Damian."

\*\*\*\*\*

*Betrayal at House on the Hill is spread across the dining room table of Viva House. I attempt to listen to Claude explain the rules, but can't quit giggling with Kellan and Claude's girlfriend, Charleigh.*

*"Guys, this is serious, this is how you win!" Claude exclaims through a grin.*

*"I know, but Charlie's face is cracking me up, he's so over it!" Charleigh retorts.*

*I smile. "Oh, I didn't realize I was being that transparent. But it's so many rules, guys. And if this happens you do this, but if this happens you can't do that anymore, so you have to do this. I mean, shit. Clearly, I don't like rules, but I said I'd play, so I'll play."*

*"You know this is the best sober house you've ever been in, Charlie," Kellan quips.*

*"Oh, for sure it is. I don't feel like I'm living real life right now, you know? Like one day I was drunk in an apartment in Kansas City, and then the next morning I was in Orange County, California, hopping from one mansion to another."*

*"Kinda makes you glad you stayed, huh? I know I am," Charleigh*

*says from across me.  She grew up in Arkansas and migrated to Orange County a couple of years ago to get sober; she now works in treatment and has remained clean since moving.*

"You know, I am. It's surreal, but I am," I answer.

*Claude gives up momentarily and wanders to the pantry.*

"I was court-ordered to go to treatment in Cali and stay out of Arizona for a year, and I'm so thankful for it! What made you decide to stay, Charlie?" Kellan asks, twirling his beanie on his finger.

"Honestly, it was a series of conversations I had with a night tech at the rehab I was at before coming to Simple. A year or so back he was in an eerily similar situation, and rather than go back home to the East coast, he opted to stay out West, and he's been sober ever since. He helped me navigate my pending court cases and apartment lease, and I just saw no reason to go back to Missouri.

"And I mean, I know it's not Missouri that is my problem. Missouri is quite lovely, actually, and really doesn't get enough credit. But I'm too versed there, too patterned and triggered. And I understand that I am everywhere I go, but why not be by these waves, yo?"

*Claude, a California native, whoops from the pantry.*

I brush a tear from my cheek and close my book. A passage reminded me of a night spent at Viva and it's as if a vice is clenching my heart. It's astounding how quickly one decision can sweep away months of work and planning.

"Are you okay?" a nurse asks.

"Oh, yeah. I forgot to blink," I lie. Please don't add another day to my sentence.

\*\*\*\*\*

"Here are your clean towels and scrubs. If you want to put the clothes you're wearing into this paper bag, we'll wash them overnight and you can wear them tomorrow. I'll leave you to shower," the nurse says, closing the door.

It is mid-afternoon, and I have just moved from the basement to the fifth floor, room 5212. Sitting on the bed with my knees to my chest, I take everything in. It is a large room, with a desk and chair, a bathroom, and a window overlooking a title loan company and fast food chains. Everything is white or tan, made of durable, safe plastic, and smells of cleaner.

I shudder and then shake my arms out. Standing, I walk the short distance to the bathroom and swing open the padded half-door, which is attached to the wall by Velcro. Staring back at myself in the streaked mirror, I see a lost boy, but not the fun kind from Neverland. I see the kind who self-sabotages and poisons.

Suddenly, I am filled with great sympathy for this wretched boy gazing at me. He needs serious help. I should probably do something.

I smile at him and hug myself.

"Hey, it's okay. I forgive you. I love you."

The words fall out of my mouth without any thought, and I am rooted to the spot, mesmerized by my reflection, holding myself. Time passes, footsteps shuffle in the hall outside, and the light leaves with the setting sun. Silence rings in the room.

"Okay, you're cracking up, bud. But am I, though? You've always felt very Gemini, very much two people in one body. And you spent an intensive month in California trying to decode the light wolf from the dark wolf. You should embrace your duality. You should really just...do something, dude."

Yawning, I turn on the shower and sigh. When are they going to give me more pills for sleep?

227

*I dream the sky is a dusky purple as I climb out of a 2004 VW Bug. It is a suburban street, with beautiful cookie-cutter homes placed in a row, and cars parked neatly in their drives. I jump to the front door and ring the doorbell.*

*Clara Bow opens the door, and I know she's dead but also alive, the two worlds overlapping. She evokes the full spirit of a Flapper, with her Jazz baby dancing, and I follow her down a winding staircase into a stadium. My friends and family zip around and above me in tiny racing cars attached to rails, which wind and climb the entirety of the stadium like ivy.*

*In the middle, there is a dance floor lit by a Disco ball. A coat rack appears so I grab a tuxedo jacket and step onto the floor. I begin a lyrical dance to a song that I'm also singing. It is beautifully haunting and I glow, literally, as everyone applauds from their cars once I'm finished. I smile and pounce toward the glass dome at the top of the stadium, shattering through and landing on a grassy cliff's edge towering over the Black Sea.*

*A large, knobby tree grows at the tip of the ledge, just before the drop-off. Instead of leaves or flowers, statuesque women dressed as Geishas hang upside down. A man dressed in black, with a pencil mustache and monocle, strolls toward me. He has a ghoulish, hellish leer and icy air scratches my face.*

*He stops near me, and I smell death and decay.*

*"Three you must kill. Three's fate, you decide. Should three you decide to spare, three will be collected from you. May your arrows be true and sure," he sneers, handing me a crossbow from The Hundred Years War.*

*The sky turns blood red and the waves froth and rage.*

Sitting up in bed, I rub my eyes, unnerved. I do not understand these dreams. They are viscerally terrifying and most likely a message from my subconscious, yet I cannot work it out. My guilt is creating weird disturbances in my sleep, and all I want to do is get blackout. Which is a selfish, terrible idea, but at least I could get some shut-eye.

*****

I rest my book on my chest, vacantly scanning the room. It's almost dinner time, which means my chances of discharging today are zero. As of tomorrow, this will be my longest stint yet, at five days. I am nearing the end of my thrilling novel, having savored it for as long as possible. As usual, it has been greater than just a story for me: I have found the message impactful, and I am enlightened for escaping to its pages.

Escape. The word rolls over in my head.

"Escape," I say aloud softly. "Es-cop-a."

What am I trying to escape from, and where am I trying to escape to? The question sears in my mind and my eyes narrow.

"Well, that's probably the answer to it all right there, Charlie. What are you trying to escape from?"

My thoughts drift.

*Sealing the lid on my disposable cup, I round the corner to Nate's office. I meet with him twice a week, as my counselor at Simple, and his style is so refreshing, a step away from the traditional "session" meetings. I should let him know that.*

*He grins up at me from his laptop.*

*"How ya doing, Chuck?"*

*"Bro, we've gone over this, Chuck is my Dad's name," I say,*

229

*exasperated.*

*"I know, that's why I do it. So how's the job search going?" he asks.*
*He winks, then closes his laptop and gives me his full attention. I*
*also like this about Nate.*

*"Really well. I have a phone interview with a bank I worked for*
*back in Missouri next week. I was there for a little over two years,*
*and my numbers were always good, so I don't think there should be*
*any reason I don't get the job."*

*"Awesome!" Nate exclaims. "Banking, huh? That's good money!"*

*"Yeah, it can be. It's just, I don't know how keen I am on jumping*
*back into my old life, you know? Like, yeah, I can get a job in*
*banking, but it feels like that's a great way to let old behaviors creep*
*back in. And I've done that, back in Missouri. I'd like to do something*
*different, but it's a safe choice, so I applied."*

*Nate studies me for a moment.*

*"Let's talk, again, about this aversion to your past, when you lived*
*in the Midwest. You know you can't just cut that part of your life*
*out, right? It's got its uses, man."*

*I lean my head back on the chair.*

*"Ugh, gross. I know. I know. And I don't want to cut it out, I just*
*want to be free of its gravity. I want to escape it."*

*Nate shakes his head, softly smiling. "Oh, Charlie. There's no*
*escaping it, bud. It's your life. You know that, come on."*

Nate's meaning finally resonates within me. I want to escape
my past because I'm ashamed of it. But by running from my
existing shame, I keep creating new shame, and at this point,
I'm drowning in it. Wallowing, more like.

"So stop. I think it really is that easy."

Strange, how stopping can go from being the hardest decision
to the easiest decision with the tiniest shift of perspective.

"Your problem is following through, Charlie. Don't just lay here, melodramatically, and figure it out in a damn psych ward, *do* something! But I don't even know how I would begin to do that."

I should probably stop talking aloud to myself. Is that how they get you?

Roaming the hall of my floor, I spot the doctor walking to my room. Quickening my step, I call out to him.

"Right here, Doctor."

He smiles and his brown eyes are kind.

"Hello, Charles," he says, stepping into my room and cracking the door. "How are you feeling?"

"I feel positive and optimistic," I say brightly. I'm playing the game now; I want out and I want vodka, my epiphanies be damned. "Honestly, I think it's best that I've stayed this long, my time here has really given me clarity."

Well, that part's true, at least.

"Excellent," he answers, flipping through charts in my file. "No suicidal or homicidal thoughts, I see, and a plan for discharge."

"Yes, I took that upon myself and submitted it to Damian, my case manager."

"Very good. So do you feel safe to leave here?"

I nod slowly, feigning thought. "You know, yes, I think I do. I've made contact with my family, and we have a solid plan to get me home and taken care of."

Lies and acting. Thank you, theatre degree.

"Very good. I will speak with your case manager and we should be able to have you discharged early tomorrow morning."

231

"Sounds like a plan," I say modestly, while internally rejoicing. A bottle is now mere hours away. Fuck escaping, fuck shame. Fuck it all, I get to drink soon!

*I dream of a gravel alleyway surrounded by dingy houses. I grip the wheel in the driver's seat of a busted old car as Brodie throws herself into the passenger seat and slams the door. It's midnight, with streetlights casting scattered halos of light. The air is cold and we're beyond panic; we've just escaped a locked house, and must now flee for our lives.*

*I reverse the car and we speed down the alleyway, merging onto a highway, where it is sunny and mid-afternoon. Brodie rolls down her window and grabs an ornately carved silver pistol from the glovebox.*

*We have a turnoff coming up, onto a narrow dirt road, and there are people hidden in the bushes, waiting to re-capture us. Brodie will need to shoot them while I take the sharp turn and floor it.*

*I slow a bit, anticipating the shift of force, and the sunlight glints off Brodie's silver pistol before she begins firing out her window. I see her bullets make an impact and bodies fall in the tree line. The car slides into the turn, and just before it can fall into a gorge, I fling open the driver's door and push it back onto the road with all my might. Jumping, I land in the driver's seat and put the pedal to the metal. Brodie leans slightly out her window and fires off one last shot. I glance in the rearview mirror, no one breaks through the dust.*

*We are safe.*

My eyes flicker open. The hall is uncannily quiet, it must be early morning. Kicking the covers off with my foot, I slide my shoes on and open my door to find the clock protruding from the wall—4:03 in the morning. Stretching, I step out and walk to the nurse's window.

Three or four sit at computers or on their phones, unaware of my presence. I scan the large hanging monitors, which are easy enough to figure out. Room number with the first two of the patient's last name, the doctor assigned, case manager, and discharge date. I quickly find my line: there is no discharge date. It is blank, like most others. I find one other patient with a discharge date displaying today, and notice their doctor is the same as mine. Did they get patients confused? My blood runs cold and I clear my throat.

"Good morning, ma'am," I say pleasantly to the nearest nurse. I will not cause a scene, I just need information.

She is wearing light purple scrubs and a plaited braid down her back. She lays down her phone.

"Good morning, how can I help you?"

"May I have some water, please? And I was wondering if I'm still on track to discharge today, is that something you can help me with?"

"Sure thing, I can help with both. Let me grab you some water and check your file. What's your name?"

"Charles Gray," I smile politely, folding my hands behind my back. After a moment, she returns with a cup of water.

"I didn't see anything in your notes about discharging today," she slides my water through the window. "Is that what your doctor or case manager advised you?"

I take a sip of water, inwardly freaking the fuck out.

"Hmm, there must've been some sort of mix-up. Yeah, the

doctor and I discussed it last night and he advised I would be leaving sometime this morning. I figured it'd be closer to noon since it takes a bit of time to get everything ready."

I scratch my ear, my mind buzzing with panic. I have to drink, I can't wait any longer for a bottle. I can feel my hands wanting to shake, but now is not the time for anger or fear. Right now, I need to turn on the charm.

"Oh, dear. Well, goodness. I better get this figured out, huh? Would you please leave a note for my case manager asking him to meet me when he's in? It's Damian, and I know he's super busy, but I'm thinking we can get this sorted out real quick. I would really, really appreciate it." I finish with a cute chuckle.

"Sure thing, hun," she says.

My right leg bounces uncontrollably as I sit on the edge of my bed. It is 9:50 in the morning and I've yet to hear from my case manager. Continuing to ask the nurses will only cause annoyance, so I wait. And spiral out of control. Captured from the wild prairies of a liquor store and caged in a psych ward, I need to break free. My entire being is screaming for a bottle and I feel as though I will split in two from the anxiety.

Naturally, I am not thinking beyond obtaining a bottle. Once I have some drink in me, though, I'll be able to form a plan. Honestly, I'm not too far from home at this point. I could try hitchhiking.

I laugh to myself and lean back on the bed. In the event I do not discharge today, I will fake a massive panic attack for some Ativan. And a nicotine patch. It will need to be enough to make me sleep through the night, though.

Gasping, I bolt out of bed and square off with myself in the mirror. Having shaved, showered, and eaten, I see traces of my old self, except for the eyes. They're still hollow and icy. I turn my head from side to side, watching.

"Is this who you want to be, then? A psych ward hopping pill junkie?"

*"Why are we parking all the way over here?" I ask as Jason, our night tech at Viva, stops the van on a side street several blocks away from our AA meeting.*

*"What? Is it too far to walk for Prince Charles?" he teases, grinning.*

*Jason is by far our most interesting and vibrant night tech. He's just over forty, tall, thin and bald, with colorful and detailed sleeves running down both arms. With the collapse of the economy a decade or so back, he lost an amazing job as a graphic designer, but funneled that into a rewarding job opportunity in recovery. He has about twenty years of sobriety under his belt, and his approach is quite lighthearted.*

*"It is, actually," I banter. "I mean, isn't my insurance paying your wages? As your employer, I am requesting to be driven closer."*

*"You would, you fucking bastard!" he exclaims, and we belly-laugh.*

*"But seriously, can we drive closer?" Kellan asks from the front seat.*

*"Now you, you're just lazy," Jason quips, sliding the van door closed.*

*Kellan whines as we cross the street. "I'll probably be hit by a truck crossing this street. And let me tell you something, my Mom will not be happy about that."*

*"Kellan, no. I don't have time for that," Jason says.*

*"Yeah, no, you're too busy tryna get Audra's dick," I say over my shoulder to Jason.*

*"Charlie, that doesn't even make sense," he sputters, a perplexed expression on his face.*

"Sure it does," Kellan chimes in, passing us as we near the meeting hall. "You're just very narrow-minded and simple, Jason. But it's okay, we still appreciate you."

The three of us giggle as we enter the hall and tread up the steep staircase. This is an excellent AA meeting in the Newport Beach area, but only Jason takes us here. It is his Home Group, and the crowd is younger and more relaxed. The atmosphere reminds me a bit of the CA meetings we attended at Reflections.

As Jason wanders off to mingle, Kellan and I step into the meeting room and find a seat near the window. I've learned it is important to find a window seat, as the building does not have air conditioning, and California AA meetings last an hour and a half. It was a shock the first time I attended a meeting out here. Not only do they clap for everything, but the meetings are longer. Reluctantly, I've grown to understand the value of both.

"Are you going to pick up your ninety-day coin?" Kellan asks.

"I dunno. I've made it this far only once before and I picked up a coin that time, then shortly after I relapsed. So maybe this time I won't, like it would jinx it or something if I picked one up."

"I don't think that's how it works, but okay. Is your Sponsor not making you pick one up?"

"No," I say, walking toward the coffee pot. "Alex isn't exactly traditional when it comes to Sponsorship. It's really nice, actually. We text every day and it doesn't feel as formal as calling someone at a scheduled time."

"Hmm, must be nice. I'm still in trouble because I haven't found one yet."

"It's because you're lazy, remember?" I smile.

I watch as the regulars drift in and take their usual seats. By now, most of them recognize me as one of Jason's guys, but I haven't actually talked to many people. I prefer to stay on the sidelines and observe. In my early days, it was important for me to speak at meetings, an indication that I was serious and wanted to change. But, in hindsight, that was artifice, though I don't think I realized it at the time. I think I had myself fooled, even then.

Kellan nudges me and slyly points to a very attractive Latino taking a seat near the door.

I smile and nod. "You're getting good at this, Kellan. Yes, he's hot."

He beams. "Now you pick one for me!"

"Okay, sure," I sigh, feigning exasperation.

I scan the growing crowd, finding a sweet girl with fair skin and light pink hair. She has one sleeve of tattoos and a nose piercing.

"Her," I say and flick my eyes.

Kellan locates her and his jaw drops.

"Let me tell you something, you're getting good at this, too. She's amazing, I love her."

As the meeting begins, I lean back in my chair and listen to others share about their day. It is relaxing, sitting in this space with my fellows, talking and poking fun at our addictions. Meetings have become a place in which I can reset and recharge. I am able to recenter myself and leave with purpose. Very rarely does this have to do with the topic or something another has shared; rather, it is the vibe and culture which spark me. The sheer will and determination to keep going, no matter what.

Kellan rests his elbows on his knees and stares at the floor during most of the meeting. He does have an honest desire to quit drugs and the treacherous lifestyle born from it, however, it is small and underfed. The pull of heroin and meth is still too strong, which I completely understand. It's more than just a high for us, it's an escape to a place where we can be free and happy. Where we can be our true selves. Or so we've been seduced to think. I'm still working on that one.

*I do hope we can stick together, though. We're good for one another. Our addictions differ, allowing us the capability to talk each other out of a relapse. I don't want to bang heroin and he's not down to guzzle vodka. Which is perfect.*

*Jason joins us at the top of the stairs after the closing Serenity Prayer and we begin our trek back to the van. He is quite chipper.*

*"Have a nice, impactful meeting with Audra, did ya, Jason? Really helping her stay sober there?" Kellan burns at Jason.*

*"At least I look up from the floor and at the girls. Charlie gets more action with women than you do!"*

*"It's because I'm so beautiful," I say in a matter-of-fact, deadpan tone.*

*They both groan and roll their eyes at me.*

I blink and I'm back.

"No, no this isn't who I want to be. This isn't who I am. God? Anyone?" I sigh and stare out the window. "Please help. I don't know what to do."

There is a knock on my door and I spring up from bed.

"Come in," I say.

Damian opens the door, my file in his hands.

"Good morning, Charles."

"Morning, Damian," I answer, steeling myself.

"Sorry it took me so long to get to you, but I really appreciate your patience. A night nurse said you wanted to discharge today?"

"Mm-hmm. I talked with the Doc yesterday and we both felt it was time."

"Alright, let me check with Dr. Ahmad. I agree that you're doing very well. Is there anything you need from me now, though?"

"No, I'm feeling very optimistic about leaving, whether it be today or tomorrow. I've decided to go with the flow, you know? It's so exhausting fighting the tide all the time, man." I chuckle at him and scratch my ear.

"That's a great outlook! I'm glad to hear that," he smiles.

"Thanks," I gush. Fake. All of it.

"Okay, well I'm off, I'll get back with you early this afternoon, though."

"Right on," I answer as he closes my door.

I take a long breath and steady myself. That was complete bullshit and I want to storm out of here in a rabid fury and flee to the nearest liquor store. But that will only earn me a Thorazine shot and an extended stay. So I fume internally. In my mind, I burn the hospital to the ground while chugging a gallon of vodka.

"My, you are troubled," I muse.

Hearing the call for lunch, I step outside of my room and join the herd filing down the hall to the group/recreation room. I have spent as little time here as possible, participating in a minimum of one group a day. Smiling politely and chattering idly show I'm content, adjusted, and ready for the world again.

"Charles!" I hear Damian call my name from behind me.

I turn, my heart beating like a drum.

"What's up, Damian?" I ask, careful to sound casual.

"I was able to talk with Dr. Ahmad, and we're in agreement that you're ready for discharge this afternoon. If you want to grab some lunch, we'll start working on the papers and a ride for you. It should only take a couple of hours. Now, where will you be going?"

I do somersaults in my head. "The Greyhound station, I can get a ticket from there and head home to Missouri."

He scribbles this on a note. "Sounds good, I'll come to chat with you in a little while. Enjoy lunch."

"Thanks."

I have no intention of eating anything, it will get in the way of my vodka. Which I will have the luxury of drinking in a few short hours. My spirits are lifted and I feel bright again. Oh, finally! After all this shit, I need a fucking drink.

Clutching my voucher for the cab driver, I flop into his backseat and pass it to him. He looks at it and then at me.

"Greyhound station, yes?"

"Yes, thank you," I answer and gleefully watch out the window as we depart the hospital awning. Bye, Felicia.

As we approach the station, I seize my moment.

"Is there a cigarette or liquor store nearby? Before the Greyhound? You can stop there."

"You want to change your stop to a liquor store?" he asks, meeting my eyes through the rearview mirror.

I nod, determined. "Yes, please."

He slows down and turns left, onto a street of pawnshops and discount cigarette shops. My oasis.

"This will do," I say. "Thank you."

"Thank you, have a good day."

Crawling out of his cab, I scan the shops for one with liquor in its title. It does not take long to find my selection, and my heart rate doubles as I open its screeching door. Roaming the rows of booze, searching for a fifth, I am reminded of a group with Poppy at Simple. It's as though a warning is being set off.

*She sits cross-legged and casual, her bangles chiming. Group is smaller today, more intimate. She shakes her head, listening, and then clears her throat.*

*"So, if you'll notice, each of you are explaining a moment that sounds different but is actually the same. Sure, the circumstances are different, but the decision that fueled each circumstance is the same. You chose to use. Or drink. There was a moment, a choice, and you decided 'you know what, fuck it! To hell with them all, I'm doing what I want, when I want, because I'm a grown-ass woman.' That's what I thought. And did. Over and over, until it nearly killed me. But one day, I was able to say 'no, I don't think I will this time.' I was able to choose life over the drugs."*

*"But what if it happens so suddenly that it's like you're not even making a choice? I mean, for me, it's like the thought pops into my head, and before I know it, I'm chugging vodka. I have no moment of 'should I do this?' I have the thought, and then my body takes action. What should I do about that?" I question earnestly.*

*"There's thought there, Charlie. You just don't want to see it. But that whole time your body is taking action and getting the vodka, there's thought."*

*"That's not how it feels in the moment. It feels like autopilot. But I guess if I take it a step further, in those moments of buying vodka, I refuse to listen to those thoughts, or I rationalize them away. They're not productive for my drinking, so I silence them."*

*Poppy levels with me. "How about you try listening to them if you're ever presented with the situation again? Try it, I bet you it will work out to your benefit."*

Part of me wishes I would walk out of the store, find a phone, and call Trella. I wish I could heed Poppy's advice, act logically and rationally, but the truth is, I don't want to; a larger, louder part of me wants the fire of vodka in my belly. Drunk, dark wolf Charlie wants to hide and ignore life. He wins out and I find a cheap pint and grape soda. At least I downgraded to a pint.

As I walk behind the store and find a covered space near the dumpster, my legs feel weak and heavy. I shouldn't be doing this, every fiber of my being tells me as every nerve sears back, aching to be numbed. It will slow me down and put me in a fog. It will lift me up and help me stay motivated. It will dull my senses and hinder my decision-making. It will make me happy and hopeful.

Fuck. This. Shit!

Two hours later I sit at a bus stop near Walmart and smoke a cigarette. I have finished my pint and the dizzying effects of the drink have taken effect. I am free again, although if I'm being honest, I feel more caged than free. Caged by a bottle that determines when and where I can feel free. Cages, everywhere. Taking a long drag, I decide my next move.

I will indeed call Trella and ask if she would be willing to make the drive to Wichita and pick me up. She's always there for me, no matter how depraved I become. I don't feel she will ever turn her back on me, and would only wish me to come home and heal.

With my liquid courage, I smile at an elderly lady entering the bus stop. Surely my cigarette smoke and cinnamon gum cover most of the vodka dragon breath. Surely.

"Excuse me, ma'am? May I ask you a question?" I continue to smile.

"Sure," she says. She wears a bright pink jumpsuit and has perfectly coiffed hair. I think she is sweet.

"May I borrow your phone for a moment, please? I would like to call my Aunt and see if she will pick me up. I was mugged and they took my phone and wallet."

The lie falls out before I can stop it, and I send out a fleeting prayer that I haven't laid out the course of my future, but without a wallet and phone to give.

She gives me a sympathetic look. "Oh, that's awful! Sure, you can use mine real quick."

"Oh, thank you so much!"

"Here you go, hun," she says and hands over her phone.

"Awesome, thanks!"

I dial Trella's number, careful to stay near the lady but also give myself some privacy. The phone rings twice and my heart beats wildly.

"Hello?" she answers.

Her voice pierces me like an arrow and my vision glazes over with tears.

"Oh, Trella," I say weakly. "It's me, I'm in Wichita at a bus stop by a Walmart. Can you please come and get me?"

"Oh my God, I'm so happy to hear from you! I'm so happy you're okay! You scared the shit out of me, Charlie Gray!" she cries, her voice breaking with tears.

"I know, I've been terrible and I am so sorry I put you through this. Really, I am, it's so unfair of me to keep you in the dark, guessing where I am."

"Yes, it was! And yes, I'll come pick you up, can you text me the address to the Walmart you're at?"

Relief pours over me. Trella has come to my rescue yet again.

"I will, but I have to give this nice lady her phone back so you won't be able to reach me once I've texted." I hesitate, then decide I've lied to her long enough. "I'm already drunk and should be that way for a while, so there's no chance of me wandering off in search of booze. I promise, Trella, I will stay put."

"Good. Please do, I'll leave here shortly and head your way. I love you."

I fall to pieces. "I love you, too. So much! Thank you, I'll see you soon."

I hear tears through her voice. "See you soon!"

As I hand the phone back to the lady, she grabs my hand and gently smiles.

"You're in a bad way now, huh? It sounds like you need to listen to yourself and stay put." She gives me a reproachful, sardonic, and kind look, all wrapped into one.

I chortle through my tears. "I think you're right, ma'am. I think I will listen, just this time."

It grows chillier as sundown draws closer. Having started my journey in California, I am wearing only a tee-shirt, a hoodie covered by a zip-up hoodie, and a pair of jeans. I do have on warm socks and shoes, and for that I am thankful. At some point, I will need to migrate inside Walmart, but for now, I'll draw the least amount of attention at the bus stop. At least no one can smell my dragon vodka breath from here.

As I watch people come and go from the parking lot, I think back over my life. While I cannot complain about my basic human needs being met, I am quite lacking in any substance, or purpose.

Since college, rather than become a working actor, I have racked up four DUI's, three trips to jail and two drunken rear-ends. I have received treatment at six rehabs, and spent time in at least twenty detox facilities, with another twenty or more trips to a psych ward. To try and keep myself sober, I've lived in five different sober houses and participated in the gamut of recovery: Alcoholics Anonymous, SMART Recovery, CBT/DBT and EMDR, religion, meditation mixed with wellness, and holistic living all while engaging in long-term, intensive therapy with a psychiatrist *and* an addiction counselor.

My body has been beaten and bruised along the way, as well. Wrecking my car, I fractured my neck in three places and collapsed my lung; a black eye and a few lacerations rounded out the damage. I was found hanging upside down, attempting to asphyxiate. About a year later, my drinking became so heavy that I actually atrophied in my bed. I had to scoot on my stomach to the freezer and drink vodka while hunched on the freezer door. Obviously, I was severely dehydrated and malnourished, in desperate need of an intervention. Thankfully, my Dad rushed me to the ER, where the doctor informed us that my liver was comparable to that of a seventy-year-old. I've come back from several bouts of extreme alcoholic hypertension, and the visible scar of a busted blood vessel on my left cheek serves as my constant reminder of the havoc I've inflicted on myself.

Yet to the bottle I've continued to scamper. It runs deeper than choice or desire, deeper than genetics or predisposition, and I believe I'm beginning to understand why I've so frequently heard a spiritual awakening is necessary for recovery. Am I ready to allow a force greater than myself to take the wheel? Not God, per se, but an energy, reciprocity, that I haven't allowed myself to tap into. A Higher Power, as it's called. Have I found my first conception of a Higher Power?

Something has to give, for I cannot go on like this any longer. I deserve a better life. Everyone does. Please let this be the last time Trella has to rescue me. Please help.

# 12

# A Brighter Shade of Gray

*July 2020*
*Clinton, Missouri*
*34 Years Old*

Pacing the floor of my apartment, I alternate between rubbing my neck and wringing my hands. My heart flutters and I can feel sweat beading on my brow. I don't want to drink, but I want to drink. I don't want to get hammered, call 911 and flee to Kansas City for a bout of insanity, but I do want to flee the expanse of my mind. My stomach lurches and I feel my mouth water.

"Oh, chitty-chitty, bang, bang. Shitty-shitty, bang, bang. Shitty-shitty-shitty," I sing, tapping my tooth with my finger.

I walk to the vanity in my bedroom and the air around me is still. Silence rings in my ears and my breath is clipped. I pull at the collar of my shirt and swallow, afraid to meet my eye in the mirror. I haven't slipped in a while, and am hesitant to manipulate myself into giving permission. I have mastered the art of manipulation so entirely that I'm now able to string myself along, as well.

Slowly, I look at my reflection.

"Turn on some music and dance. Clean your kitchen. Take out the trash and scrub the bathtub. Do all of that, right now."

I nod at myself and open Spotify, rush to my first playlist, and let San Holo take me away. I slink my neck to the music, letting my shoulders roll with my hips. Snapping and twisting, I make my way to the kitchen and begin moving the dirty dishes in the sink to the dishwasher, stacking to the beat. Why have I never done this before?

As I work on my chores around the apartment, it dawns on me I've simply implemented a skill taught at several rehabs, and spoken about in many AA meetings. I've distracted myself through an urge, or craving, and proven that I *can* do it. I can ride the wave and win, if only I fully engage myself in another task. The imagery of my duality flutters to the forefront of my mind and I pause, understanding. Finding a way to repair the disconnect between my head and my heart could be my deliverance. Seeking ways to divert, entertain, and motivate *both* parts of myself will bring salvation.

"And be open to help," I whisper.

A thought occurs, that perhaps my head and heart have been in constant competition, vying to be the leader. However, in all honesty, neither is fit to lead. I'm either all logic or all emotion, with a tendency toward emotion. For many years, it is clear, I have lived one lie after another and in judgment of myself; without offering any recommendation or solution, constantly feeding the concept that I'm uniquely troubled and afflicted. Separating myself from this disparaging thinking is like shrugging a weight off my shoulders. Why have I not thought to combine the powers of my head and my heart, to put myself and self-love first?

Wouldn't it be better for me to approach my situation with some grace and understanding? A dash of sympathy and an eye to the past for consultation? Couldn't I be a much better person if I forgave my past transgressions and worked toward building a brighter, more fulfilling future? Why should I remain bogged down in shame and regret when it reaps nothing but sorrow? How can I let myself wallow in torture when I could bloom and shine, finding a new beauty to life? Don't I remember the infinite possibility of my youth, when something as simple as a song or sunset would send my soul to uncharted depths? Won't my life be more amazing and epic than anything I could concoct in my most dizzying blackouts, if only I try? Certainly, I no longer wish to rob myself of a vibrant, technicolor life? Certainly.

I need to mix all of my learned lessons into a recovery gumbo, for they're all sending the same message: forgive yourself, Charlie. Love yourself, Charlie. Find your purpose and seek it like you sought the vodka bottle. Give this back to others, find the awe in life and help others to see it, too. It will be what fulfills you. Find your spark, your zest, a reason to stay off the bottle regardless of the number of days. This will help you finally understand and immerse yourself in faith and gratitude.

"Huh," I cluck, coming to a stop in my hall. "I really like this energy, this vibe, man. I'm not sure where it's coming from but I'm definitely down to cultivate this shit."

Straightening my blankets for bed, I pause and peer around my room, smiling. Not only have I staved off drinking a couple of times now, but I have found clarity and hope, too. I have begun to fully understand what I was only on the brink of understanding in my last psych ward. My dreams are beginning to make sense, a subconscious indication of my desire for an alternate avenue, a better lane of life. A return to myself and Brodie.

I will need to change my perception and intention, that much is obvious. Rather than focus on the fact I have nothing, I can focus on the fact I'm free to build. I have open parameters to explore. Perhaps I have squandered the last ten years, but that doesn't mean I haven't learned lessons. If nothing else, I've amassed a wealth of life experience, which should be shared. The universe has sent me many gifts, it simply took years for me to hear and decipher its message: to guide others from spending ten years of their life sailing the seas of a vodka bottle, or a pipe, or a bag of chips. Whatever it may be, I must send forward what has been given to me, or I will lose it. Is that AA? I'm not sure, but I *like* it.

Switching on my fan, I slide into bed and take three breaths, exhaling slowly. It is a trick I've observed others do over the years, and it actually works wonders. Before closing my eyes, I decide to send up a prayer, to whoever may be listening.

"Thank you. Please help."

*September 2020*
*Calhoun, Missouri*
*34 Years Old*

Gravel crunches soothingly under our feet as Brod and I hike the Katy Trail. Once a railroad, it now serves as a bike and jogging path covered by lush trees and bushes. Benches are placed every half mile and the foliage is well maintained, providing the ideal space for a leisurely stroll. Sun breaks through the leaves in chaotic patches as the wind gently blows.

This is our first excursion together since she moved back home in May, and I'm beyond grateful to spend time with her, just the two of us. The Gray kids, back in Clintonia. Who could have predicted?

"Oh, it's so beautiful today!" Brod cries excitedly. "I'm so happy it stopped raining, I was needing some sun!"

"Me, too! I needed to get outside of my walls for a minute. You know, it's crazy, but ever since I moved home and stopped drinking, I can't get enough of nature. I'd forgotten how much I love it!"

"That's so good, Bub!" she smiles.

Our relationship has mended itself organically, through normal, everyday acts. Nothing slick, no formal conversation or tearful apology. A living amends, as it's called. I have become a positive, active presence in her life in an attempt to draw out the poison I'd released over the years.

Brodie *needed* her big brother back, plain and simple. She *needed* me to show up, to listen, to laugh, and to advise. She *needed* me to be the fun, carefree influence of her youth. She *needed* me to love myself so that I could love her. Her patience truly is a virtue and I intend to reward it tenfold. She is a part of me, we're cut from the same cloth, and weathered the same storms; it feels as though I'm fully awakened, now that the fracture between us has healed.

Walking her down the aisle with my Dad in July was a moment of unity the three of us will share for the rest of our lives. I am the luckiest drunk of them all, that I could put the bottle down and partake in this life, with my family and friends. That I no longer feel left out or sullen. While I'm by no means naive or swollen with pride, I do believe these events have fostered a sense of dedication to my sobriety I'd yet to achieve until now. Forces greater than me are moving and I'm enjoying letting it take control of the reins. Surrendering, I believe is the term. How silly of me, to know these things for years, yet dismiss them as frivolous statements for the weak-minded. I chuckle to myself.

"What're you giggling about?" Brod asks.

"Just how silly I was all those years," I answer. "Silly and stubborn."

"You *feel* different now, though. I mean, there have been times before, when I thought you were really about to get sober, but this, right now, feels different from that, even. I feel like you're not trying to prove anything, you're just really embracing and loving life and what it has to offer. You're calm, and it's doing you a lot of good, I think."

"Yeah, I had to stop getting into tizzies over everything. I just needed to slow down, look around, and enjoy life, you know? Remember who I was. But without a vodka bottle."

"I'm so proud of you, Bub," she says earnestly.

"I'm so proud of you, Brod! Of the amazing woman you've become, of how wise you've grown!"

We giggle, grateful to be happy in each other's company after so many years of heartache.

"Isn't it just *so fitting* that we're both back in Clinton and all this is happening, though?" I chortle.

"I think it's perfect, honestly. It seems like it's right where we both need to be. It's so nice, with Tay back, too. And Trella and Dad and Kathy and Sarah and Chris and Dena and *everyone*. It feels safe and, well, like home, you know what I mean?"

I nod. "I know exactly what you mean. And it's heartwarming. It's like a damn Hallmark movie and I love it so much. It reminds me of our days at the house on the hill, being back here with you and Tay."

We walk in silence for a long span of time, listening to the chatter of the birds and the whispers of the leaves. I welcome the scent of pine, of home, like a long drink of water on a hot day.

"I'm so ready for Christmas!" I burst.

"Oh my gosh, me too! We haven't had one with the whole family in a couple of years and it's going to be so nice!"

"And all the food! How glorious!" I chime. "I think I want to put a tree up soon."

Brod cackles. "Wait until after Halloween, 'cause your Halloween decorations are so cute!"

I beam. "They are, aren't they? It was so fun to decorate!"

As we near a crossing, Brod pivots and steers us back in the direction of her car. She glances over at me, her face content.

"Keep doing what you're doing," she says.

"Will do," I answer simply and from the heart.

*November 2020*
*Clinton, Missouri*
*34 Years Old*

Gazing out my patio door, I wait for Kellan's phone call. We've messaged the last several days and he doesn't sound well. It was surreal, to be on the other side of the message, the one who hasn't relapsed. The one who has kept going, making moves and finding myself. I've never been 'the one,' for I was always crawling in and out of vodka bottles. It is a foreign and exciting feeling, much more so than drinking.

Lemongrass and tea tree oil perfume the air and I inhale

deeply, finally content with my life. I honestly thought this day would never come, the day where I am able to love and respect myself again. The day where I stopped condemning myself in mirrors. The day where I felt a sense of pride. It's astounding, and early twenties Charlie would have quite a task, wrapping his head around the fact that Clinton, Missouri is where he'd find his recovery. This is where my "come to Jesus," "ah-ha" moment happened, and I am thoroughly amused it took my hometown to pull it from me. Amused and grateful. Amused and humbled. Amused and changed. Amused and better; not cured, better.

Kellan's FaceTime beeps through and I grin.

"What's up, bud?" I ask, assessing him. Same messy dark hair, same beanie; pallor skin, and sunken eyes, though. Regardless, he beams back at me.

"Hey, man! I just got out of detox," he sounds sheepish and I feel a pang of compassion.

"Hey, well at least you went *and* stayed, dude! That's a huge accomplishment! How long were you out?" I ask.

"About two months, but it wasn't too bad. I kept my job and my sober house didn't kick me out, just sent me to detox."

He walks down the street, palm tree leaves passing overhead, and I hear the cars on the highway in the background. The sky is clear and blue, and I long for California.

"You still in Newport Beach?"

"Yup, not with Simple but one of their sister centers," he answers.

"Good, is it nice?"

"It's not as nice as Viva, but it's not bad, either. I miss Viva. I miss you, man," he smiles into his phone, forlorn, and I hate that we're so far away.

"I miss you too, man. I really do. I think about you guys a lot. That was such a shaping, momentous time in my life—traveling to California and meeting everyone, especially you. It changed me. And I'm just now seeing and feeling the full effects."

He steps under the shade of a tree and lights a stubby menthol.

"So you're sober, then? Right on. How?" he chuckles, dejected. His eyes are full of despair and I know, in my core, the fragility of his mental and emotional state, for I lived in that space for years.

"You know, honestly, it was my only option. And what I mean is it was my only option with myself. Obviously, my life had been indicating for a long time that it was my only option, but I've never listened to that message. It's been sent for years, and I've never listened.

"But I looked around and saw that I had *absolutely nothing*. Nothing within me, no material possessions. Nothing. I felt hollow and void of emotion. It was bleak, Kellan, and I had never felt that cold, that deadened. I wanted to be left alone in a dark room forever. I wanted to hide and drink myself to death. For real, I'm not saying that flippantly. But I also knew I had to separate myself from thinking like this, that if I *were* to drink myself to death, I'd be taking the easy way out. You know, letting myself down as usual. And then, for once, *finally*, I saw *my* place and *vodka's* place in all of this. But I was able to see it without guilt or anger or fear—I was able to see it objectively. As if I were viewing someone else's life. And it was crazy, bud! There was this picture in my head of a cart that had careened off its railway, and I simply nudged it back on track. Like, *I* was the cart.

"And then I was able to reach a conclusion without feeling any particular way: I needed a purpose, a goal, anything. But it had to be beyond sobriety, it had to be something I could work toward *even if* I relapsed. A reason to continue to get back on the horse. I needed to be single-minded about something *other* than sobriety. Which I know isn't advised in AA, but then again, AA alone didn't keep me sober.

"And I don't mean that AA is wrong, or doesn't work. Because it *does* work. I mean that I had to take every lesson, from every form of therapy I'd been exposed to, and understand that it was all telling me the same thing: I was the only one who could make myself better, I would need support, and I would need a purpose, a reason. Anything to give my life merit and meaning.

"So I found a goal, I've become very immersed in energies, and I got the fuck over myself. I dunno, now that I think about it, maybe I just needed to get over myself."

I laugh softly and watch Kellan's face; he appears pensive.

"So what was your goal?" he asks after a moment.

"To write, actually. To share my story with other gay alcoholics, and alcoholics and addicts in general. And their family and friends, anyone who has been impacted by the vicious disease of addiction. In any form. I was always searching for something to identify with, something to compare myself to, something to track myself against. And I know that's not healthy, but it's reality. Healthy takes time and reality is always here, now, you know?"

Kellan nods his agreement.

"So I thought, why not tell the story of the boy who couldn't quit drinking and going to rehabs and psych wards and jails. Until he did. Maybe, that way, I can save someone a little time. I mean, I know there is no magic cure or program or pill or shot or anything like that, but I do know I could help people chop a few years off their sentence. I was floundering for *so long*, I just wish I would have found something to latch on to sooner, but maybe I wasn't meant to."

"And you feel like writing is what's kept you sober?" his voice is low, intrigued.

I stand and pace my living room.

"Part of it, yes. Writing alone has not kept me sober, although it has been super cathartic. And the purpose of my writing, the creativity, has given me *so much more* than a vodka bottle had in a *long* time. It helped me gain a new perspective on life, a more mindful, present mindset. I realized I *really don't want* to die a drunk. Especially a drunk who contributes nothing to the betterment of mankind. Like, what's the point? Working on my story gave me a great headspace, where I decided to choose happiness, to make healthy decisions for once. It really just helped me choose myself again."

Silence rings as we lock eyes. His fill with tears and he looks down, ashamed.

"But all I wanna do is get high, Charlie. Like, I get what you're saying, and I understand and agree and wish I could do it myself, but I can't. I just wanna get high *and* do all that!"

"I see your point, because it's valid and how I felt until very recently. But once I started working, in a sober state of mind, and things started to feel better, I found myself *not* wanting to drink. Even if no one knew and I was able to hide it, I didn't *want* to because I had finally found something better. You just have to find something better, man. I mean, I know it sounds silly and cliché, but what have you always dreamed of doing?"

"I'm not sure, I've been doing drugs for so long," he answers genuinely.

I guffaw. "Oh that's so honest, I love it! And I get it, man! But somewhere within you, there's a light waiting to shine, you just need to find the switch. And I guess the most important thing would be that you have to keep trying, no matter how many times you relapse. Just keep trying. You shouldn't beat yourself up too much along the way, either, and *really use* the tools we were taught in all of our many programs. Just get up and do it, day after day, and then *that* becomes your routine. Find something you're passionate about doing, and make *it* part of your routine. I dunno, that's what I had to do and it's worked, bud. It *really* has."

"Pearls of wisdom by Charlie," Kellan teases.

"Sorry, I know you wanted a pearl necklace, but this will have to do."

We erupt in laughter.

"Do you think you'll stay sober?" he asks as we sigh.

"Isn't that the billion-dollar question? Do I hope to stay sober? Yes. Do I think if I continue to nurture and cultivate my spirit with nourishment from varying interests of life that I'll stand a better chance of staying sober? Yes. Yes, I do. I think if I choose to view life through a dark looking-glass, then that is what I will reap. Maybe it's not the same for everyone, but that's how it is for me. I have to put out what I want, in order for it to find its way back to me. And I no longer want to aid and pander to the forces of evil, bro! I'm Dumbledore's man, through and through."

Kellan gives me a lopsided grin. "You sound so fresh and spunky, dude. I really hope this works out for you, you've just got the *best vibe* right now."

"Shucks, man. You do, too! It's just so hard for us to see that about ourselves. I often think it's because when we're out there using and drinking, we see only our savage bits, our primal, aggressive behavior. We forget that we're also kind and loving and gracious. We have to stop throwing out the good just because we really hate the bad. It's *insanity.*"

"Come back to California," he pleads.

"If only, man. If only. But I've still got community service to figure out and probation to finish up. I'll probably be in Missouri for a while."

Kellan rubs his eyes. "Oh, man, I really need to get to my new sober house. Can I call you later tonight, though? After I've moved in?"

"Sure," I answer.

After hanging up the phone with Kellan, I pour a glass of water from the faucet and lean against the sink. For the first time in my life, I've actually meant what I said regarding sobriety. While I've been able to "talk the talk" for a while, it's never come from my heart and soul. I lacked conviction and didn't care. A greater change has occurred within me than I thought possible, and from that, a new seed of hope is planted.

*April 2021*
*Windsor, Missouri*
*34 Years Old*

Crisp air flows through the windows of Kendra's Jeep as we cruise gravel roads, backroading, as it's called. She's taking me to the car wash, which is not a car wash at all, but a creek at the end of a winding dirt road. I turn to her and smile.

"Are you sure you're not taking me to some gay boy beating in these backwoods?" I tease and we laugh.

We met seven months ago when I began working for Show Me RV, a dealership in my hometown. I went to high school with an owner and he mercifully snatched me up from Walmart and placed me in his office. It was an amazing blessing and one of my miracles from coming home. Kendra is, for all intents and purposes, my supervisor, but we don't put too much stock in that.

She is a kindred spirit and a gift from fate; it is a mutual feeling. Kendra and I were both a bit stagnant before we met, however, we've remedied that quite thoroughly. We'd only known one another for a couple of months when we decided to go skydiving. It was at that moment, when booking the jump, we realized there was a stronger connection than an ordinary friendship.

I am in awe of the woman she is at such a young age. At twenty-five, I was in the beginning stages of my descent into madness, while *she's* a homeowner with a kayak and motorcycle. We provide excellent balance for another, though. She's introduced me to TikTok and put me back in touch with my silly bone, and I've opened her eyes to a more holistic lifestyle.

"It's so beautiful and lush right now," I gush, watching as green meadows pass by. "See, this is why I think a retreat could work perfectly in the Midwest. I know there's no mountains or waves, but these fields is pretty AF, I think. There's something very comforting in them, maybe because I grew up around here?"

Kendra nods. "No, I can see that. They are beautiful, and the woods and the creeks, too. It's just a different type of beauty."

"You know, I think being back in this type of nature has helped me stay sober. It's helped me reconnect to who I used to be. Before the vodka and the insanity. It's reminded me of the carefree, hopeful boy that I once was and it's been easier to fall back in love with myself, remembering him. I mean, he never really went away, you know? I just kept locking him in the basement."

"That's so sweet, Charlie! It's so strange to hear you talk about your life before meeting me because all I've ever seen is who you are *now*. But I feel like you're exactly what I needed. 'Cause you know, I do believe everything happens for a reason, whether it be frustrating, heartbreaking, happy, scary, etcetera. *Whatever* it may be, I believe it has all happened to me for a reason.

"And I am so grateful that you came into my life and there are so many good things that have come from it so far. Like, opening my eyes to meditation and just overall searching for a happier, more content version of myself. I mean, *everyone* deserves a person like you in their life and I'm glad you're that person for me." She smiles at me, her radiance amplified by the setting sun.

"Oh my God, you *are* going to kill me, that's why you're being so nice! You're gonna make me cry, Kendra! I think that's the sweetest thing anyone has ever said to me, and I've had some sweet things said!" I chortle.

"It's all true," she says.

"You know," I sigh and give her a wink. "Even though you're a stinky old girl, I feel the same way about you, too."

A wave of gratitude washes over me as I drive home and my eyes sting with tears. For the first time in a decade, I am bubbling over with a sense of purpose and fulfillment. In finding my light, I have created the ability to help others find theirs. Kendra was correct, everything does happen for a reason. I have survived my alcoholism these many years so that I may share my strength with others.

My perception of the world was molded as a result of being struck by the disease of alcoholism. Born with the benefits of a white male in a comfortable, middle-class family, I have had the chance to step beyond my privilege and see the gruesome underbelly of life and addiction. It is quite fair to say I have been changed for the better by it. My compassion and understanding of mankind increased *because* of my affliction; it softened my rough edges. I am able to recognize how fragile we are as human beings, and how delicately we need to treat one another.

Traveling the country through institutions of recovery has shown me that love and tolerance must be the language above all. Division, judgment, and contempt only bring humanity to its knees. We must cease general observations and fully immerse ourselves in the plight of our brothers and sisters, otherwise what separates us from the beasts? Shouldn't we learn to love broader, to condition ourselves to see that unconditional love rings louder than any spout of hate?

"Oh, *lofty*," I chuckle and glance at myself in the rear view mirror. "But you're on the right track, bud."

*June 2021*
*Springfield, Missouri*
*35 Years Old*

Lighting a cigarette, I gaze around Ransom's gigantic backyard, awestruck.

"So this is *all yours*, Ransom?" Anne asks with pride and wonder in her voice.

"Yup, it sure is. And Rebekah, you remember my sister?" Ransom's blue eyes flicker to mine.

"Of course I remember Rebekah, how is she?"

"She's great, she bought the house next door, and that's her backyard there. All the way to the treeline, too."

"Oh. My. *Lanta*, Ransom! This is amazing! I'm so proud of you!" I gush, surveying his massive spread of land. Nearly two acres each, with a chain fence dividing the properties. The previous owners maintained the grounds, and it is free of bushes and weeds, enclosed by tall trees, and shady.

"Yeah, it's gonna make business a whole lot easier," he muses, gesturing to three rows of saplings growing in old tires.

"Oh, are you going to grow more of these?" Anne walks toward them, some are nearly four feet tall while others hover around two feet.

"Uh-huh, for my nursery," Ransom answers, smiling broadly.

I take a few steps toward his treeline, moving my secondhand smoke downwind. A lump is rising in my throat, and I need a moment to collect myself, as well. Had someone told me on my birthday last year that I would be spending my *next* birthday with my best friends from college, I would have laughed sadly in their face. At the time, I did not think it was possible, for I had forsaken those dearest to me in my alcoholism. But recovery is full of amazing gifts, and one of those is spending my thirty-fifth birthday with some of my most important people.

Plucking up the courage in April, I reached out to Anne. As each day passed and I remained sober, it became more and more clear I needed her back in my life. I admire and love Anne in a way I have never loved another human being. We met on the brink of adulthood, and have experienced several of my fondest memories together. It was through reconnecting with Anne that my other companions from Drury re-entered my atmosphere, and I am ecstatic to have the gang assembled again. Today, Anne and I shall hang with Ransom, and then crash at his place while he heads out to Wichita for a tree climbing competition. Tomorrow afternoon, we shall be reunited with

Keith for lunch, where the three of us will FaceTime Bert in Switzerland. He grew to be a very pedigreed man, with many degrees and doctorates, and a teaching gig in Europe. Oh, my old friend Bert. I am extremely proud to be his friend. I am extremely proud to have all of them in my life, for we are a great group. I am a better man by knowing them.

Snuffing my cigarette in his burn pile, I tread closer to Anne and Ransom.

"So business is going well, huh? What exactly do you do again?" I ask.

"I prune, remove, and plant trees," he says simply.

"So you're living a dream of yours, huh? Ransom, you're so cool, you just went out and did it!"

Anne giggles. "He's licensed and insured, too! All grown up and *everything!*"

"Oh my goodness, look at all of us! Anne's a *voice-over actress*, Bert teaches in *Switzerland*, Keith is a *friggin' scientist* in Arizona, *Ransom's* saving the trees and I'm sober! We're *all* so cool!"

We chuckle together.

"It really is cool, though, isn't it?" Anne says softly. "And you're more than sober, Charlie, your blog is helping so many people."

A warm, tingly feeling pricks over me. "Thank you, Lassie. It's so nice to be helpful, for once. It's so nice to know I'm easing people's pain somewhat."

She pats my shoulder and we turn to go back inside Ransom's house.

"Lassie, I have a present that I've wanted to give you for a couple of years now," Anne says, plopping down on Ransom's bed with me. "Remember a few summers ago, when you were gonna fly

264

down and see me in Dallas?"

I furrow my eyebrows in consternation and a vague memory surfaces. One in which I missed my flight and went into drunken hiding for days. "Oh, Lassie, yes, I think I do."

"Well, when you never showed up, I got so worried, and the airline wouldn't give me any information, so I was kinda left in the dark. Anyways, I was gonna give it to you that day and I've kept it all these years, but I feel like now is the perfect time to open it." She beams at me, beautiful as ever.

"Anne, I'm so sorry I did that. I'm so sorry that *happened*."

She is my best friend, the funniest girl I've ever met, and I never meant to hurt her. It stings knowing that she was hurt by my love for the drink.

"Oh, it's alright, Charlie, really. We've moved on, and you're in such a good place right now, none of that other stuff from before even matters."

I am filled with emotion and want to grab her and weep, but contain myself with a grin.

"Let's have it open, then!" I chirp.

As I untie the bag and pull out the tissue paper, I see a small book with a slick, glossy cover. *Hippies and Crackheads* a novel by Margaret Thatcher. The cover image is my Drury gang walking down a path, taken from behind, and of their backs. Anne, our usual photographer, must have captured it one day on a nature walk. I burst with laughter and my soul is moved. I am sheer joy.

"Oh, Lassie, this is *everything* right now!" I exclaim. "Hippies and crackheads, what a lovely title!"

"You thought of it," she chortles.

"Oh, did I?"

Flipping through the pages, I find photos and quotes from

our escapades throughout college. I am reminded of people and places I hadn't thought about in ages, and it is the most fun I've had in months. Anne and I reminisce for an hour or so, then she heads off to bed down the hall.

As I stare out Ransom's window before laying down, I take a moment to realize how far I've come on my journey. I allow myself the tiniest congratulation, for learning to live a more authentic life. For learning, accepting, and embracing my identity. For truly working on myself, for healing. I take a breath of relief and close my eyes.

"Thank you. Please help."

# About the Author

Charlie Gray is a recovering alcoholic sharing the experience of addiction, relapse, and recovery in his debut memoir, *At Least I'm Not The Frog: A Zany Memoir of Alcoholism & Recovery*. Living eleven long years as a high-functioning alcoholic, he attended a plethora of treatment centers, detox facilities, psychiatric wards, and hospitals across the United States. His story offers unique insight into the method and mind of a chronically relapsing alcoholic, and the tools necessary to combat such an affliction.

Charlie resides in his quaint hometown in Missouri, with his family, friends, and cat, Klaus. These days, he can usually be found searching for epic, inspiring moments or updating his blog on maintaining sobriety and clarity, aptly titled *At Least I'm Not The Frog II*.

**You can connect with me on:**
- https://www.atleastimnotthefrog.com
- https://www.facebook.com/atleastimnotthefrog